William Alexander

Notes and Sketches

Illustrative of Northern rural Life in the eighteenth Century

William Alexander

Notes and Sketches
Illustrative of Northern rural Life in the eighteenth Century

ISBN/EAN: 9783337058890

Printed in Europe, USA, Canada, Australia, Japan

Cover: Foto ©ninafisch / pixelio.de

More available books at **www.hansebooks.com**

NOTES AND SKETCHES

ILLUSTRATIVE OF

NORTHERN RURAL LIFE

IN THE

EIGHTEENTH CENTURY

BY THE AUTHOR OF
JOHNNY GIBB OF GUSHETNEUK

EDINBURGH
DAVID DOUGLAS
1877

PREFACE.

THE NOTES AND SKETCHES of which the present small volume consists have not been written upon any systematic plan. The nucleus of the whole was a paper read several years ago before an audience of decent country folks, who, it was thought, might listen with some interest to matters connected with the social and industrial life of those who had preceded them, and lived under conditions as to occupation and the daily round of duty, corresponding as nearly as might be with their own. The object in view then met with at least the amount of success that had been expected; and the paper with variations—or rather, perhaps, part of it with additions—was, at intervals, repeated to other similar audiences. And thus the essay grew in bulk. The style is admittedly not altogether that which would have been adopted had publication been in view at the outset, the paper having been shaped mainly to suit the original purpose for which the materials were gathered. The sources of information were various, and are generally indicated in the text. Of the books chiefly consulted a list has been given in the Appendix (1) in preference to an excessive multiplication of foot notes. And it occasionally happens that a statement made, or an opinion expressed, is the result of a comparison of two or more authorities rather than the unqualified averment of a single individual.

In acknowledging his obligations to several friends who have supplied information on particular points, the author feels it right to say that he has been specially indebted to Mr. Alexander Cruickshank, M.A., whose unwearied industry in the collection of facts and statistics is not more marked than his unselfish readiness to make his stores of knowledge available to others.

The sketch of a twelve oxen plough, which forms the frontispiece, is from the skilful and accurate pencil of Mr. Andrew Gibb, F.S.A., Scot.; and was taken from the specimen in Marischal College Buildings mentioned at page 33. The beam remained entire at date of drawing; the stilts, &c, had to be somewhat helped out from the parts of them still extant, and a certain measure of traditional knowledge. And as the plough is drawn to scale, readers interested in such matters, and who care to do so, will be able to compare its size and the proportion of parts with those of the improved plough of the present time.

ABERDEEN, *April*, 1877.

CONTENTS.

CHAPTER.		PAGE.
I.	INTRODUCTORY—STAGNATION OF AGRICULTURE DURING THE EIGHTEENTH CENTURY,	1
II.	TOPOGRAPHICAL AND SOCIAL,	7
III.	RURAL OCCUPATION—OLD LAND MEASURES,	13
IV.	CULTIVATION OF THE SOIL, 1700-1800,	19
V.	FIRST IMPROVERS—AN EARLY AGRICULTURAL ESSAY,	24
VI.	IMPLEMENTS OF THE FARM—THE TWAL OWSEN PLOUGH,	32
VII.	RESULTS OF CULTIVATION—PERIODS OF FAMINE,	41
VIII.	THE BAD HARVEST OF 1782—EFFECTS IN TOWN AND COUNTY OF ABERDEEN,	48
IX.	LIVE STOCK—EARLY IMPROVERS—HIGHLAND REIVERS,	60
X.	LIVE STOCK—CATTLE DEALING AND DROVING,	68
XI.	COUNTRY FAIRS—THEIR ORIGIN AND CHARACTER,	77
XII.	ROADS AND ROAD-MAKING—STATUTE LABOUR—FIRST TURNPIKES,	83
XIII.	IMPROVED LOCOMOTION—THE EDINBURGH FLY—SCORGIE'S CARAVAN,	92
XIV.	EARLY AGRICULTURAL IMPROVERS IN ABERDEEN AND KINCARDINESHIRES,	101
XV.	CHARLES HACKET OF INVERAMSAY,	108
XVI.	AN AGRICULTURAL TOUR—ANDREW WIGHT, SURVEYOR—DR. JAMES ANDERSON,	116
XVII.	DOMESTIC LIFE AND SOCIAL HABITS—DRESS—FOOD—DRINK,	127
XVIII.	DOMESTIC INDUSTRIES AND OUT-DOOR LABOUR,	134

CONTENTS.

CHAPTER.	PAGE.
XIX. THE MILL AND THE MILLER—THIRLAGE—FETCHING HOME THE MILLSTONE—MULTURES,	146
XX. CRAFTSMEN, ITINERANT AND OTHER—JOCK YOUNG AND TIB DOO,	154
XXI. VAGRANT LIFE—FLETCHER OF SALTOUN'S OPINIONS—TIBBIE CAMPBELL,	162
XXII. POPULAR AMUSEMENTS—COCK-FIGHTING—FOOT-BALL—WAD-SHOOTING,	172
XXIII. SMUGGLING, LOWLAND AND HIGHLAND—PHILIP KENNEDY THE SMUGGLER—MALCOLM GILLESPIE THE GAUGER,	182
XXIV. THE PROPHET OF BETHELNIE—STATE OF MEDICAL PRACTICE—SUPERSTITIOUS BELIEFS,	192
XXV. THE KIRK-SESSION AND ITS DUTIES—LAYING A GHOST—TIBBIE MORTIMER AND GEORDIE WATT,	200
XXVI. IN CONCLUSION — SUMMARY, SOCIAL, MORAL, AND RELIGIOUS,	208
APPENDIX,	215

NOTES AND SKETCHES,

ILLUSTRATIVE OF

NORTHERN RURAL LIFE IN THE EIGHTEENTH CENTURY.

INTRODUCTORY—GENERAL STAGNATION OF AGRICULTURE DURING THE EIGHTEENTH CENTURY.

IN the annals of Scottish agriculture, and specially of agriculture as it concerned that limited district in the north-eastern part of Scotland to which the jottings that follow will be chiefly confined, the eighteenth century was, throughout almost its whole course, a period of remarkable stagnation. It opened inauspiciously, in so far as the close of the preceding century had been marked by a series of very ungenial seasons, which brought with them disastrously deficient harvests, and want of food, amounting in many parts to absolute famine. The method of tillage, too, had seen no improvement from time immemorial; and as a natural consequence of this, the land, even in ordinary seasons, had in many cases come to yield not more, but less than it had yielded in the time that had gone before. The system pursued was one of exhaustion, and the cultivated part of the soil was to a large extent getting quite worn out. The native cattle were small, ill-grown animals; and they were correspondingly ill fed.

The spirit of enterprise was not yet abroad. For the first thirty years of the century, that is from 1700 to 1730, "the medium price of lands sold in the county of Aberdeen did not," we are told, "exceed sixteen years' purchase of the then low rents." It was not always that the lairds could find tenants willing to "keep in the rigs" at a merely nominal rent, until resort was had to the practice of stocking farms as occasion required on "steelbow," a technical term, the signification of which was that the landlord provided a "stocking" of cattle, corn, and implements, and the tenant became bound to return to him articles equal in quantity and quality at the end of his lease, if he could not free himself sooner. A man, if he were so minded, might readily obtain a "tack" on very easy terms, so far as a money or other payment was concerned; and that tack to last not for his own lifetime only, but for the period of one or two lives thereafter of such persons as he chose to name.

And small in amount as the money payments to rental were, they were not always, nor indeed generally, made off the produce of the land. It was chiefly through the manufacture of home-spun cloths, and the knitting of stockings for exportation that money came into the hands of the smaller tenants, sub-tenants, and cottar folks; and it was chiefly through them that it reached both the principal tenant and the proprietor, other sources of revenue hardly existing for either, in so far as local industry was concerned.

The roads they had were roads only by courtesy. Wheeled vehicles were scarcely known, and would have been but little serviceable if they had been more plentiful. The best frequented lines of road were not much else than mere tracks, that had taken their form from the hoof-marks of the cattle that traversed them; a few stones being sometimes roughly thrown into the bottom of a soft bit, forming a kind of rude causeway, sometimes not. And thus came the story of a certain man and his mare. As he plodded along, driving the animal before him, with the pack saddle on her back, the wary beast boggled at a particular part in the road, where she had "laired" on a previous occasion, and fairly refused to go on. But the mare had overlooked the fact that it was now in the drought of summer, whereas it had formerly been raw winter. And her master, failing to persuade her that it was safe to hold on her way, exclaimed "Wae-worth ye, beastie; yer memory's a hantle better than your jeedgment."

The people dwelt almost of necessity much amongst themselves, living in a simple, homely style, on the produce of their own cultivation. Observant strangers, in speaking of diversities in manners, and style of speech, among the common people, professed to note specific differences, if not between the inhabitants of one parish and the inhabitants of another, certainly between those of one district and those of other districts in the same shire; and it might be, in some instances, not half-a-dozen miles apart. The state of matters was not unfavourable to the growth of certain virtues, such as neighbourliness, social sympathy, and the like. And along with these there was almost necessarily contractedness of view and lack of the spirit of progress. It was equally natural that there should exist a considerable tinge of superstitious feeling, manifesting itself in such forms as the prevailing beliefs in fairies, ghosts, witches, and water kelpies, as well as in a sort of character who seems to have held a midway place between the fully developed warlock, who had his commission directly from the Prince of Darkness, and the seer, or person originally gifted, more or less, with superhuman power which enabled him to cope with certain bodily ailments and various other of the ills that afflict humanity.

Among the peasantry generally, as indeed amongst other classes of society during the same period, religious feeling was in a rather dormant state. The prevailing sentiment was pretty much that which, at a later era, came to be described by the term "moderate," understood in its worst sense. The "Seceder," when, in due time, he became an existing entity, here and there, was ordinarily regarded, and described as a pestilent fanatic simply; the "Missionar'," who in his turn was held in similar repute, did not come on the scene till a later date. It is not very easy, and might not be altogether wise, to pronounce an explicit judgment on the social morality of the period, comparatively viewed. In the north-eastern part of Scotland the great religious movements that accompanied and followed the Reformation, down to the Revolution of 1688, did not pervade the commonalty to the same extent, nor stir their feelings to a like depth, as in districts further southward. How far this may have been significant of, or have tended to promote, obtuseness of moral feeling in a comparatively rude state of society, we do not profess to say. But in so far as local records lead us, there does not at any rate appear to be much ground to believe that the social morality of the eighteenth century was in many of its phases of a higher or purer type than that of the century that has followed it.

By the middle of the eighteenth century, and even a little before it, the subject of improvement in agriculture had engaged the attention of men of intelligence; chiefly men of some position, who, while they had a direct interest in the subject as landed proprietors, were in several cases also actively engaged in professional life or in commerce. Some of these to advanced theorising added successful practice in such matters as turnip cultivation and the establishment of a rotation of crops; and notably also in the planting of timber trees. But it took long time till their example, in the matter of improved husbandry, was generally followed by the tenants, who were, as a rule, equally devoid of means and of the spirit of enterprise. Prejudice in favour of the old system and against the new was strong, too; and in some cases manifested itself in direct attempts to obstruct or defeat efforts toward improvement. Nor need we be altogether surprised at this. The time had not long gone by, when the highest agricultural wisdom merely sought to conserve the experience of the past as a creed for the present, and a guide in the future.

And the changes mooted must have seemed exceedingly revolutionary. It was not at an early date in the century, but towards the latter part of it—somewhere between the years 1770 and 1780—that a decent woman in the district of Garioch, in Aberdeenshire, found herself left a widow, with two sons coming toward man's estate. The family had cultivated the same farm for several generations, perfectly contented with their lot. It was a good farm; but under a constant succession of cereal crops, with no variation except from oats to bere every third or fourth crop, even good "intoon" land did not improve; and now the elder son and heir to the "tack"—like a headstrong young man, and disregarding the example of his seniors—would follow the new fashion of husbandry, which some of the neighbouring lairds had begun to practise. His mother was sadly distressed at the idea; but what availed it that she had the sympathy of her younger and more timorous son if the other would have his way; his latest extravagance was the determination to apply lime-shells as a quickening manure to the exhausted and inert "rigs." The perplexed widow could only send for a neighbour farmer of acknowledged sagacity and prudence to decide what ought to be done. The neighbour came, duly took note of what was going on, and, seeing the hopelessness of the case, proceeded to discharge his office of counsellor faithfully; and of course, very adversely to the youthful improver, winding up with this deliverance—" Weel, 'oman, I dinna believe that that loon 'll halt till he herry ye oot at the door, an' syne gae to the sodgers." The result of this "finding" was that the hot-headed young man threw up his birthright and was paid off with the sum of £30 sterling, his cannier brother assuming the office of farmer in his stead. The wilful young man did not go to the soldiers, it may be said, but betook himself to the county town for the purpose of acquiring as perfectly as he could the handicraft of the blacksmith, then in a rather primitive state in country districts. And having fairly mastered his business at a somewhat mature stage of his life, he set up his "smiddy," building his fire wholly of coals in place of home-made charcoal, and otherwise prosecuting his calling in accordance with his own advanced notions: although it was not he, but his son, who followed in succession to him in the same business, whose services came to be in repute in the first quarter of the present century as the only blacksmith over a wide district who understood, and could, with his own hand, fit up all the iron work of the thrashing mill and winnowing machine, then coming into general use, and if need were of the "meal mill" as well.

Generally, the latent energies of the people, which in the early part of the eighteenth century had been starved down by the meagre style in which physical life was sustained on the one hand, and the discouragement to enterprise found in the existence of heritable jurisdictions and the repressive fiscal system of the time on the other, had been only partially stirred at its close. Old customs; old habits of life, thought, and speech; antiquated implements, and obsolete modes of operation still kept their place with a wonderful tenacity; and the march of improvement, clogged as it was by sundry extraneous impediments, the weight of which we have difficulty under our greatly altered conditions in realising, was yet but slow and halting.

CHAPTER II.

TOPOGRAPHICAL AND SOCIAL—ABERDEENSHIRE POLL BOOK—A PICTURE FROM IT—HEATHER AND DUB BUILDINGS—AN OLD FASHIONED HAMLET.

For the purpose of arriving at a reasonably distinct notion of our country districts in their general features a century or a century and a-half ago, we shall do well to bear in mind that, along with the prevailing paucity of passable roads and absence of bridges on the larger streams, much of the surface of the land remained in its natural state. Cultivation was more picturesque than systematic in its developments; bogs, "mosses," and marshes continued undrained, covering in the aggregate a greater extent of the superficies of the country than it is easy now to realise. Natural forest grew in some places now bare enough of trees, but thousands of acres of the most valuable timber-land planted in the latter half of the eighteenth century had, prior to that date, produced little but stunted heather and clumps of broom.

If we go on to inquire how the rural population were distributed and how they were occupied, the contrast between the life of the people then, and what it has become since, is found to very marked. There is perhaps no county in Scotland in which materials fitted to illustrate this point are more abundant than in Aberdeenshire. By the aid of the *Poll Book** alone, and a

---

* The "List of Polable Persons within the shire of Aberdeen," printed by the gentlemen of the county in 1842, with the sanction of the Spalding Club, and under the editorial care of Dr. John Stuart, from MS. in the possession of General Gordon of Cairness, is almost unique in its way. In the year 1693, and again in 1695, a poll-tax was imposed by the Government of the time on all adults, for the purpose of paying off arrears due to the army, &c. The tax consisted of 6s. Scots per head, on each grown-up person, male

certain measure of local knowledge, the attentive topographic student might readily call up to the mind's eye quite a distinct picture of any given locality. He would be able not only to form an estimate, very nearly correct, of the actual population of any particular parish 180 years ago; but could also ascertain how that population was employed, and how it was located—the forms of occupation corresponding to a great extent with those which had obtained for some hundreds of years, as we shall afterwards see. He would find the Poll List for the parish headed by the laird and his family and servants; then, apart from them, the tenants and sub-tenants, with generally a group, more or less numerous, under some principal tenant, of cottars and their wives, of "grassmen" and their wives; and occasionally a "lone" woman or two in a "mailt house." Such was the more specifically farm establishment in which the relation of the various members of the small community to each other were readily intelligible. At the next place we have the hamlet. Here were congregated sundry minor farmers, along with the weaver or "wabster," and the tailor and smith, each of whom usually had his croft or piece of land to till, and his "lair" in the moss to furnish him with fuel. The two latter, important enough functionaries in their respective spheres, do not figure so frequently in the Poll Lists as we, with our modern notions, might expect. The people were not given to variety in "changeable suits of apparel" to the like extent that their descendants are. The common male dress consisted chiefly of coarse

---

and female, and 6s. additional if the man had a trade, such as that of a tailor or smith. And if he had property he had to pay a fortieth part of its value; while if he chose to call himself a "gentleman," his poll was £3 Scots. Pretty stiff all this no doubt, considering the value of money at the time; and so apparently thought those immediately concerned, for it was with great difficulty they could be got to pay the poll-tax. The Poll Book gives complete lists of the adult persons in each parish. Comprehensive as was the poll-tax of 1696, it produced in Aberdeenshire only the sum of £28,148 7s. 1d. Scots, or £2,345 13s. 7d. sterling.

woollen, home-spun, and home tailored, with a scanty supply of linen, and thus comparatively little professional tailoring was needed. As for the blacksmith, with scarcely a particle of iron in the plough or any other farm implement, and no horse shoeing to speak of—even where he was capable of doing it, which was not always the case—he could meet the wants of a very wide district. It was necessary, indeed, that he should do so ere he could find employment; and, in some cases, the smith had his "sucken" bound to attend his smiddy just as the miller, who had his place on every laird's land, had his "bun' sucken" up to a much later date—the minister of a Highland parish, indeed, states that by an "immemorial assessment," the smiths in his region were paid in meal by the farmers, they being in some cases also entitled to "the head of every cow slaughtered in the parish." At the hamlet, too, we should find the "chapman" or "pack-merchant," a very important member of the trading community in those days; who could indeed have commanded a good deal more of ready cash, in most cases, than the ordinary class of farmers could. The "stocks" of individual chapmen are valued in the Poll Lists, in some cases, at as high a figure as 500 merks; and in a few instances at even more than that; and taking into account the relative value of money, 500 merks then was probably quite as large a capital, relatively, as many dealers in soft goods can boast of now who exhibit their wares by the medium of a grand shop front, in place of undoing the pack on the old kitchen "deece." In addition to the classes named, the "herd" figures pretty regularly in the lists. He was not seldom a grown-up person of the male sex; perhaps some one who had been lamed of a hand or arm, or who was of more or less deficient intellect. And his mode of living was apt to be dependant and precarious; "herd in summer, but begs his meat in winter," and "herd on charity, his winter maintenance being gratis," are definitions of this official that repeatedly occur. In any case the "herd" was an indispensable functionary. And we now and then find in the lists such people as the "tinkler," the "horner," the "pewterer," and more rarely the "pyper;" designations which sufficiently explain the occupations of those who bore them.

Let us attempt to sketch the general features in the outward aspect of one of these hamlets, or "clachans," as they were called in the Highlands. The site of the hamlet had at first been determined, perhaps, by the presence of a gushing spring of "caller" water, or the vicinity of some "wimplin burnie;" or by the fertility of the soil at that particular spot; for men did not then ordinarily resort to such artificial means as the use of the suction pump to supply them with one of the essentials of life, nor did they contemplate setting themselves deliberately down to reclaim barren moors and hillsides for the sake of the other. They rather chose those situations where it was likeliest that bread would be given them without extra toil, and where their water would be sure so long as perennial fountains, fed in hills and heights, should seek the gladsome daylight where undulating hollows and rifts in earth's surface allowed it. It thus came to pass that the hamlet, in respect of site, had frequently a fair share of the elements of natural beauty; and in time, these came usually to be enhanced by the presence of some goodly trees clustering about the place.

The walls of the straw-thatched cottages or huts were composed, in the upper part at least, of "feal" or turf; or it might be "heather and dub," or mud and straw. The roofing "cupples," firmly embedded in the walls at bottom, were fastened with wooden pins a-top to a short cross bar, the roof-tree extending from end to end of the house over this bar, and between the points of the cupple legs. Stout binders, formed of saplings sawn up the middle, were placed horizontally down the rib of the roof, and over these again transversely the "watlin," consisting of smaller sticks split with a wedge. The "watlin," which, with the cupple legs and binders, was quite visible from the interior, carried the "divots," and these latter the "thack," ordinarily fastened on with "strae rapes." Each house consisted of a "but" and a "ben," with little variation in the character or extent of accommodation embraced.

In certain districts the style of building described was known as "Auchenhalrig," from its having been first used at a place of that name in Morayshire. Of the Auchenhalrig walls and the mode of constructing them, a detailed description informs us that :—"This work is built of small stones and mud, or clay, mixed with straw. The proportions of these materials required to make a rood of thirty-six square yards are . . . about thirty cart loads of stones, ten cart loads of clay or mud, and twenty-four stones weight of good fresh straw." The straw and mud being properly worked together, "twenty-two inches are sufficient thickness for a wall of seven feet high—if higher, they should be two feet thick—carried up perpendicularly the same as other walls, and care should be taken never to build more than two or three feet in height in any one part in the same day; if raised more, the wall is apt to swell, for which there is no remedy but to pull it down and rebuild." These walls were "equal to the weight of any roof commonly put on mason work," and would, "when properly built, and kept well under thatch, last for more than a century."

Here then, in our hamlet, we have a number, varying from four or five to a dozen, of these homely yet tolerably comfortable houses, with their walls of rude "concrete"—some with their adjuncts of barn and byre—planted down in a miscellaneous sort of way, as if they had dropt from the clouds, or been scattered broadcast over the knoll by Titanic hands. A winding road, or track rather, partly fenced in by round-headed "feal dykes," not in the best state of repair, leads up to the hamlet. This road expands into "the toon loan," and loses itself somewhere about the "head of the toon" at this end; most likely it loses itself at the other end among "the rigs outbye;" or, at farthest, about the margin of the "moss," where peats, or more likely "sods" only, are dug as fuel for the community. About the place we find here and there an exceedingly rustic sort of garden. In these "yards," which occur in no regular order—are so placed, in fact, that a stranger could hardly guess from the position of any one of them to which of the indwellers it belonged—may be found, besides certain useful vegetables, as "kail," green or red, and "syboes," a few old fashioned herbs and flowers. Some clusters of rich scented honeysuckle, a plant of hardy southernwood, peppermint, and wormwood; with, mayhap, also a slip or two of "smeird docken," the sovereign virtues of whose smooth green leaves, in respect of sore fingers or broken shins, commend it to careful consideration. And, as already indicated, in almost every case we find trees about the hamlet. A few ashes about the loan head, some rough scrubby elder (or "bourtree") bushes about the corners of the gardens, and, it may be, a plane-tree enriching the scene with its mass of dark-green foliage. Then, in some favoured corner there is the rowan tree, or possibly a pair of these growing side by side like twin sisters with their arms interlaced. They have yielded many a slip for crosses to put above the byre-door, on Rood even, to fend the bestial from "uncanny fowk." For, as we know,

> Rowan tree and red thread,
> Keep the witches fae their speed.

Such, in a general way, was the outward aspect of the hamlet and its surroundings.

CHAPTER III.

RURAL OCCUPATION—OLD LAND MEASURES—THE PLOUGH-GATE AND DAVOCH—EARLY LAND LAWS—EMANCIPATION OF THE NATIVI OR SERFS—REMAINS OF EARLY OCCUPATION IN SEVENTEENTH AND EIGHTEENTH CENTURIES.

In early notices of agricultural matters, we now and again stumble upon such expressions relative to the measurements of land as "oxgate," "ploughgate," "forty-shilling land," and somewhat more rarely, "davoch." By the learned industry of Mr. Cosmo Innes, it has been settled "beyond reasonable doubt," that an oxgate meant 13 acres. A ploughgate consisted of 104 acres—it and the forty-shilling land being equivalents—and the davoch was "as much as *four ploughs* could till in a year."* There was, too, the "husband land," which consisted of 26 acres, being the extent of land held by a single husbandman. Each husbandman furnished two oxen to the common plough, and, with the four pairs thus supplied, the ploughgate, which was a joint occupancy, was tilled. This principle of joint holdings, which found its extreme development in the "run rig" system, where two tenants cultivated alternate ridges on the same field, was well fitted to breed difficulties in the practical business of cultivation; and so the overlords had rules of "good neighbourhood" established, under which the several tenants were bound to perform their respective shares of the farm labour at the sight of "birley men" chosen by themselves.

---

* Strathbogie was of old divided into forty-eight davochs, each containing as much as *four ploughs* could till in a year. (*Antiq. Shires*, vol. IV.) Hence the phrase "the aucht-an'-forty dauch."

There are examples as early as the 13th century * of a land tenure, and regulations of the kind just indicated. It has been truly enough said that the Church in those early times was the great cultivator of the land as well as the great improver of the arts. While the rude unlettered barons devoted much of their energies to breaking each other's skulls and despoiling each other's possessions, the monks, so long as they continued to be men of moral lives and simple tastes, promoted husbandry to very good purpose, both as actual cultivators and as good and merciful landlords. The complete agricultural economy under and in connection with the monastery would consist, first, of the grange or farmstead, where were gathered the cattle, implements, stores, and so on, required in the cultivation of the land; as well as the serfs, or carles, who did the actual work, and their families. The whole would be overlooked by a lay brother, who rendered his accounts to the cellarer of the monastery. Outside the grange there dwelt the "cottars," each with a little bit of land, for which he paid some money rent, with certain services in seedtime and harvest. Beyond these again lived the "husbandmen," of whom we have heard, who paid each half-a-merk in money rent, with a variety of personal services, including four days' reaping in harvest of the man, his wife, and all their children; carrying home a certain quantity of peats yearly at the fitting season, and so forth.

The agriculture of the fourteenth and fifteenth centuries was prosecuted with more success and intelligence, all things considered, than we are apt to imagine. Various enactments of the Scottish Parliament in the fifteenth century indicate an enlightened and earnest regard for the interests of the cultivator. Leases in some sort date from the fourteenth century; and we find an Act of James II. (1449) conferring a tenant

---

* Rental of Monastery of Kelso, 1200.—*Legal Antiq.*

right adapted to the time in a single comprehensive sentence, thus—" For the safety and favour of the puir pepil that labouris the grunde, that all tenants having tacks for a term of years shall enjoy their tacks to the ish of their terms, suppose the lords sell or analy their lands." Another statute of James I. (1424), titled " Of bigging of ruikes in trees," in respect that the said ruikes "does" great "skaith upon cornes," provides for a penalty upon those who fail to despatch the young birds before they have flown from their nests. And there was a statute of the same monarch binding every man "tillan with a pleuch of aucht oxen" to sow a certain quantity of wheat, pease, and beans yearly. Mr. Innes points out, as an interesting and creditable fact in the history of the social life of the rural population, that the amelioration of the condition of the *nativi* or serfs belonging to the land was accomplished voluntarily during the fourteenth and fifteenth centuries. "From the thirteenth century, when the serfs must have formed a large proportion of the population; when gifts of serfs and sales of serfs, and claims of runaway slaves, are of as frequent occurrence as any transactions connected with land—between that century and the end of the fifteenth, hereditary slavery had ceased among us without any legislative act." From the beginning of the sixteenth century, the serf, formerly an important adjunct of the glebe, has disappeared, and we have a free agricultural class; a rather remarkable result, certainly, to be wrought out naturally and without the intervention of Parliament.

During the sixteenth, seventeenth, and greater part of the eighteenth century, we can trace the general features of the old rural economy. Lord Forbes's rental, of date 1532, quoted by Mr. Innes, shows the land divided into ploughs, each of eight oxen: the ploughgate being "sometimes let to four tenants, each of whom contributed the work of his pair of oxen to the common plough. These joint tenants were bound to keep *good neighbourhood*," in the way already explained in carrying on the common tillage operations. Again, in the rental of the Bishopric of Aberdeen (date 1511), under the conditions of sub-letting on the lands of Fetternear, "a crofter was bound to build one rood of the fold for every cow which he had in the town of his master. The tenants were answerable for the conduct of their crofters in the grazing of their cows and in other things that belonged to good neighbourhood." Probably, as time went on, and the Church lands had passed to other owners, the prevailing regulations were neither better systematised nor more regularly enforced, but rather the opposite. The mode in which the Church lands were dealt with at the Reformation did not reflect credit on those more immediately concerned. John Knox, in his History, speaks of some of the "nobilitie" who "had greadelie gripped to the possessionis of the Kirk," and done other selfish deeds despite the rebukes of the preachers; and in point of fact a number of the ostensible lay adherents of the Reformation, upon conveyances from the prelates, or in their office as "commendators," unscrupulously seized the temporalities of the Church, and, with equal indecency, turned out the old occupants of the land as they saw fit in order that they might fill their places with a subservient following of their own friends and dependants. These were hardly the men to encourage and foster honest industry in any shape; and for a time the peaceable and industrious cultivators of the soil, in many cases, suffered not a little injustice and oppression at their hands. Still, in its main features, the agricultural economy of the country seems to have undergone but little change for a very long period. At the earliest date to which we have referred, the different grades in the rural community had recognition; and their relations to each other, from the landowning class of ecclesiastics, barons, or lairds, and principal occupiers, to the humble cottar, who mainly represented labour, were distinctly understood. And so it continued to be up to a time less than a hundred years ago. It was, indeed, left to the enlightened nineteenth century to adopt the principle of segregating classes; to foster a policy that allowed the tenant occupier to grasp his holding, and too often in selfishly seeking to extend its boundaries, rid himself of all trammels of "good neighbourhood" by pushing the manual tiller of the soil off the manor altogether, even as a cottar occupier.

In the records of a Garioch Kirk-Session, under date 1720, I find an incidental illustration of the rural economy then in operation. Certain neighbours were "delated" to appear before the Session for "breach and prophanation of the Sabbath, by beating and blooding on ane other." A principal in the "scandal," on being interrogated, declared that "he had neither beat nor bled any person;" but that the two sons of his neighbour, who was "possessor of *one of the ploughs* of Twadam, had that Sabbath morning singled by their father's cattle from the cattle of the other *three ploughs*, and brought them from the common fold, thorow the midest of his corns, to feed them in places where no cattle were wont to graze; and that all the cattle of the other three ploughs had broke the fold to come after them;" whereupon he interposed. Thus far the two sides substantially agreed. A divergence of testimony occurred concerning the precise intentions of the first narrator in the scuffle that ensued between him and one of the young men for possession of a cudgel carried by the latter, he averring that his single object was to "turn the cattle from among his corns," while the two brothers, who had severely pommelled their assailant, asserted that it was to "strick" his opponent "withal." A couple of independent witnesses deponed to the facts, but declined to give an opinion on the merits, whereon the session found them all guilty, and appointed them to be publicly rebuked.

The noticeable point here is the four ploughs working

jointly, as we find them at any time during the four hundred and fifty years preceding 1720, and presumably also the common pasture, with the common fold, wherein each husbandman put his cattle along with cattle belonging to the others, each occupier having however his own arable rigs.

Up to a considerably later date the practice of "run rig" cultivation was pursued more or less; and for its smooth working "good neighbourhood" must certainly have been essential. It was a curious system, and gave scope for queer, and at times amusing results. A good story enough was wont to be told some sixty odd years ago, of two neighbours on a farm in the lower part of Aberdeenshire—Eastertown and Westertown let us say. Their "hyeucks" had "kempit" side by side through the hairst till only one run-rig field was left to "shear." It was gloamin, and the harvest moon beginning to peep over the eastern hills when Wastie descried a form, which he judged to be that of his pawky neighbour Eastie, passing along the head-rig on the skyline, and stooping down at every dozen paces. "Ay, an' ye wud like to hae klyock first," thought Wastie to himself as he quietly followed the trail to find that Eastie was with great pains sticking up "a bit knablick stane" at the top of every second rig, the rigs so marked being of course those that belonged to himself. With equal care he lifted each of these marks and transferred it to the next alternate rig, and then slipped leisurely home to bed to await the result next morning. It was precisely as Wastie had anticipated. At the hour appointed, Eastie's "hyeucks" had gone out to take "klyock" by the light of the moon, and so have the pleasure of accomplishing a stolen march on Wastie. They had duly shorn their "stent;" only that through the small piece of dexterous manipulation of the way marks just mentioned, daylight revealed the fact that it was Wastie who had got "klyock"—not Eastie!

CHAPTER IV.

CULTIVATION OF THE SOIL, 1700—1800—ORDINARY MODES OF CROPPING AND THE RESULTS.

An English tourist who visited Scotland in 1702, speaks thus of the general aspect of the country at that date:—" The surface was generally unenclosed ; oats and barley the chief grain products ; wheat little cultivated; little hay made for winter, the horses then feeding chiefly on straw and oats." " The people of the Lowlands partly depended on the Highlands for cattle to eat, and the Highlanders, in turn, carried back corn, of which their own country did not grow a sufficiency."

In even the best cultivated parts of the south of Scotland, "the arable land ran in narrow slips," with " stony wastes between, like the moraines of a glacier." " The scanty manure was conveyed to the field by manual labour ; and the unpleasant scene has often been attested by English travellers, of the crofter's wife carrying the unseemly burden on her back." " The hay meadow was a marsh where rank natural grasses grew, mixed with rushes and other aquatic plants ; and the sour wet ground not only remained undrained, but was deemed peculiarly valuable from the abundance with which it yielded this coarse fodder." * It has been averred that "nine-tenths of

---

* The natural meadows of this country may be all comprehended under the denomination of swamps and morasses, of which there are specimens in almost every farm. Formerly these produced the only hay in the country, and they are still, almost exclusively, applied to the same purpose. It was from hay of this kind that

the corn produced in the country was raised within five miles of the coast." This may probably be accepted as rather a loose statement, yet cultivation was mainly confined to the lands that lay along the courses of rivers and streams, while in the interior wide areas of unbroken waste land prevailed extensively. It was not till near the end of last century that blackfaced sheep were introduced into the Highlands. The only use previously made of the hill pasture, apart from feeding wild animals, was to feed the small black cattle sent thither during the summer months.

A precise and detailed account of the modes of tillage practised in the north of Scotland toward the close of the seventeenth century occurs in a letter written by Alexander Garden of Troup, and the date of which is 1683.* Mr. Garden, in describing the usual course of husbandry, says—" The husbandman keeps in some of his ground constantly under corne and bear, dunging it every thrie years, and, for his pains, if he reap the fourth corne he is satisfied." That is to say, if he has four returns of the seed sown he is satisfied. This, Mr. Garden informs us, was the "intown." "Our outfields," he says, "when they have been grass four or five years, are plowed up, and letting them lie a summer thus ploughed, we plow them over again, and sow them the next spring; and in our best outfields if we reap the fourth or fifth corn the first year we are satisfied. Yea, the third is very well thought off." Then he tells us that they took at least three corn crops in succession off the outfield, and if the cattle had been folded upon it before being

---

the Duke of Cumberland's cavalry were supplied in 1746, when in Aberdeen, on his march to the north, in pursuit of the rebel army. Even this miserable forage was not obtained without much labour; part of it being furnished from the swamps among the woods of Fetteresso, at the distance of 16 miles, by, at that time, a very bad road.—*General View of the Agriculture of Kincardineshire; by George Robertson.* 1807.

* *Spalding Club* Collections in the shires of Aberdeen and Banff.

broken up it was considered fit to carry another crop before it required to lie in grass again. The laying out in grass consisted, of course, of merely letting the land alone without ploughing or sowing in a corn crop, till the surface grew green with whatever species of weeds were indigenous to the soil. A specific description, applicable to a somewhat later date, sets forth that when the "outfields" would no longer pay for seed and labour, "they were then allowed to remain in a state of absolute sterility, producing little else than thistles and other weeds, till, after having been rested in this state for some years, the farmer thought proper to bring them again under cultivation, when, from the mode of management before described, a few scanty crops were obtained."

Before adverting to individual views of agricultural improvement, as held by persons taking a prominent interest in the subject, a brief glance at the general state of cultivation during the century may be taken. And it is a curious illustration of the slow rate of progress in those days to find that when the close of the eighteenth century was almost come, though not a few energetic improvers had arisen and set a better example, exactly the same modes of tillage were in almost universal use over a great part of the country, as at the beginning of that century. Of this we have abundant evidence in the pages of the *Old Statistical Account of Scotland*, begun to be published in 1791, and actually completed in 1798, in twenty volumes, through the heroic perseverance of Sir John Sinclair, by whom it was originated, and its publication superintended, the reports for the several parishes being drawn up chiefly by the ministers. The detailed testimony of one of these witnesses may be accepted as nearly sufficient ; and we take the statement of the minister of Alford, in Aberdeenshire, who is very definite and copious. Writing in 1795, he says :—
" The infield or intown lands are constantly in white

crops, unless where the farm has very little or very bad pasture, and then, perhaps, a ridge or two is left untilled, to throw up the weeds which ages have nourished in it to maintain the farmer's cattle. One third of it is manured regularly with all the dung of one year's gathering; and thus, in three years, all the infield on a farm has been once dunged." This, it will be observed, is precisely the practice that was followed a hundred years earlier, as detailed by the Laird of Troup. The writer goes on to state that "the infield land is generally an excellent soil, full of manure, but stocked with destructive weeds, of which wild oats and knot-grass are among the worst. The average produce in tolerable seasons will not," he says, "exceed from 4 to 5 bolls per acre." In regard to the management of outfield land, the "most proper way," we are told, was to have it divided into eleven parts which were folded upon in succession. The cropping is thus described :—" In spring oats are sown, and as soon as the crop is off the ground, it is again ploughed for a second, and so on until it has borne five successive crops of oats; and then it is left five years lea to throw up whatever poor grass such worn out soil will produce. The first two years the grass is as bad as possible, and though during the other three it thickens, yet, even at the best, it gives but a scanty bite to the cattle." As to the grain produce of the outfields, it is said " the first three crops are nearly alike, and will rarely run beyond four bolls per acre on an average; and for the last two years they dwindle down to betwixt two and three, and often less. The produce of the untoathed fields is much inferior in quantity as well as quality; and, indeed, the return from faughs in grain will seldom defray the expense of labour and seed; and the farmers are tempted to plough them though it is to their own loss, merely for the sake of the small quantity of straw which they yield."

Another of the Old Statistical writers speaking of

outfield tillage, says, after the land had grown the *sixth* grain crop in succession, " it was seldom before the fourth year that it got a green surface." The minister of Birse speaks of some portions of the ground having been cropped continuously, with an occasional dunging, without having been allowed " any rest for a century." The minister of a Buchan parish says :—" A rotation of crops is not yet established in this district. While the heritor only plows where he cannot get grass to grow any longer, the tenant sometimes plows as long as corn of any kind will grow." Another minister, who had made some inquiry on the subject, got this statement from one farmer—" On my farm there was a field of four acres which, for twenty-five years during my residence there, yielded alternately full crops of grain, viz., beans, peas, and oats, without any manure. I have reason to think my predecessor for five or seven years employed it in the same manner." This rare field always grew a conspicuously rich crop however ; but " another farmer candidly told me," says the writer, " that from twelve bolls of oats which he sowed last crop, there was only produced twenty bolls ; and of crop 1793 he had not three returns."

Samples of fields which had grown ten, fifteen, or twenty grain crops in succession with little or no manuring were not confined to a single district, nor to a single county ; for we hear of them in Banff and Kincardineshires, as well as in Aberdeenshire, toward the close of the century. It was in the first named county, and in the parish of Alvah, that fields to which lime had been applied, were reckoned fit to yield from twelve to nineteen crops of oats in succession. And it was to Kincardineshire the old school farmer belonged, who, on being complimented on the good appearance of his crop, said—" It's nae marvel, for it's only the auchteent crap sin' it gat gweedin' (dunging)." In some of the old leases, it was formally stipulated that " there shall not be more than *five* crops of oats in succession."

CHAPTER V.

FIRST IMPROVERS—A SMALL SOCIETY OF FARMERS IN BUCHAN—AN EARLY AGRICULTURAL ESSAY.

IT is believed the very first person to introduce agricultural improvements effectively into the north of Scotland was an English lady—Elizabeth Mordaunt —who was married to the eldest son of the Duke of Gordon in 1706, the year before the Union. She was a daughter of the Earl of Peterborough, himself a great improver, and she brought down to the Duke of Gordon's estates " English ploughs, with men to work them, and who were acquainted with fallowing—heretofore utterly unknown in Scotland." She taught the Morayshire people how to make hay, and set them the example of planting moors and sowing foreign grasses. About ten years later the Earl of Haddington began to plant extensively, and introduced other improvements, including sowing clover and other grass seeds. Nearly contemporaneous with him was Sir Archibald Grant, second baronet of Monymusk, who writes— " Soon after the Union, husbandry and manufactures were in low esteem. Turnips raised in fields for cattle by the Earl of Rothes, and very few others, were wondered at. Wheat was almost confined to East Lothian. Enclosures were few and planting very little ; no repair of roads, all bad, and very few wheel carriages."

On July 13th, in the year 1723, there was instituted " the Society of Improvers in the Knowledge of Agriculture in Scotland." Its membership included 42 peers and 260 commoners, of whom 4 peers and

25 commoners belonged to Aberdeenshire. This society, which assumed the character of a national institution, published its transactions occasionally for the information of its members. Only seven years later a local society was established, which embraced in its membership a good many names of note, such as those of Alexander Lord Pitsligo, the Hon. Alexander Fraser of Strichen, one of the senators of the College of Justice; Sir James Elphinstone of Logie; James Ferguson of Pitfour; Alexander Garden of Troup; James Gordon of Ellon; Ernest Lesley of Balquhain; George Skene of Skene; and William Urquhart of Meldrum. The title they appear to have assumed was that of " A small Society of Farmers in Buchan," and an Essay published by them in 1735, which presents in good set terms their notions concerning the main points of practical husbandry, is somewhat of a curiosity in its way, were it only for the graphic picture it gives of the difficulties the farmer had to struggle with in keeping down weeds when he had not the advantage of green crops to clean the land, but grew cereals year after year. The Essay extends to ten separate Articles, treating of the different crops, and the appropriate cultivation; and varieties of soil, each article being subdivided into several Rules. In their modest preface the authors say that the essay " contains nothing purely speculative, but a plain and genuine relation of our practice, as we have learned from tradition, and our own repeated experience, put into method to ease our memories, and for the instruction of beginners."

These worthy men were thus content scrupulously to adhere to the modes of farming they had learnt by " tradition"; and in place of hunting after novelty or change in the way of alleged improvement, they only sought to stereotype established practice, and put on record well-proved methods for their own convenience and the behoof of posterity. The land, they go on to say, was divided, in the common course of husbandry, into "bear land, bear root, and awal bear root." They first give rules for the ploughing of the bear land; a "break" followed by a "clean furrow;" the latter, which covered in the dung, being given as late as possible—at the end of April or beginning of May—in order to prevent that growth which "infallibly disheartens the field for corn, when it gets footing by ploughing bear land early." The "growth" here spoken of, in other words, the weeds in the land, formed evidently a serious matter of consideration. And thus, while the farmer is advised to sow immediately after the last furrow, he is also advised to let the newly-sown field lie at first half harrowed, and then cross-harrow it when the seed has begun to take root; for, say the essayists, when the weeds—"yarrs, skellachs, gules, and others"—begin to spring, "it will be fit to crush them with the harrow." "After the brier blade falls, the corn makes no progress till the stock be formed; the weeds taking advantage of this delay, advance with incredible celerity, and unless they be crushed at this juncture they soon overtop the brier, and maintain their victory till they render the corn both thin and feeble; but a judicious management of the harrow will set back the weeds and give the brier, which in that season naturally grows up very quickly, the advantage over them, and having again recovered the former loss, it will preserve its distance to the end."

Harrowing down weeds among the briard, then, is strongly recommended; and "because they cannot be suppressed at once, they ought to be torn up as oft as they appear until the brier begin to recover after stocking." No method yet tried had proved so effectual with the weeds as this of tearing them up with iron-tined harrows; "and," say the essayists, "if any one apprehends loss by the harrowing his brier, we do assure him that that scruple is contrary to experience, several of our own number having followed the above directions with great success."

Thus far of harrowing down weeds among the springing corn. But even the free use of the harrow among the briard was not quite enough at all times. Of course it was when it came to the *awal*, or second crop after bear, that the contest between the crop and the weeds for possession of the ground became most serious. And then, evidently, it not unfrequently assumed the form of something very like a life-and-death struggle; became a question, in short, whether the weeds, with which the land was so densely stocked, or the corn was to be the predominant crop. The roots of the weeds " being turned deeper down in ploughing" formed one reason why the bear-root crop " sometimes escapes their clutches. But if they miss the one, the other, to wit, the *awal*, is sure to feel the weight of their revenge." Our essayists, in speaking of the management of the *awal* crop, repeat their advice about the use of the harrow among the briard in order to check the weeds; and after observing that " it will be fit to harrow down the weeds about the time of stocking," they add, " and if, after all, the weeds happen to prevail, it may be eaten up with beasts betwixt the beginning and middle of May." A truly sage advice it may be said; yet, it was given in all sincerity. For it was the case that the knot-grass and other weeds were often so deeply rooted as to " baffle the harrow, however carefully applied." So say our authorities. And that being the case, " it is very reasonably advised to eat both weeds and briard up with beasts to bring them upon one level." And this being done, the chances were, we are assured, that the grain would in all probability " soon overtop the weeds."

The essayists give specific directions how this rather nice agricultural operation might be best performed. " The animals that are fittest to be employed in this affair," say they, "are young nolt, because they cut cleverly, without disturbing the root, whereas old or ill-toothed beasts very often pull up the brier by the roots. Horses and sheep are not so fit to be put upon this expedition, unless they be carefully kept or tethered upon the field; for, although their teeth be sharp, yet we evidently observe them to eat the corn and leave the grass untouched, which is directly contrary to the design; and this their aversion is probably raised from the roughness of grass in respect of the smooth and sweet blade of corn." "This experiment," it is added, "will no doubt much offend the timorous and unthinking part of mankind; however, it hath often proven very beneficial both for keeping back the weeds and preventing the lying of corns before they be full."

But even after the awal crop had, by the friendly aid of the harrow and the young nolt's teeth, battled through the initiatory stages, and come off victorious over "yarrs," "skellachs," "sorrel," and all their aiders and abettors, it had yet another enemy to contend with—viz., the wild oats, which, while they did comparatively little harm among the two former crops, in the awal, we are told, "do very notable mischief to their neighbour corn; for the wild grows up much faster, and ripens much sooner than the tame, and thereby exhausts the nutriment thereof. This never misses to render it both weak and thin, and therefore 'tis well worth the owner's pains to endeavour by all means to prevent this imminent danger of his corns, which will in a great measure be done by cropping the wild oats how soon they come out of the hose, who appear always about eight days before the tame. Thus is Providence so kind as to tack that to their nature which is the mean of their own destruction. Any one that is careful may perform this work, with the hook in one hand, and grasp the crops with the other, which will be good entertainment for cows; or, if he hath no mind to take the trouble to preserve them, let him fix a sharp-toothed hook in the end of a small pole or hazel rod, and strike them down therewith, which is more expeditious, though less profitable." But there was a possibility that all these rules —rules which, their authors quietly insinuate, reason and experience alike recommend—might fail of the desired end; and such contingency was not left out of view. For, it is added, "If a field be so backward that it does not answer by following the foregoing rules, it will be fit to lay it down in grass until it contract a body, which will take five years to ly."

It were scarcely profitable to follow the essayists through the detailed rules for tillage applicable to infield and out-field, and the method of toth-folding, and so on. For the bear crop we note that "Ebb tilling is recommended to retain the dung as near the seed as possible, and the remainder of the mold is to ly in the meantime to contract a body." For the first crop after bear, "Let it be ploughed with competent sap both deep and tight"—the "two good reasons" for the deep furrow being "to bury the grass roots," and "that the rested mold which lay idle underneath last year may appear to act its part." Indeed, the Society, in the case of out-field, at least, seem to have had some vague kind of notion that each succeeding furrow should go a little deeper than the one given the previous year, till, as they say, "the pan" were reached. The "fauch" is justly declared to be "in all respects inferior to dung, seeing it adds no benefit to the soil for the future, but only extorts, as it were, by violence whatever productive qualities Providence has bestowed upon it." And then they lay down one or two general principles which we may carry along with us; thus:—"If we look into the common way of managing husbandry, especially in those parts where nature has been less liberal of her favours, we will have just reason to reprove the inadvertancy of some in bestowing their labour without any prospect of an adequate return, and condemn the inhuman practice of others for wounding so unmercifully the sides of our common mother earth, without ever offering any medicine. There is no excuse can be made to alleviate the severity of this censure, except it be the prevailing humour of landlords in exacting what they possibly can of their dependants, and they, as the phrase is, must put at the rigs. However, it were a far more equal way for masters to allow their fellow-creatures a reasonable subsistence, their lands, in the meantime being improven, as well as greater justice done to their own children, to succeed to a thriving tenantry and well-managed ground. This would be a sure way to raise a more plentiful fortune, and transmit their memory with more honour to posterity, than the heaping up a store of money by those means that have such an affinity to extortion, and seldom enrich the third heir."

One fancies that in these latter sentiments he hears the voice of some nineteenth century radical, rather than that of the aristocratic members of the small society of Buchan farmers of a hundred and forty years ago.

We take a step onward and listen to the advice obtained in a particular case by an ardent improver. About the year 1757, Sir Archibald Grant had addressed a set of queries to the hon. the "Society of Improvers in the Knowledge of Agriculture in Scotland," concerning the most advantageous way of managing a field of sixteen acres, said to be "of good black soil," "abundantly dry, or can easily be made so." It had produced clover and ryegrass for three years, but could not be longer pastured. The advice Sir Archibald receives for the treatment of the field—and it is given in the month of January—is to plough with all convenient speed, "that it may have got three furs betwixt and the latter end of April or beginning of May." Pease were then to be sown, the object being to manure the field, and when they came to be in full bloom, they were to be pressed flat to the ground with a roller, or in absence of such an implement, with harrows thrown upon their backs, or "an old door may be used." The land was then to be twice ploughed, and sown out with twelve pounds of clover and two bushels of ryegrass seeds to an acre.

CHAPTER VI.

IMPLEMENTS OF THE FARM—THE TWAL OWSEN PLOUGH—THE SOAM AND TEAM—WOODEN HARROWS AND FIR TETHERS—CURRACHS — THE BOBBIN JOHN.

IN exhibiting the advanced state of Scottish agriculture at the present day, as compared with the agriculture of last century, one could scarcely find a readier or more effective method of illustration than that of contrasting the implements of the farm then and now. Alongside the two horse swing plough, fashioned of iron, and marked by accurate proportion of parts, and absolutely artistic finish in the workmanship, we should have to place the large uncouth wooden implement, devised for the draught of eight, ten, or twelve oxen; with "beam" so disproportionately long, and "stilts" so relatively short, that collision with some big "earth-fast" stone in the opening furrow, really threatened, at times, to throw the hapless ploughman's heels, if not against the seven stars—as a local Munchausen averred, had once happened at the cost of nearly obliterating one of their number from the firmament—certainly, to an elevation, at least equal to that of his head. Against the steam threshing machine, with its complete dressing apparatus, there would stand the primitive flail; and the equally primitive hand riddle and "wecht," for use in winnowing the corn between the open barn doors by the natural wind of heaven; and so on through the remaining implements of the farm.

Concerning the twelve oxen plough, Dr. James Anderson, (of whom some particulars are given further on) says:—" The plough itself is beyond description bad; and it is of so little consequence to perpetuate the memory of what can never be imitated elsewhere, that I shall omit the description of it. I shall only observe that it makes rather a triangular rut in the ground than a furrow, leaving the soil for the most part equally fast on both sides of it, so that if all the loosened earth were stripped from a plowed field, it would remain nearly in this form ∧∧∧∧∧ only, it would sometimes happen that a gap would be made in these protuberances." Yet, rude as the plough was and imperfect its equipments, under the steady persevering pull of the team of great sinewy oxen of six or seven years old, so long as it could be kept in the ground, it made a large if unshapely furrow, turning over or pushing aside a mass of soft earth, and clearing away obstacles, such as "earth fast" stones that stood in the way, aye and until the soam broke or other part of the gearing gave way.

The plough wright, when his services were needed, went to the farm, and if he was an early riser, and his wood looked out beforehand, would contrive to build a plough in sufficient time for the ploughman and "gaudman" to take their team a-field. The implement he had to construct was hardly more elaborate, though it may be safely believed a good deal clumsier, than that which had been used by the Israelites when they dwelt in the Land of Canaan. And certainly it was much inferior in design and material to the plough of the ancient Romans, described by Pliny, as in use in his time. The tools the plough-wright used were a saw, an axe, an adze, and a large forming iron and wimble. The only parts made of iron were the coulter and "sock;" and the "cheek-rack" or bridle (if such there were). The mould board was of wood, and the frame was kept together chiefly by sturdy wooden pins. An expert wright could make three ploughs in a day, working diligently; and he was paid eightpence to a shilling for each. For wood and workmanship, the plough seldom cost above four shillings; and the iron furnishings did not exceed that amount, so that the total outlay for a completed implement was under ten shillings.

It was not till the century was pretty well advanced, that iron-tined harrows came to be commonly used. The tines or teeth, as well as the frame work, were of wood: and while oxen were used for the plough, the harrowing was done by horses, as were the carriages needed in connection with the farm. When improving lairds endeavoured to reform the style of the ploughs, and the method of ploughing, they were met by two obstacles. One was "want of experience among country servants in the management of horses;" the other the fact that the wrights and smiths, in place of adequately imitating the improved ploughs put before them—as those of James Small, the father of the swing plough, on the basis of which others have improved so much—invariably continued to bring them nearer and nearer to their own defective models. And it was with a view to overcome such obstacles that in some cases, along with Small's ploughs, expert ploughmen were also brought from East Lothian to Aberdeenshire, to set an example in working them.

The extinction as an operative agency of the old plough, with its team of ten or twelve oxen, was quite gradual. In 1770, it was still in all but universal use; twenty years thereafter it had to a certain extent given place to a better fashioned implement and a lighter team, the first modifications of the team being to four pairs of oxen and one pair of horses pulling together, the horses being next to the plough; then to two pairs of horses in a team, and so on. In Cromar, the Garioch, and other districts of Aberdeenshire, the "twal owsen" plough was pretty common so late as 1792; and in exceptional cases it was in use a few years after the commencement of the present century. The late Dr. Cruickshank, of Marischal College, Aberdeen, remembered seeing such a plough at work in the parish of Culsalmond, so late as the autumn of 1807; and it did not go finally out of use in this part of the country till about 1815 or 1816.

A specimen of this cumbrous implement used after 1784, by Mr. Stephen, tenant of Millden, Belhelvie, was exhibited at the Aberdeen Show of the Highland Society in 1858, when its uncouth appearance made it an object of great interest and curiosity to those of the living generation of farmers and ploughmen who were present to inspect it. It was thereafter presented to the authorities of Marischal College by its possessor, Mr. Craighead, presumably for preservation in the Museum. No particular care would seem to have been bestowed on the interesting relic (the only remaining specimen of this particular kind of plough so far as we are aware), until sometime ago it was found to be literally crumbling into dust, and past all hope of staying the progress of decay.

The draught equipment was as primitive as the plough itself. The "soam" already spoken of—an iron chain, fastened to the cheek-rack, or to a simple staple fixed in the beam on the right hand side some distance from the point—ran along between the pairs of oxen all the way to the "fore yoke."* A yoke lay across the necks of each pair of oxen; and a "bow," consisting of a piece of ash, birch, or willow, bent to the proper shape, surrounded every separate ox's neck. The points of the bows were stuck upward through

---

* The names of the six pairs of oxen as fully given in Dr. Pratt's *Buchan*, with illustrative diagram, were—foremost pair, on wyner, and wyner; second do. on-steer draught, and steer-draught; 3d do. fore-throck on land and fore-throck in fur; 4th do. mid-throck on land and mid-throck in fur; 5th do. hind-throck on land, and hind-throck in fur; 6th pair, fit on land, and fit in fur.

the yoke, and securely pinned in that position. A "brecham," or pad of dried "sprots," rushes, straw, or strips "tyave" of moss fir roots, intervened between the neck of the ox and the bow, to prevent friction in the draught. The more important animals in the team were the "fit owsen" and the "wyners." Connected with the yoke of the former pair, which, of course, were nearest the plough, was a short series of elongated links, or staffs, for raising or lowering the "soam" according as more or less "yird" was required by the ploughman. And a "fit o' lan'" ox was not considered fully trained in his function till he had learnt to lower his neck when the ploughman cried "jouk," at such times as he wanted the plough to go a little deeper for the moment. The wyners again occupied an important position, in so far as the turning of the unwieldy team on a moderate width of end-rig depended on their easing the draught off gradually and featly. And then, as the young oxen were always trained in the steer draught immediately behind them, it depended chiefly upon the trustworthiness of the veteran wyners that these juniors should be kept steady, and prevented running into untimeous and uncanny escapades, even to the extent of breaking their harness at times, and scampering off from the draught altogether.

A tolerably vivid idea of the harnessing and draught equipments of the time will be obtained, when it is kept in mind that, apart from the plough soam, there was no iron chain ordinarily in use. The "theets," or traces, used in harrowing, were made either of dried "sprots" or rushes, or of twisted fir roots—hempen rope being a little-known commodity. Thin "splits" of fir taken off logs that had been dug up in mosses and twisted into a sort of rope, because they stood wet well without rotting, were "preferred above all others for tethering horses in the field," as well as for draught purposes. "These ropes of a proper length," we are told, were "sold ready made under the name of fir tethers"; and, it is added, "when no longer fit to be used as a tether, they are employed as candle fir." For tethering purposes there was also the home made hair rope, the materials of which were supplied from the tails of the cattle.

It is not to be supposed that either the fir or "rashen" traces were capable of sustaining very great tension; and they were the less severely tried from the fact that the horses were small, potbellied, ill-fed, and consequently rather pithless animals. One is not so sure about even the soam, by which the whole eight, ten, or twelve oxen hung on. At any rate the story told of a certain smith, would seem to indicate that his notion of the strain which the welded links ought to be capable of bearing, had not been very enlarged. He had just mended a break in the soam from the Mains farm, and the "herd loon" took his way home therewith from the smiddy. Tired of other modes of conveying his rather onerous burden, the herd took to dragging it after him, when, unluckily the soam snapped again. On being told of this fresh disaster, and discovering the ordeal to which the soam had been subjected by the herd, the smith exclaimed —"Sorra set ye laddie, fat need ye 'a trail't it!"

The style of work accomplished by the great wooden plough has been already spoken of. The furrow opened was large and uncouth; and in their wide way of talking, the old fellows spoke of the ploughman occasionally turning down a refractory bit, which the rude mould board had failed to lay over "wi' the tap o's shooder." The "rigs" they made were crooked like an elongated S; and from the practice of "feering" always in the crown of the rig and "gathering" to the same point, the tendency was to pile up the ploughed land in a series of long narrow mounds. And thus it was that when the principle of straight furrows, and level rigs began to have place, the laird of Rothney, in Insch, endeavoured to persuade his ploughman to adopt the new mode, only to find him impervious to reasoning and obstinately determined on adhering to his old practice. At this the laird lost temper and turned away with the exclamation, "Augh min! It's been some confoun'it idiot like you 't's cairn't up the hill o' Dunnydeer there!"

The ordinary carriages of the farm were accomplished by means of "currachs" or creels of wicker work —hung from a "crook saddle"—one on each side of the horse. Dung was carried from the farmyard in these, and in harvest they bore home the sheaves to the stackyard. In loading it was needful to fill the two currachs simultaneously to keep them balanced. When one man filled more promptly than his fellow of any heavy material, he gained an advantage in depressing his own creel and correspondingly elevating that on the other side of the horse. Hence the phrase "coupin' the creels" upon one, came to be a sort of "byeword," which has hardly yet died out in certain localities. When corn or meal had to be taken to or from the mill, or conveyed away for sale, a sack or "lade" was put across each horse's back, and the animals followed one another in single file, the "halter tow" of the second horse tied to the tail of the first; and so on: a mode of transport that was still in use in the remoter parts of Aberdeen and Banffshires at the end of last century, as many as a dozen horses being occasionally to be seen following in single file, each bearing its lade. It was not that wheeled conveyances were utterly unknown. Carts and wheelbarrows too had been invented long before. But the cart was a clumsy vehicle indeed. It was made entirely of wood, including the axle-tree. As in the case of the plough, no plane was used to smoothe the surface of the wood in any part. In the "tumbling cart," in place of the wheels turning round on the axle, the axle-tree itself turned round. There were no iron bushes in the naves of the wheels, and as no grease was used the movement of the cart was apt to be accompanied by a noise more shrill than pleasant.

But the state of the roads, or rather the absence of "roads before they were made" did not favour wheeled conveyances. Up to fully the date of "the Forty-five" one or two carts in a parish would seem to have been all that existed. Toward the close of the century they had become much more abundant over the country, though, as just indicated, the currach still held its place to a moderate extent. The minister of New Deer (*Old Stat. Ac.*) says "when the present incumbent was settled, in 1737, there was not a cart but his own in the parish; nor were there roads which could be travelled in many places. Then, and for many years after, there was but one carrier who went weekly to Aberdeen with a horse and packets; sometimes he even went with nothing but a back creel, and brought what merchandise and provision were at the time necessary. Now (1793), there is sufficient employment for three or four carriers, who go each with a cart and two horses." Similar statements are made by various others. Two-wheeled carts became common in most lowland districts during the last quarter of the eighteenth century.

Of the primitive character of the farm implements generally, near the close of the eighteenth century, an incidental illustration may be given from the pages of a witness already cited. Dr. James Anderson, who was a keen improver and reformer of old things generally, credits his patron, Mr. Udny of Udny, with a useful invention in implements. That gentleman, who filled the office of a commissioner of excise, was an earnest agricultural improver. He was an early and successful cultivator of the turnip, and his invention was an improved sower—cost eightpence to a shilling. It was a perforated tin box with a wooden handle—neither more nor less than a "Bobbin' John," which was carried along in the hand over the drill top and shaken to throw out the seed. Its capabilities as a sower are strongly lauded by Dr. Anderson, by whom it is averred that many hundreds of persons who could neither have purchased nor used a fine apparatus, had, by the possession of it, been induced to enter keenly into the cultivation of turnips. And he held that; " To induce such persons to go forward on a small scale is an object of much greater consequence than to have kings and princes, and the great men of the earth, displaying with a pompous parade a complicated apparatus which would prove the ruin of a poor man to attempt to purchase." And so, when the century was near its close, an implement like the ordinary turnip sower for horse haulage, had evidently been regarded, even by men of advanced ideas, as rather an elaborate piece of mechanism.

CHAPTER VII.

RESULTS OF CULTIVATION—PERIODS OF FAMINE—KING WILLIAM'S DEAR YEARS—PICTURES OF THE TIME BY PATRICK WALKER AND FLETCHER OF SALTOUN—EFFECTS OF FAMINE IN THE NORTH—LANDS DESOLATED.

WHEN we keep fully in view the prevailing system of tillage and the implements with which the work was accomplished, it is not difficult to understand how the results in the way of produce must often enough have been sufficiently poor to be some way short of satisfactory to the tiller. The difficulty rather is to understand how the soil in certain cases could have been kept under tillage on any terms. We have already seen something of the struggle that went on between the arable farmer and the indigenous "growth" that sought to re-assert its right to the possession of the soil; and it was undoubtedly creditable to the sheer hardihood of our forefathers that they did not oftener than actually happened give way before the perversity of those less fertile parts of the stubborn glebe that yet owned their full share of the effects of the primeval curse, and allow the land to run again into a state of nature. In ordinary times the products of cultivation in the form of crops raised and reaped for the sustenance of man and beast were frequently but meagre. It is, however, when we look at what we find recorded regarding seasons of dearth, or absolute famine, from failure of the crops, or their destruction through inclement weather, that we most readily obtain a distinct picture of the harder conditions of life in what has been occasionally spoken of as "the good old times."

The concluding seven years of the seventeenth century (1693-1700) were years of dearth over the greater part of Scotland, though some of the northern districts suffered earlier and more severely than many other parts of the country. The pinch of famine had begun to be felt in various parts of Aberdeenshire and Banffshire, in 1693, while it was not till 1695 that the crop in certain of the southern and western counties was "stricken in one night" by an easterly fog, "and gat little more good of the ground." These were "King William's dear years." In accordance with the fiscal system of the time, an Act had been passed in 1672 forbidding the importation of meal while the price in Scotland remained below a certain rate. And an order of Council had actually been issued for "staving" grain, unlawfully brought from Carrickfergus in two vessels in 1695; the vessels themselves to be handed over to the person—Sir Duncan Campbell of Auchinbreck—who had seized them on their way to a Scottish port. But now, when one season after another was only threatening the "misgiving and blasting of the present crop to the increase of that distress whereby the kingdom is already afflicted," it was found expedient to allow the importation of meal from Ireland. And not only so, for in 1698 exportation of grain was strictly prohibited; and various emphatic edicts were issued against "forestalling" and "regrating." A solemn fast was ordered on 9th March, 1699—as fasts had been appointed in some of the previous years—on account of "the lamentable stroke of dearth and scarcity;" while "King William, his kindness is not to be forgotten," offered all who would transport victual to Scotland, that they might do it custom free, and have twenty pence off each boll."

The pictures we have of the sufferings endured at

this time are very lamentable. It was represented in Edinburgh in 1696, that if extraneous supplies of victual were not speedily received in Aberdeenshire "a good part of that and the next county [Banff] will undoubtedly starve." This was in July, and George Fergusson, a generous baillie of Oldmeldrum, and a member of a family long well known in that region, with Alexander Smith, writer in Edinburgh, proposed to purchase 1000 or 1200 bolls of corn and bear, to sell to the people at a price to be fixed by the authorities, they having no desire of profit, "but allenarly the keeping of the poor in the said shire from starving." They wished their cargo protected from the risk of French privateers on its way to Aberdeen; and the Privy Council agreed to recommend their petition to that effect to the Lords of the Treasury.

"These manifold unheard-of judgments," says Patrick Walker, the Packman, "continued seven years, not always alike, but the seasons, summer and winter, so cold and barren, and the wonted heat of the sun so much withholden, that it was discernible upon the cattle, flying fowls and insects decaying, that seldom a fly or cleg was to be seen; our harvests not in the ordinary months; many shearing in November and December; yea, some in January and February; many contracting their deaths, and losing the use of their feet and hands shearing and working in frost and snow; and, after all, some of it standing still and rotting upon the ground, and much of it for little use either to man or beast, and which had no taste or colour of meal."

"Meal became so scarce," adds Patrick, "that it was sold at two shillings a peck; and many could not get it. It was not then with many, 'Where will we get siller?' but 'Where shall we get meal for siller?'" "Deaths and burials were so many and common that the living were wearied with the burying of the dead. I have seen corpses drawn on sleds. Many got neither coffin nor winding-sheet. I was one of four who carried the corpse of a young woman a mile of way, and when we came to the grave an honest poor man came and said —'You must go and help to bury my son; he has lain dead these two days; otherwise I shall be obliged to bury him in my own yard.' Many . . . did eat, but were neither satisfied nor nourished; and some of them said to me that they could mind nothing but meat, and were nothing better by it, and that they were utterly unconcerned about their souls, whether they went to heaven or hell. The nearer and sorer these plagues seized, the sadder were their effects, that took away all natural and relative affections—so that husbands had no sympathy for their wives, nor wives for their husbands: parents for their children, nor children for their parents." "These and other things" made the worthy man "doubt if ever any of Adam's race were in a more deplorable condition;" but "the crowning plague of all" was that, though many were cast down, few were humbled; there was "great murmuring, but little mourning;" "the great part turned more gospel-proof and judgment-proof."

The picture given in part, applies to the south-west of Scotland. It is singularly like that supplied by several writers of the state of things at the same period in some parts of the county of Aberdeen. Concerning the district, of which Turriff forms the centre, the misery of the people was very great— "One Thomson, wadsetter, of Hairmoss, driven from his home by want, was found dead near the shore with a piece of raw flesh in his mouth." Of sixteen families that resided on the farm of Littertie, thirteen were extinguished. On the estate of Greens, three families (the proprietor's included) only, survived. A number of farms, being entirely desolated, were converted into a sheep walk by the Erroll family, to whom they belonged. "The inhabitants of the parish in general," it is added, "were diminished by death to one-half, or, as some affirm, to one fourth." "Until the year 1709 many farms were waste." The minister of Keith-hall parish, in writing of this time, says, "many died; in particular, ten Highlanders in a neighbouring parish, that of Kemnay, so that the Kirk-Session got a bier made to carry them to the grave, not being able to afford coffins for such a number." And we read of other parts of the county being "almost depopulated" by those years of famine. In illustrating the moral effects of the prevailing physical misery, a writer already quoted says, "when the means of saving the living and of burying the dead began to fail, natural affection was in a great measure suspended. A fellow, George Allan, having carried his deceased father upon his back half way from his home to the churchyard, threw down the corpse at the door of a farmer, with these words, 'I can carry my father no farther. For God's sake bury his body; but, if you choose not to take that trouble, you may place it, if you please, on the dyke of your kailyard as a guard against the sheep.'"

It may be observed, in connection with the state of matters indicated rather than described, that while in those seven years there were some seasons "not altogether unfriendly to vegetation," and while the failure of the crops was only partial in its range, yet so miserable were the means of communication from want of roads, as well as want of wheeled vehicles, that, though the inhabitants of some districts of Aberdeenshire were comparatively well off, those in other districts were, at the very same time dying of absolute starvation. The minister of Turriff says of the inhabitants of his parish, that most of them, "reduced to misery, had neither money to purchase nor horses to carry" victual from the Formartine and Buchan district, where, we are told, "seed and bread abounded."

Andrew Fletcher of Saltoun, in describing the misery

of "the ill years," states that, in 1698, in addition to those " very meanly provided for by the Church boxes," there were in Scotland " two hundred thousand people begging from door to door." He says the number had perhaps been doubled by "the present distress," which it is likely was quite true, though his gross estimate is probably higher than the actual number. Of the general aspect of things, Fletcher says it was fitted to stir the mind with the two powerful emotions of terror and compassion—" because from unwholesome food diseases are so multiplied among the poor people, that if some course be not taken, this famine may very probably be followed by a plague." And what man was there, if he had any compassion, who would not grudge himself " every nice bit, and every delicate morsel he puts in his mouth, when he considers that so many are already dead, and so many at that minute struggling with death, not for want of bread but of grains," which he was credibly informed had been used by some families in the preceding year. The least unnecessary expenditure on household things or personal finery must, he adds, " reproach us with our barbarity, so long as people born with natural endowments, perhaps not inferior to our own, and fellow-citizens, perish for want of things absolutely necessary to life."

It throws a curious light on the legislation of the time to find that, in 1701, only a year or two after this terrible suffering from actual famine, a Government commission was issued commanding that all loads of grain which might be brought from Ireland into the west of Scotland should be staved and sunk.

The next most remarkable year of scarcity was 1740. A great frost, with " deep and untimely snow," occurred in early spring. The principal rivers in Scotland were frozen over, water mills stopped, and ships frozen in in some of the harbours. Loch Lomond was frozen over from Luss to Buchanan, so as to bear men and cattle. The Forth was frozen over above

Alloa, and there was a crust of ice even at Queensferry. The Thames in that year was covered with ice as far down as Billingsgate, and a fair was held on the ice. A bad summer followed. The inclemency of the season brought about failure in the crop and distress on the common people, leading to bread riots in Edinburgh and Leith—the populace attacking certain mills, granaries, and meal shops—and the necessity of "large contributions" "from the rich to keep the poor alive." At this time day-labourers and others in Aberdeenshire, "stout men," thankfully accepted "twopence each per day in full for their work."

A natural consequence of these years of famine was to throw agriculture backward by utterly impoverishing a large proportion of those of the tenant farmer class who had managed to escape extermination. The civil wars of the previous century had been very adverse to agriculture in Scotland; and now, in 1700, at the close of the "seven ill years," the landowners were fain to bribe tenants of substance with a yoke of oxen, or other part of the farm furnishings, to extend their holdings by leasing one or more adjoining farms that had become vacant. Sometimes they obtained tenants in sufficient number; sometimes not. And in the latter case arable areas, here and there, went again into a state of nature; to remain so for an indefinite time, as testified by traces of "baulk" and "burrel" rigs in various places not under the plough within living recollection; nor indeed in exceptional instances until this day. And of so little value was land in Aberdeenshire at the period under notice, that there were instances of "considerable tracts of corn lands being so totally abandoned as to be allowed to pass from one proprietor to another merely by a prescriptive title of occupancy for upwards of forty years without a challenge."

CHAPTER VIII.

THE BAD HARVEST OF 1782—THE ACTION TAKEN BY THE TOWN AND COUNTY OF ABERDEEN TO MEET THE FAMINE.

In 1782, the harvest was unusually late, even for a time when from imperfect cultivation and similar causes the normal period of ripening of crops was apt to be put well into the autumn. The season had been a very backward one throughout; and the harvest of that year in Aberdeenshire is said to have been the worst on record. The summer was so cold and rainy that most of the oat crop was only beginning to shoot in the end of August. Early and severe frosts came soon after, the first in the middle of September which damaged some part of the grain then in the milky stage, so as to render it unfit for seed. And again we read, that on the night of the 5th of October, "when growing oats and barley were still generally green" "a frost, armed almost with the vigour of a Greenland climate, desolated in one night the hope of the husbandman." At the end of October, when but little of the crop had been cut, a snowstorm of extraordinary severity for the season ensued. Snow lay a foot deep in many places, and the storm continued for a fortnight. After it had passed away, the crop, still green but now past hope of proper ripening, was cut as it best could be in the continued cold and wet, though portions remained uncut at 28th November. Hardly any of the crop was got carried to the stackyard in the usual way, but was first put up on the fields in small "huicks," which could not be finally "led"

The Bad Harvest of 1782.

home till December, when two weeks of dry "open" weather occurred. Of the crop generally, the statement is made that while—" the fields yielded not one-third of an ordinary crop," the oatmeal, " dark in colour, was acid and disagreeable to the taste." Neither potatoes nor turnips had yet come so prominently into use as they were destined to do : but potatoes where grown were damaged by the frost, and turnips were a very poor crop. Even the produce of the garden was, we are told, " destitute of its usual nourishment."

And the famine was not local in the narrow sense. Owing to the high price to which grain had risen in the month of November, the Scotch ports, generally, were by that time opened for importation of corn upon paying the low duties. Sir William Forbes and his fellow-bankers offered the Lord Provost of Edinburgh to advance £2000 free of interest for six months, his lordship and the Town Council having it in view " to procure a supply of corn for the advantage of the poorer sort of the community," and they having it " much at heart" " to facilitate so very useful a plan." The Lord Advocate, in whose mind " very serious apprehensions had arose relative to the supply of provisions for the lower class of the inhabitants of Scotland for the ensuing year," had previously written to the Provost suggesting the propriety of people contributing according to their means in order to keep the markets " from rising to any immoderate height." The Lord Advocate is persuaded the Lord Provost and his brethren will take the requisite steps in the matter ; and as his excuse for troubling him, requests that in case he should be absent from Scotland when any plan is in agitation, his lordship " would dispose of him to the extent of £100 " for promoting the same.

At the meeting of Aberdeen Town Council held on 8th November, the Provost represented that " the state and condition of the country was universally allowed to be alarming ; and that, notwithstanding the advanced season of the year, a very large part of the crop was in many parts still uncut down, and consequently in imminent hazard." At same time, there was " but a very small quantity of meal in town for supply of the inhabitants." The chief magistrate further stated that his Monthly Committee had thought it right to confer with some of the principal traders as to a speedy supply of meal, and a subscription had been set on foot "with considerable success." What further happened was, that the Council voted a donation of three hundred guineas out of the town's funds to aid the citizens' subscription. A " proper person," Robert Gibbons to wit, was next appointed to proceed southward to purchase grain or meal to the extent of 1000 bolls, to be got through British or foreign ports ; only it was the determination of the general meeting by which the appointment was made " that the encouragement to be given for importing grain be confined to grain imported for the sole purpose of being converted into meal."

This was in November, and as stated early in that month. By and by matters were getting more serious, and the pinch of actual famine seemed likely to be felt with some severity. On the last day of December, 1782, the famishing country people " could get no meal in Aberdeen, as the citizens were afraid of a famine, and a poor man in the district of Garioch could find none in the country the day after." In November oatmeal sold at thirteen pence to fifteen pence a peck ; at the market held on the first Friday of January, 1783, it rose to " the enormous price of twenty pence per peck." In that month the Aberdeen Bank and the Bank of Scotland offered each an advance of £3000 for twelve months, free of interest, " for the relief of the poor in both the new and old town," which advances were accepted, and no doubt largely used, as we find that by the beginning of the month of March £900 had been "given off by the magistrates" to importers of grain, and a committee of nineteen, who had been appointed for " managing and conducting the business of the subscription," were authorised to intromit with the balance yet remaining.

So early as 29th October, the Commissioners of Supply for the County of Aberdeen had met and taken into consideration the alarming state of the country from "the almost certain appearance of scarcity," and the likelihood of dearth before next harvest. And being persuaded that meal of all sorts would not only be very dear, but in many parts of the country hardly to be got at any price, it was agreed that in the circumstances it would be a great injury to the poor "to give the smallest encouragement to any practice that might make their bread still scarcer and dearer." The commissioners accordingly declared formally that they were "resolved to punish in the most exemplary manner all persons who should be convicted of privately and illegally distilling spirits from grain;" and they hoped the officers of Excise would exert themselves in discovering all transgressors of that class.

Circular letters were soon after sent out to the parish ministers, asking them to give in reports on the state and condition of the crop, "how soon the corns are got in,"a method that was followed in some of the neighbouring counties as well. At another meeting held on 6th December, it was found that answers had been received from very few of the ministers, owing, it may be, to the fact that at that date the crop in many cases had not been got in.

On the 23rd day of December, 1782, a meeting of the proprietors and principal inhabitants of Aberdeenshire was held, the Sheriff of the county, Mr. Robert Turner, being put in the chair. The expressed object of the meeting was "to take under consideration not only the present state of the country and the crop of this year, but also to consider of what may be done for the ensuing year, especially regarding the capital article of seed." The facts stated by individuals at this meeting from their own knowledge were, we are assured, "of a nature too singular to be allowed to fall into oblivion. At that time it appeared that great quantities of corn in many parts of the country were still to cut down. Some gentlemen who lived in the best parts of the county gave it as their opinion that a boll of the best oats might give about half a boll of meal." But others, "especially in the higher parts of the county" were of opinion that "it would require three bolls of the best oats to give one boll of meal ; and many instances were produced where it had not yielded one-fourth of that proportion. From about thirty trials in the lands of Mounie, which is one of the earliest places in the Garioch, it was found to require three bolls of oats to give one boll of meal on an average."

It was computed, in short, that from lateness, bad weather, destruction by rooks, heating, and other casualties, one-fourth of the crop was lost before it could be got in, and that between waste and actual deficiency little more than one-fifth of the usual quantity could be used for meal.

The computation made was, that while in an ordinary year each 100 bolls of grain grown might be reckoned in this way :—25 bolls for seed, and 75 bolls for as many bolls of meal ; each hundred bolls of crop 1782, must be reckoned thus—30 bolls for seed and 25 bolls for waste, leaving 45 bolls, which would average only $18\frac{1}{2}$ bolls of meal. The inhabitants of the county were computed at 131,000, and the calculated allowance of oatmeal to these was 300,000 bolls. "It was admitted that the county used to supply its whole inhabitants with corn in an ordinary year, and no more, as it appeared from the Custom-house books, that the exports and imports, including transportation coastwise in both cases, were nearly equal on an average of years." Instead of 300,000 bolls, the data submitted showed only 79,000, say 80,000 bolls, making a deficiency of 220,000 bolls. The crops in the southern parts of the island had not suffered nearly so much; and hence flour imported from England became comparatively so plentiful in Aberdeen as to be cheaper than oatmeal; one result of which was that the Governors of Robert Gordon's Hospital ordered coarse flour to be used in that Institution instead of oatmeal.

To meet a deficiency of the character indicated was no slight matter. A somewhat sanguine narrator of the occurrences of the time (Dr James Anderson) speaks of the "unanimous resolution" of the meeting of proprietors and principal inhabitants, that "all ranks" should abstain from malting bear. The usual annual yield of that grain, we are told, was estimated at 80,000 bolls. Half of this, it was thought, could be made into meal, yielding say 60,000 bolls. The estimated "saving in consequence of scarcity" (in other words, the depth of the hunger bite) was put at 35,000 bolls; accelerating next harvest by early sowing, "and mealing it as soon as possible," might, it was thought, be equal to 25,000 bolls; and, as the past harvest, by its lateness, had shortened the period of waiting, a favourable season, with very prompt resort to early potatoes, might give another gain of a month, or say 25,000 bolls. This would leave the actual deficiency in the meal supply of the county at 75,000 bolls. And this estimate, it is added, was pretty near the actual state of the case. The total importation was about 80,000 bolls.

The sentiments of the County Meeting found ostensible expression in a minute remarkable for its unusual length and the copiousness of its style.* It sets forth that in order to prevent the inhabitants from experiencing a total want of food before another crop can be brought to maturity, it is a matter of necessity "that every individual shall observe the most frugal economy in regard to provisions; that the smallest article which

---

* If a guess might be hazarded on the point, the internal evidence would seem to indicate that this minute had been drafted by Dr. James Anderson.

can be employed as the food of man be not on any
occasion applied to other uses, or lost through neglect
or inattention." And in the way of practical enforce-
ment, it is argued that " with this view, all dogs, unless
those of great use and value, should be instantly put to
death. At a time like the present, when the whole
produce of the country is not sufficient to sustain the
life of the inhabitants themselves, it must," says the
minute, " be deemed a heinous crime to suffer any part
of that food to be consumed by vile animals. Those
who must have useful dogs, and those of higher rank
who can afford to keep dogs of value, ought to procure
from abroad as much grain at least as would serve to
sustain them till a new crop can be brought to market.
Persons in lower circumstances who, regardless of the
duties they owe to themselves and society, persist in
keeping these animals, should be accounted enemies of
mankind. They cannot in justice lay claim to the
sympathising benevolence of their fellow-creatures, and
their dogs ought to be destroyed by order of the civil
magistrates and Justices of the Peace."

For the like reasons it was thought right that no
corn that could be converted into meal should be given
to horses. "Good hay and straw, with whins, where
these can be had, will sustain, during the winter season,
horses which are moderately worked. And in regard
to chaise horses, which at present too much abound, it
is believed the necessity of the times will greatly
diminish their employment; and it is hoped that those
who, through disease or otherwise, are under the
necessity of employing them, will permit them to be so
gently driven as not to hurt them, though greatly
stinted in their usual allowance of corn." It was
strongly urged that people should refuse to sell for
horse corn what was fit to be made into oatmeal. Innkeepers might get a supply from abroad; and it
behoved them to devise the means of so obtaining it.

One of the numerous "resolves," and which bears on

the question of malting bear, already spoken of, seems rather in the nature of a simple recommendation. It runs thus:—" To show an example of moderation in the use of the necessaries of life to those of inferior degree, it will be highly commendable, in all gentlemen and others, not only to give over entirely for a time the use of home-made spirits, but also, in as far as health permits, to abstain from the use of malt liquors of every kind that shall be brewed from grain in this country, and also prohibit their servants from using it as drink, permitting no malt liquor in their families but merely as *kitchen* (that is as a nourishing and palatable addition) to bread or other dry food where milk cannot be had; and in that case to allow no more at each meal than shall appear to be indispensably necessary." Following on this other provident and precautionary measures were suggested. Gentlemen were recommended to make exact survey of " all the corns" on their respective estates, to ascertain what stacks contained stuff in a state sufficient for seed, and have these "marked off and appropriated to that purpose alone;" to promote the sowing of bear in place of oats as coming earlier to harvest; and, in particular, that a subscription should be opened to import early potatoes for seed, " especially the early Henley," which, it seems came two months sooner to maturity than the other varieties. And as early Dutch turnips came "into eating in May and June," these would be found highly useful. Moreover, " the meal of the present crop, on account of its bad quality, will, with too much certainty, subject those who must live entirely upon it to various disorders; and nothing it has been said, proves more efficacious to remove this species of disorder than turnip." To all this is added the recommendation that, to render next crop as abundant as might be, farmers should prepare only the best of their land for sowing—(proprietors sanctioning departure from the usual rules of husbandry)—disregarding " that which would yield but a poor return."

The general conclusion of the meeting was expressed in this wise—" But when all this shall be done there will still remain a frightful deficiency, which must in one way or another be made up, or many of the poor will inevitably perish for want." It was agreed to petition Government to give a bounty on importation of grain; and other measures of purely local application were adopted, including that of printing and circulating the resolutions of the meeting, a step that appears to have so far re-opened the question; for at a meeting of Commissioners of Supply in January 31, 1783, with Sir William Forbes as preses, Mr. Turner of Menie had the question put formally—" Whether or not the resolutions of the said meeting, which had been printed and dispersed, were not hurtful both to the town and county of Aberdeen, and the fears of want therein exaggerated?" A majority of votes decided the question in the affirmative; but in order that the sense of the county might be more fully ascertained, an adjourned meeting " of landed gentlemen and freeholders" was held on 14th February; and they agreed "that the dread of so fatal a want, as had been formerly suggested, was groundless, but were sensible that the crop had proved remarkably deficient, and therefore made no doubt that this would become an object of most serious consideration and attention to every gentleman in the county."

Beyond question there was famine in the land; and there is abundant evidence that but for extraneous supplies, death from want would have been far from an uncommon experience. The estimate of crop, as we have seen, gave less than a third of the crop of an ordinary year in quantity; and in an ordinary year they grew only enough to meet their own wants—precisely what the generation of a hundred years earlier had done. And the quality of such crop as they had was bad, being greatly lacking in wholesomeness and nourishment. Well might it be that, as put by one of the local chroniclers, a man evidently exercised in the construction of sentences—"Temperance stern but friendly established her reign on the solid base of necessity." But the pressure of dearth went much deeper than this; and but for the importation of bread stuffs already spoken of, and which took the shape, to a considerable extent, of grants by Government of oatmeal and peasemeal, or rather of pease to be ground into meal, there is no reason to doubt the statement that "numbers would have perished."

Neither of the two adjoining counties seems to have suffered quite so severely. The parish reports asked for and obtained by the Commissioners of Supply for Banffshire in the late autumn of 1782, led them to conclude that "the condition of the crop was not so bad as was apprehended." In Kincardineshire a portion of the cereal crop was wheat, which gave better results comparatively than the oat crop; and the farmers ground it in the ordinary corn mills, using it for porridge, while they made cakes of the oatmeal and bearmeal.

In country districts the distribution of these grants of meal was a duty that fell to the Kirk-sessions, who, as a rule, did their part with a creditable amount of shrewdness and humane feeling. Here, in brief, are the arrangements in a large parish in a central Aberdeenshire Presbytery, and which may be taken as typical of the county parishes generally. On Wednesday, 8th January, 1783, a fast was observed according to the Presbytery's appointment, and the occasion no doubt carried with it more of a practical aspect than "fasts" frequently do. On April 13th, the Session, "considering the deplorable situation of the parish through the dearth and scarcity of meal, and being well informed that even they who cannot properly be ranked amongst the poor, find very great difficulty in getting meal even when they have money to pay for it," resolved "to bespeak fourty bolls of pease on their own account." They held a bond of a principal heritor for a certain amount, and, he being out of the country at the time, "the interest could not be uplifted till his return;" but several "generous and charitable" individuals made offer of sums without interest to pay for the pease purchased; and others "cheerfully promised" their assistance in fetching the purchase home. The price of the pease was £1 2s (sterling) per boll; and as the carts told off to convey the "fourty bolls" numbered fourteen double and three single carts, the separate loads would not be very large even for a twenty mile journey. The quantity of peasemeal yielded was "not fully sixty bolls," and as the cost, including milling and drying, was £44 16s. 8d., the Session found they could not sell their peasemeal under 1s. per peck. What happened next was that, under supervision of the elders, appointed to the duty in turn, over forty bolls were sold, and four bolls given away gratis early in May. It was not till July that five bolls of meal were got from "the Royal bounty;" and between that and the beginning of November it seems to have been a continued struggle with want. One or two further doles were got from the Government grant; while the Session, in addition to distributing the remainder of their own purchase, bought a further supply of oatmeal when harvest had come to distribute among poor people who, from the long distress, were unable to supply themselves even after the price had fallen.

The "ill years 1782-3" had the effect of ruining many farmers in Aberdeenshire, and some landlords as well; and a good deal of emigration to America followed. And while a further result was to stimulate improvement by the introduction of earlier and better varieties of grain, and greater attention to green crops, the necessities of the time greatly promoted the granting of long leases during the immediately succeeding years. Previously the leases given had been of varying length, seven, nine, twelve, fifteen, or nineteen years being terms occasionally granted indifferently by the same proprietor. The prevailing poverty on both sides made it an object now to secure substantial tenants; and thus, when a man, possessed of a few hundred pounds came in the way, he was encouraged in the idea of permanency of occupation by the offer of a lease not merely for his lifetime, but for the period of one or two lives in succession after his own, he naming his successors. Some of these leases granted soon after 1782 had not finally expired in 1860.

CHAPTER IX.

LIVE STOCK—EARLY IMPROVERS—ROB ROY AS A CATTLE DEALER—HIGHLAND REIVERS—THE BLACK WATCH—VALUE OF CATTLE PLUNDERED.

"The places in this country which produce sheep and black cattle have no provision for them in winter during the snows, having neither hay nor straw, nor any enclosure to shelter them on the grass from the cold easterly winds in the spring; so that the beasts are in a dying condition, and the grass consumed by those destructive winds, till the warm weather, about the middle of June, come to the relief of both." These words were written of date 1698, and they present a vivid and graphic, as well as, in the main, a truthful sketch of the conditions under which the live stock of the country existed about the close of the seventeenth and beginning of the eighteenth century. At that time the native breeds of both cattle and sheep were poor in character and poorly kept. Improvement in the rearing of neat stock seems to have begun in the south-western corner of the land. Sir David Dunbar of Baldoon, in Galloway, the very tragic story of whose wooing and wedding furnished Sir Walter Scott with the central incidents in "The Bride of Lammermoor," and who was himself killed in 1682, was "an active improver of the wretched rural economy of his day." And amongst other things, he formed a famous park, two and a-half miles in length and one and a-half in breadth, which could "keep in it summer and winter a thousand bestial." Part of these, we are told, he bought from the country, and part were of his own breed, "for he hath nearly two hundred milch kine, which, for the most part, have calves yearly." Sir David sold yearly to drovers, or sent to St. Faith's and other fairs in England, about eighteen or twenty score of bestial. "Those of his own breed," the chronicler adds, "at four years old are very large; yea, so large that in August or September, 1682, nine and fifty of that sort, which would have yielded between £5 and £6 sterling the piece, were seized upon in England for Irish cattle; and because the person to whom they were intrusted had not witnesses there ready at the precise hour to swear that they were seen calved in Scotland, they were, by sentence of Sir J. L. and some others, who knew well enough that they were bred in Scotland, knocked on the head and killed."

This extract throws a somewhat curious light on both the cattle trade and the political economy of the time. Whether the Baldoon cattle were the ancestors of the native "Galloways" of the present day, we know not; possibly they were. But it does seem rather odd that a set of English magistrates (as presumably Sir J. L. and his friends had been) should seize upon a number of them and have them killed upon the mere suspicion, or pretence rather, of their being Irish cattle. The offence, even though it had been proved, would not seem a very grievous one, there having apparently been no dread of contagious cattle diseases then. But not only did Ireland possess a superior breed of cattle at that time; it was also against the law to import them into Scotland. We find Sir David Dunbar's successor at Baldoon petitioning the Privy Council for permission to import from Ireland "six score young cows of the largest breed," for making up his stock in the park of Baldoon; he "giving security that he would import no more, and employ these for no other end."

Various others followed the example set at Baldoon,

and a considerable trade in droving cattle from Galloway and other parts of Scotland to England seems to have sprung up. Sir George Campbell of Cessnock, in Ayrshire, had also a park "furnished with 'ane great brood of cattle' and a superior brood of horses, both from Ireland," and he, too, asks permission to import from the Green Isle.

The Union between England and Scotland, which took place in 1707, gave a stimulus to various branches of manufactures and trade, and among other things to the trade in cattle, which then began to be sent southward in greater numbers and from further distances off than before; the profits derived leading certain gentlemen, members of families who considered commerce in any shape rather below them, to become cattle-dealers. Amongst these was the Hon. Patrick Ogilvie, brother of Lord Seafield. Seafield, as Chancellor of Scotland, had taken an active part in bringing about the Union, a measure very unpopular at the time north of the Border. And accordingly, on the Chancellor remonstrating with his brother, on his undignified business of cattle dealer, the latter drily replied, "Better sell nowte than sell nations."

In a sketch given of a great cattle fair at Crieff, in 1723, it is said there were at least 30,000 cattle sold there, most of them to English drovers, who paid down above 30,000 guineas in ready money to the Highlanders; "a sum they had never seen before." The Highlanders, it is added, "hired themselves out for a shilling a day, to drive the cattle to England, and to return home at their own charges." The connection of the Highlanders with the cattle business was not always quite so accommodating or creditable as this. Yet it is somewhat curious to find that the famous Rob Roy Macgregor, cattle lifter and outlaw, began his career as a legitimate cattle dealer, buying cattle in this very Crieff market and other fairs, and droving them to England. The first public notice we have of him was his being advertised as a fraudulent bankrupt, who, having been "intrusted by several noblemen and gentlemen with considerable sums for buying cows for them in the Highlands, has treacherously gone off with the money to the value of £1000 sterling, which he carries along with him." The real explanation was understood to be that Rob had been placed in serious pecuniary difficulties by the defalcations of a subordinate agent or partner, and to avoid the penalty of a harsh law, desired to keep out of the way for the time. But the Duke of Montrose, who had advanced money, as a sort of sleeping partner with Macgregor, having got Rob's wife and family turned out of his poor property of Inversnaid, Rob took to the rough country round Ben Lomond as his retreat, assumed the outlaw's life, and took sweet revenge by pouncing down as occasion served upon the Duke's Lowland farms, and making booty of meal and cattle; and on one occasion of his factor, along with the rents he was engaged in collecting.

But Rob Roy was not the originator of the practice of cattle lifting, any more than he was the last that lived by it. A contemporary description of the Highlanders of this time, and which is more forcible than complimentary, speaks of them as "a people who are all gentlemen, only because they will not work; and who, in everything, are more contemptible than the vilest slaves, except that they always carry arms, because, for the most part, they live upon robbery." And truly the Highlander's habits gave not a little countenance to the accusation. Long before Rob Roy's day, the unceremonious Celts were wont to come down in force upon the Lowlands, and carry off "spreaths" of cattle and other goods. We read of such expeditions as that made in 1689, by a dozen wild Lochaber men, who had come down to the heart of Aberdeenshire—more than one hundred miles—and "lifted" six score black cattle. They were pursued by a body of nearly 50 horsemen, well mounted, and armed, and each carrying bags of meal and other provisions, both for their own support, and to offer in ransom for the cattle, if peaceful negotiations could be carried through. On through the hills, over marshes, rocks, and heather, the spirited horsemen followed, under their leader; and guided by a herd boy whom they encountered, they traced the robbers by Loch Erricht side into the heart of their own country. At nightfall, they came upon them at Dalunchart, encamped and busily engaged roasting a portion of the flesh of one of the cattle they had stolen. They offered, after some parley, to give each of the freebooters a bag of meal and a pair of shoes in ransom for the cattle. The Highlanders treated such an offer for cattle driven so far and with so much trouble with contempt; the herd was gathered in, and the fight began in deep earnest, the result being that the Lochaber men were all shot down, killed or wounded, except three, who escaped unhurt to tell the tale; and the cattle were, of course, recovered.

In 1691 a certain Hugh Thaine, messenger, makes declaration that he is unable to go "the length of Edinburgh" from Elgin "by reason of sickness and inabilitie of bodie," from "the hard usage" he had met in Strathspey, in the wood of Abernethy. And he "supplicats" the Privy Council or other judges to "apoynt some way for redressing and punishing the abusses committed against the law and Government" upon his person and those in his company. Some Strathspey Highlanders had lifted cattle belonging to Sir Robert Gordon of Gordonstone, and Hugh, in his official capacity, had been sent to cite the Laird of Grant, as answerable for his clan: when he and three men who accompanied him "were seized upon be a pearty of armed men, who most maisterfullie and violently struck me with ther gunnes, gave me a stobbe with a durke in my shoulder, and a stroak with my owen sword; robbed me of my money, my linens, some cloathes, my sword, and provisions." They also took Hugh's letters, bound him and his company, and " allways" threatened him with " present death" for executing " the foresaid letters." They offered his life to any one of the company who would hang the rest ; and finally, having secured them with "horse roaps," left them in the wood, where they lay on the ground " in cold, hunger, and great miserie for four days and three nights." Such was the treatment of which cattle lifters deemed the myrmidons of the law fit subjects.

The thefts and depredations committed upon some lands by Rob Roy and his followers are said to have been equal to the rents of those lands. The practice of cattle lifting had indeed come to be a well-systematised business, and the freebooting Highlanders had their own code of honour in conducting it. When cattle were stolen, one means of recovery used was to send an emissary into the region where the thief was supposed to be, and offer a reward for his discovery. This reward was looked on with great abhorrence. With the high-minded Highlander, who scrupled not to rob his Lowland neighbour's byres and his girnal, *tascal money*, as he called it, was the " unclean thing," and he and his fellows would solemnly swear over their drawn dirks that they would never defile their consciences by taking any such reward from the vile " Lallander." " Black mail " was exacted with very peculiar coolness. When a district was almost ruined by the depredations of a band of thieves, their leader or some friend of his would generously propose that for a certain annual payment he would protect it from plunder. There was no help but comply, as those who refused were made special victims ; and it occasionally happened that some of the thieves themselves, living within the district, were hypocritical enough to pay black mail to keep up appearances.

In the reign of William III., there had been an armed watch established, and severe measures taken to put down this system. But for a time this had been given up, and in 1724 Government established six companies of native soldiery, consisting of 480 men of the clans believed to be loyal, to prevent these cattle robberies and suppress the disgraceful impost. The men were dressed in plain dark-coloured tartan: and hence were called the *Reicudan Dhu* or Black Watch. And such was the origin of a regiment since then highly distinguished in many a well-fought field—the gallant 42nd Highlanders. They were formed into a regular regiment in 1735 for foreign service; and a consequence of the removal of the companies from their special posts as the Black Watch was the revival of the old practice of cattle lifting, which had been pretty effectually kept down by them. The caterans in 1743 came down again into Badenoch, into Nairnshire, and Banffshire, " harrying" as they could, and not scrupling even to kill those who resisted the driving off of their cattle. And in the following year Macpherson of Cluny had to raise a body of armed retainers, and take active measures to put down the determined incursions of the Highland robbers. Down to 1745, though the Highlanders may have confined their raids to nearer home, there does not seem to have been much abatement of the practice of cattle lifting. Mr. Graham of Gartmore, writing about the close of the Rebellion, says :—" It may be safely affirmed that the horses, cows, sheep, and goats yearly stolen in that country [the Highlands generally] are in value equal to £5000, and that the expenses lost in the fruitless endeavours to recover them will not be less than £2000; that the extraordinary expense of keeping herds and servants to look more narrowly after cattle on account of stealing, otherwise not necessary, is £10,000. There is paid in black mail or watch money, openly or privately, £5000; and there is a yearly loss by under-stocking the grounds, by reason of thefts, of at least £15,000, which is altogether a loss to landlords and farmers in the Highlands of £37,000 a-year."

If Mr. Graham's statement can be accepted as even approximately correct, the business of cattle lifting had clearly been of considerable extent. At that date the animals stolen would not have exceeded £3 in average value, so that sixteen hundred at least must have been stolen annually. Only in certain cases the Highlanders apparently regarded reiving in the light of a serious duty. Captain Burt speaks of their holding the doctrine that they had a right to plunder their Lowland neighbours, particularly the Moray lairds, on the ground that their ancestors once owned the lands of these same neighbours. A letter addressed by the laird of Lochiel to the laird of Grant, the terms of which follow, bears out this view, and at same time shows that these forays were sometimes dangerous to both the aggressors and their victims:—

> RESPD. AND LOWING COUSIN.—My heartly commendations being mentioned to you. I have received your letter concerning this misfortunate accident that never fell out the like between our houses the like before in no man's days; but praised be God, I am innocent of the same, and my friends, both in respect that they went not in your bounds, *but to Murray lands, where all men taken their prey* nor knew not that Moynes was ane Graunt, but thought he was ane Murrayman, and if they knew him they would not stor his land more than the rest of your bounds in Strathspey, and, sir, I have gotten such a loss of my friends, which I hope you shall consider, for I have aught dead already and I have 12 or 13 under cure quhilk I know not who shall die or who shall live of the saming; so, sir, whosoever has gotten the greatest loss I am content that the same shall be referred to the sight of friends that loveth us both alike, and there is such a trouble here amongst us that we cannot look to the same, for the present tyme, until I witt who shall live of my men that is under cure. So not further troubling you at this tyme, sir, you shall not be offended at my friend's innocence, so I rest you.
>
> ALEXANDER CAM. of Lochyle.
>
> Glenlacharkeg, 18 October, 1645.

CHAPTER X.

LIVE STOCK—REARING IMPROVED ANIMALS—CATTLE DEALING AND DROVING.

THE great cattle fair of Crieff, so flourishing in 1723, like other institutions, had its time, and then ceased to be what it had once been. When stricter notions began to prevail regarding improved lands and rights of property therein, the Highlanders could not, as hitherto, get their cattle driven thither on the principle of free grazing all the way from their native glens—(or at any rate from the point at which they came outside the Highland border)—and market "custom," too, had begun to be exacted on the cattle offered for sale. So they found it more advantageous to make their rendezvous at Falkirk; and Crieff came to be a horse market chiefly. In the latter half of the eighteenth century, the Falkirk Trysts, where the southern dealers in cattle met the dealers from the northward, had grown to a position of great importance, owing, no doubt, to the fact that the locality was at once accessible from both the Highlands and the Lowlands, and convenient for the dealers who bought cattle to "drove" southward. Toward the close of the century, it was estimated that between 20,000 and 30,000 black cattle were offered for sale at each October Tryst; and that the cattle brought up to the three Trysts that occurred during the year would number about 60,000.

It was only after the eighteenth century was fully half gone that any considerable trade in cattle existed north of the Tay. Berwickshire, the Lothians, and

Fifeshire on the east coast, with Perthshire and the adjoining counties to the westward, had been chiefly concerned in that business at an earlier date. Farmers in the north-eastern counties—Angus, Kincardine, Aberdeen, and Banff—got oxen for the plough from the Lothians, and later from the county of Fife; the cattle they reared of their own native breed being too " sober" for the yoke. They bought them of the dealers when young; that is, when three years old, or thereby; kept them as draught cattle for the next eight or nine years, and then re-sold them to the same class of traders at the best price obtainable; though it would frequently happen, we are told, that these venerable oxen had to be parted with " at a great discount." But now that the Lothian farmers had begun to find it more to their advantage to grow wheat and other grain rather than breed live stock, the rearing of cattle became of more account with the northern Scottish farmer. In the first place, he must have oxen to enable him to plough his land; and he would by and by come to take his due part in rearing cattle for the dealer to drove southward. Some of the proprietors made spirited efforts to improve the cattle and rear stronger animals by obtaining bulls from Falkland in Fife, where a superior breed, originally from south the Tweed, existed. Other varieties were imported directly from England, but with no great success it would seem. The complaint was that there was no food to support these large-sized and somewhat delicate animals. And, indeed, until cultivation of the turnip became general (which it did in the latter part of the eighteenth century, especially during the last decade), it is rather difficult to realise the miserable style in which even the small black cattle were maintained, especially during the " wintering," when the staple of their sustenance, at its best, was oat straw, with what they could pick up by roaming over the fields. By early spring the poor animals had got into sadly reduced condition, and if severe weather continued far into the season, it was not always that the farmer could bring his whole stock to the grass in life, through lack of nutritive provender. And even when spring had fully come, the pasture on the cultivated land, furnished by the growth of indigenous grasses, was wretchedly poor. In the Cromar and some other districts of Aberdeenshire, the practice was to send the larger cattle away about the end of May to graze in the Highland glens at many miles distance, and they were brought home again about the end of August. The cost of grazing was 2s. or 3s. a-head for the summer. In the pastoral region of Cabrach, in Banffshire and Aberdeenshire, where the tenants traded in cattle as they could, they bought in sheep in early spring, and cattle a little later, to graze; and sold them off again about August. The cost of grazing black cattle about 1790 was 2s. a-head on hill pasture, and 5s. a-head on "infield" grass for the summer; not high rates; but then at three years of age and upward these same cattle ranged only from £3 to £7 a-head in value.

About 1750, when ten or twelve oxen were universally used in each plough in Aberdeenshire, "the greater part of the draught oxen came from the Lothians." Twenty years later they came from Fifeshire, but not in so great proportion; and the number reared by farmers themselves gradually increased till the disastrous year 1782, which, if it ruined many farmers, had also the effect of stimulating those who escaped ruin in the direction of improved modes. After that date, turnip cultivation, as already indicated, became more general; the plough teams were curtailed, and the oxen that composed them were almost exclusively reared at home. It is curious, however, to note the enormous proportion which the work oxen bore to other stock, so late as the date of the Old Statistical Report even. Thus, one minister of an Aberdeenshire parish, who had been at the trouble to take the bovine statistics of his diocese, as indeed a good many others did, informs us that there were in it 953 cattle; and of these no less than 346 were oxen for the plough, the number of ploughs in the parish being 65.

In connection with what has been said about the introduction of improved breeds of cattle, it has to be noted that the business of sheep farming was no whit more advanced than that of stock raising. Considerable numbers of one or two native breeds of very small size (there was a whitefaced and a blackfaced variety) were reared in the Lowlands. They were fed on the rougher and less fertile pieces of land, and were valued chiefly for their wool, which was fine, though the fleece would weigh only from 20 to 28 ozs. It was not till the patriotic Sir John Sinclair formed the British Wool Society in 1791, that the larger Cheviot variety or "long hill sheep of the East Border" was generally introduced and naturalised in the northern parts of Scotland.

In or about the year 1764 "a few dealers from Galloway and the west of Scotland" seem to have begun a sort of regular business of "droving" cattle to England. A more or less intermittent "trade" of the kind had apparently gone on for many years previous to that time. And some of these Scotch cattle, after sale in English fairs, and fattening on English pastures, would find their way to the London market; though the wants of the Navy in the matter of salt beef appear to have been at this time, and for long after, regarded as the main source of demand. In 1763 "salted beef was purchased at the average of one penny per pound." It rose in price next year; but the year after, viz., 1765, the price of black cattle fell so suddenly and badly that "the dealers in Aberdeenshire universally stopped payments." In 1766, "cattle dealers came from England, in the end of June and July, to purchase live stock for the English market" (previously they had been content to wait till they were "droved" over the Border to them). The fact indicated a rising demand; which was but temporary, however, for "a second and sudden fall of the price of black cattle towards the end of 1767, again damped the spirits of the farmers and ruined all the cattle dealers." Prices declined till 1770, when they had reached the low level that prevailed before the influence of the southern market had been felt. From that date, with occasional fluctuations—and aided by the demands of the Navy, pretty generally on a war footing in those days—prices kept higher till the short-lived peace of October, 1801, brought "a temporary fall of 25 per cent. in the price of cattle;" and thus, "for the third time" in the reign of His Majesty King George III., most of the unhappy cattle-dealers were "ruined." * By that time the price of a well-grown ox of three to four years old had risen to as high as £20, which was much more than double the price when droving southward began; though it must not be forgot that the cattle had much improved in quality and size. In the report to the Board of Agriculture for the county of Kincardine, we read that, "about the year 1740, the largest ox in the county at that time, weighing from 25 to 30 stones, could have been bought for twenty shillings, or at most a guinea;" which is less than a shilling a stone—the stone of that period being equal to about 17·4 of the present imperial lbs. They rose gradually in price till about the year 1764, when "cattle of that size, and as full-fed as the country could make them, brought from £3 to £4, or from 2s. to 2s. 8d. the stone. From this period, cattle, being somewhat better fed, not only increased in size, but were improved in condition. And from the increased demand for butcher meat, combined

---

* In his interesting book on "Cattle and Cattle Breeders," in which the process of dealing, as practised in the earlier part of the present century, is graphically described, Mr. M'Combie, M.P., tells a story of George Williamson, the senior member of a well-known family of local cattle dealers, known as the "Stately" Williamsons, and the peace of 1815:—"He was passing through Perth with a large drove of cattle. The Bells were ringing a merry peal for the peace. St. John's Wells said it was a sorrowful peal to him, for it cost him £4000."

with the gradual decline in the value of money, the price of meat in the market, by the year 1792, enabled the graziers to give at the rate of 6s. 8d. the stone." After the use of turnips had become general, " every succeeding generation " of cattle increased in size, and the statement of Messrs. Williamson was that in their time (say 1810) by the introduction of the turnip husbandry, the native breed, from better keeping, had come to weigh at least double its former weight. Up to this date, and indeed for a long while after, the ordinary farmer did not regard the fattening of cattle as a thing much in his way. He aimed rather at rearing what stock he could, to be sold in "fresh keeping condition" to the butcher or other person who chose to "feed" for the shambles, a state of matters now very completely changed.

According to the estimate of Sir John Sinclair, about 100,000 head of cattle were sent to England yearly from Scotland toward the close of the eighteenth century, and of these a considerable number were from far north districts. About 3000 were taken to the southern markets by drovers "who droved them by land" all the way from the county of Caithness, and probably 8000 to 9000 were " droved " yearly from Aberdeenshire.

Of the Highlander's way of turning out his cattle we have the following description (dated about 1730) :—" About the latter end of August or the beginning of September the cattle are brought into good order by their summer feed, and the beef is extremely sweet and succulent, which, I suppose, is owing in good part to their being reduced to such poverty in the spring, and made up again with new flesh. Now the drovers collect their herds and drive them to fairs and markets on the borders of the Lowlands, and sometimes to the north of England ; and in their passage they pay a certain tribute proportionable to the number of cattle, to the owner of the territory they pass through, which is in lieu of all reckonings for grazing."

The writer goes on to say that he had often from a distance seen great numbers of cattle driven along the sides of the mountains, but only once had been near at hand, when in a time of rain a drove of cattle were being taken over a wide river across which the drovers were ferried by a boat. "The cows were about fifty in number and took the water like spaniels; and when they were in their drivers made a hideous cry to urge them forwards; this they told me they did to keep the foremost of them from turning about, for in that case the rest would do the like, and then they would be in danger, especially the weakest of them, to be driven away and drowned by the torrent. I thought it a very odd sight to see so many noses and eyes just above water, and nothing of them more to be seen, for they had no horns, and upon the land they appeared like so many large Lincolnshire calves."

In the Lowlands the local business in cattle in each district was transacted at a few annual fairs—Lawrence Fair in the Garioch and Aikey Fair in Buchan were early established "trysts" in Aberdeenshire. And as the fairs were wide apart, in point of locality, and came but once in the season, the gathering of cattle at them was always large. If less wild and romantic than the cattle traffic in the Highlands, it was still a picturesque style of things as they gathered out here and there from upland glens; the master, plaided and bonneted, riding his hairy pony, and one or two assistants equally hairy and hardy, tramping on afoot for many miles, and keeping the small drove of shaggy Highlanders jogging leisurely along, and picking up a livelihood by the way; while the dwellers in the Lowlands came "their gate," from the haughs and braesides, with groups of black "hummlies," diversified by an occasional "bran'it" or "rigget" stirk; or it might be a few horned beasts not indisposed to butt, and be otherwise domineering amongst their fellows. The roads were not very exactly defined, and fences were little known;

so that the cattle had moderately free access to pasture by the wayside, and occasionally to such cultivated crops as might happen to be within reach. Bridges were few and far between. Where burns and rivers had to be crossed, the cattle forded them, how deep or broad soever, and so did their drivers; and when "spates" were on a "mishanter" would sometimes happen of a more or less serious kind. When the market was over, and the "drove" of eight, ten, or fifteen score made up for the journey, after the same fashion, to the dealer's pasturage; or better still for their long and leisurely travel of days and weeks to Falkirk or Hallow Fair, it was a sight to see. The "drove," as it moved along, would stretch to nearly a mile in length, with here and there a rough "cowte" of a drover stalking away among the beasts stick in hand, and his wallet slung over his shoulder. And truly the "topsman," who had the responsibility of looking after and guiding the whole to their destination needed no mean powers of generalship to do his work safely and well.

Up to the date of the Rebellion of 1745 cattle sent to the southern markets from the counties of Aberdeen and Banff were driven across the Eastern Grampians by tracks marked out from time immemorial by the continuous tread of man and beast. The chief of these primitive highways were the most easily accessible and least steep of the natural ravines among the hills; and generally these—from Tomintoul, by Corgarff, Crathie, and Braemar, to the Spital of Glenshee, Blairgowrie, and Perth; from Ballater, by the Spital of Muick, to Clova, and Kirriemuir; from Aboyne, by the Tanar, and Mount Keen, to Lochlee, and down by the Esk to Brechin; from Kincardine O'Neil or Banchory-Ternan, across the Cairn o' Mount, to Fettercairn, and Brechin; from Durris, by the Crine Corse to Drumlithie, and the Howe o' the Mearns; from Aberdeen, by the Tollohill, and Causey Port, to Stonehaven. These primitive highways rose to elevations of from four hundred feet to two thousand feet above sea level. In the post-Rebellion period, road-making was more systematically pursued; and where formally constructed highways were laid out, the drover naturally followed the line of these, though the metalled surface was trying to the hoofs of his travel-worn charge. "Droving" cattle southward from the north and north-eastern counties continued to prevail for fully the first quarter of the present century; and was gradually superseded by winter fattening of cattle for transmission, first by steamboat and latterly by railway direct to the London market.

CHAPTER XL

COUNTRY FAIRS — THEIR ORIGIN AND CHARACTER—
AIKEY FAIR.

THE old country fairs had apparently been an institution established by the Monks of the middle ages, with a view to facilitate the transaction of general business. And hence the fair came usually to be held on a saint's day. In degenerate times, indeed, it was frequently held on a Sunday. And at one time the fair was regarded quite as much in the light of a rendezvous for indulgence in such rude games and wrestlings as are celebrated in "Chirst's Kirk o' the Green"—a poem with an appreciably northern smack about it, by whomsoever written—as in that of a resort for the transaction of serious business. Hence such expressions as " Play Feersday" (Thursday), when the fair happened to be held on that day of the week, or "Play Friday," if it happened to be on a Friday ; the dominating idea being amusement. The practice common in last century, of having fairs announced outside the kirk door after service on Sundays, with a comprehensive summary given by the "crier" of the more attractive articles likely to be found thereat, gave rise to the "byeword," that such and such a thing that seemed likely to become notoriously public was "like a cried fair."

An almost invariable accompaniment of certain of the fairs was the occurrence of party fights, or personal encounters between rustic athletes fond of testing their physical prowess. These encounters, which ordinarily took place about the close of the fair, were sufficiently brutal in character, the combatants often mercilessly belabouring each other with cudgels. In no quarter perhaps were they so formidable or so systematically kept up as in the district of Cromar, where the periodical onsets between "the rough tykes of Tarland," and "the Leochel men" seem to have been as regular in their occurrence as the fairs in which the two parishes were interested ; the fight being understood always to end in one or other of the sides being driven off the field vanquished.

At the last century fair, the business transacted was of an exceedingly miscellaneous kind. Live stock was by no means the most important feature. All sorts of household furnishings—including chairs, stools, wooden ladles, "caups," and barrels and brewing "bowies," rough wicker "creels," and such like, were exhibited in quantity by the wrights and coopers and other artificers, so as the more strictly agricultural class might supply their needs in such matters. Even ploughs and harrows were taken to the fair for sale. On the other hand, those who tilled the soil had the wool of their small stocks of native sheep spun into yarn at home, and then converted into webs of "fingrams" by the weaver, to be taken to the fair and offered to such as would buy; their customers, to a large extent, were itinerant "merchants," who picked up the fingrams at the annual fairs in Aberdeenshire, and then found a market for them in other parts of Scotland, or by getting them exported abroad. And after the decline of the trade in fingrams, when spinning worsted and knitting stockings for "the factory merchant," mainly engaged the attention of women in the country, dealers in soft goods in Aberdeen and the other county towns, found it worth while to shut shop for a day or two on the occurrence of some of the principal annual fairs, in order that they might cultivate business by exhibiting prints and other fabrics there alongside the stocks of the regular packmen.

Seventy or eighty years ago Aikey Fair, which is still held annually on Aikey Brae, in the parish of Old Deer, in Buchan, was the largest fair in the North of Scotland. A legendary account of its origin is to the effect that a packman of unknown antiquity, Aul' Aikey by name, in crossing the river Ugie, on stepping stones, a mile west of the ancient "Abbey of Deir," dropped his pack. On fishing it out of the water, then slightly flooded, he proceeded some three hundred yards farther on to what is now known as Aikey Brae, which was then, as it still is, covered with short grass and heath. Here he spread out his goods to dry. The contents of the pack consisted of prints and woollens, some of them being of gaudy colours. A good many people passed during the day, and being attracted by his stock bought up all the articles in it. Aul' Aikey was charmed with the success which followed what he had regarded as a calamity—the accidental soaking of his pack. Apologising to his purchasers for the meagerness of his stock he promised to show them something better worth looking at if they would meet him next year at the same time and place. He kept his word, while the report of his gains brought others with goods for sale to the same place, and so traffic gradually increased year by year till Aikey Brae, from its central position, became a general mart for the large and populous district of Buchan.

Doubtless the story of the packman is fully as picturesque as credible. But be that as it may, the hillside called Aikey Brae, where Aikey Fair is held yearly on the Wednesday after the 19th of July, slopes to the north down to the Ugie, while between the market stance and the river runs eastward from New Maud Junction, the Peterhead branch of the Buchan and Formartine Railway. The Brae affords an extensive view of the country to the west, north, and east, including the fine grounds of Pitfour, with the mouldering ruins of the Abbey of Deir nestling amid the orchard gardens of the same seat, the grounds of Aden, and half-a-dozen miles to the north, the highest ground in Buchan—Mormond Hill—with the noted figure of a white horse occupying an acre of the surface of the south slope of the hill, the space within the outline of the animal being covered with white quartzose stones.

When their great annual fair approached the dwellers in Buchan, eastward and westward, began to bestir themselves in preparation for the most important gathering of the year. On the day preceding the fair cattle were to be seen converging from all sides to fields within easy reach of the stance. Dealers and others from a distance came, all on horseback. Thus at the ford of the Ebrie, near Arnage, some eight miles off, as many as a hundred horsemen would pass on the evening before the fair. They rode not unfrequently at full gallop. Bets on the comparative merits of their horses sometimes gave rise to racing in this sort; but there was, in addition, the prevalent notion that it involved a sort of slur to allow your neighbour to pass you on the road to the fair. On the day of the fair fifty or sixty acres of Aikey Brae were covered with human beings, cattle, horses, and various kinds of merchandise.

Aikey Fair day was regarded as the great summer holiday; and both old and young flocked to it. Indeed, it was the boast to have seen so many fairs. "Old Cairnadaillie," who died at the age of ninety-six, affirmed that he had been at ninety-one successive fairs at Aikey Brae, having been first carried there in his mother's arms. As many as 10,000 persons are said to have been sometimes present, all attired in their Sunday best. The men appeared in the old-fashioned, home-spun, woven, and tailored coat and vest, with big pockets and big buttons, knee breeches and hose, all made of the wool of sheep reared at home. They wore shoes with large buckles; and some of the rustic dandies came dressed in white trousers and vest. The women also were in their "braws," and those of the fair sex who could afford it appeared in white. They generally wore high-crowned gipsy mutches. Then, as now, in matters of dress, the common folk trode on the heels of the gentry. The latter made a point of attending the fair, and several carriages might always be seen at it. The traffic at Aikey Fair, as at other annual fairs of the period, included cattle, horses, sheep, merchandise, and chap-book literature of no very pretentious character. There was always a wonderful supply of "carvy" and coriander sweeties wherewith the lads might treat the lasses. The shows and amusements at the fair were of a very simple kind. The pipers from the country around assembled, and often a dance would be improvised on the green-sward. As time wore on there appeared the "slicht o' han' men" to divide the attention of the idle and curious.

Cattle and horses chiefly were the animals exposed for sale at the fair, very few sheep being reared in the districts around it. Most of the cattle sold in the fair were driven south by Savock of Deer, Tarves, Inverurie, Echt, Banchory, the Cairn o' Month, &c., to be fattened on the rich pastures of England. Seventy years ago as many as 6000 beasts are said to have passed through Tarves in a continuous drove, a mile long, on their way south on the day after the fair. In 1836, however, only 2200 cattle were counted on this road on the same day, while at the present day not over 250 in all appear in the fair, though in 1876 as many as 600 horses were shown.

The merchandise sold in Aikey Fair about 1800 consisted chiefly of webs of sacking, bed-tick, a variety of prints often of gaudy colours, cottons in the shape of moleskins and corduroys, of which the outer garments of working men were then mostly made; wool and yarn were also sold in large quantities. On the day before the fair there used to be a large wholesale business done in woollen cloths among merchants and others. About the period indicated there were, as now, tents in the fair for supplying refreshments. Such a thing as whisky for sale was unknown, the liquor being confined to home-brewed ale, which was much drunk, though it was rare to see any one tipsy.

CHAPTER XII.

ROADS AND ROAD-MAKING—STATUTE LABOUR—MILITARY
ROADS—FIRST TURNPIKES.

In no department of social economics has progress been more signally manifested within the comparatively recent past than in the department of roads and means of locomotion. It has been said, and truly enough, that the past half-century, or thereby, has witnessed a greater advance in the facilities for rapid locomotion than all the intervening centuries back to the era of the Pharaohs had witnessed. It is just the difference between the speed of the horse going by "posts," as was done in the days of Ahasuerus, king of Medo-Persia, and the speed of the express train in the days of Victoria, Queen of Great Britain. At the former date, they could no doubt keep up to at least eight miles an hour on a long journey; and when George Stephenson practically tested his "Rocket" engine in A.D. 1829, little if anything more had been accomplished in the way of accelerated speed; and as George had occasion to know it was not deemed credible that the speed mentioned could be safely increased to twelve miles an hour. During all the years that have elapsed since the present century began, however, the country has been traversed, to a moderate extent at least, by fairly passable roads. Over a large part of the eighteenth century it was very different. Passable roads were scarcely known; and the bulk of traffic of the heavier sort that went on (as well as mere personal touring) was almost incredibly small. Think of "the whole intercourse between Edinburgh and Glasgow" being carried on by means of "ten or twelve pack horses going and returning once a week," as we are told was the case, so late as about 1760!

It was not till 1810 that that "most eminent of road surveyors," Mr. Loudon Macadam, succeeded in getting public attention called to his improved system of road-making, by first securing the support of the Board of Agriculture through its President, Sir John Sinclair, and in virtue of that support obtaining the approval of a Parliamentary committee. And it was several years after till macadamised roads came into anything like general use. Before Macadam there was General Wade; but apart from the military roads constructed under his direction, and up to fully the date when these were "made," "the communication by land" in Scotland was "along paths which necessity had traced out, that were marked only by the footsteps of the beasts that travelled along them, unless it was in a few bad passes through bogs that could not be avoided, where a rough and narrow causeway of stones badly laid together afforded at least a solid footing to the beasts, though a very disagreeable and dangerous path to those who were obliged to use it." Such is the description of a writer, speaking of what came almost within his own personal recollection.

In the county of Aberdeen, Sir Archibald Grant of Monymusk, who began his operations as an agricultural improver about 1716, was among the first to move on the subject of road-making, as of many other improvements. In describing the condition of his paternal estate at the date mentioned, he says :—" At that time there was not one acre upon the whole esteat enclosed, nor any timber upon it, but a few elm, cycamore, and ash about a small kitchen garden adjoining to the house, and some straggling trees at some of the farm yards, with a small copswood, not inclosed and dwarfish and broused by sheep and cattle. All the farms ill-disposed and mixed, different persons having alternated ridges, not one wheel carriage on the esteat nor indeed any one road that would allow it." "In 1720 I could not in chariote get my wife from Aberdeen to Monymusk," wrote Sir Archibald. Macadam had yet to come, and the causeways had evidently been neglected. The question of road reform was just about to be taken up in earnest, however, and for probably the first time on any comprehensive plan. In that very year, 1720, after due advertisement " att the several paroch churches," the Aberdeenshire county gentlemen " met, and having read the Act of Parliament of 1719, relative to the Highways and Bridges, they unanimously agreed 'That the whole Highways and Bridges, within the said county, should be repaired, amended, and built with all convenient diligence.'" And, to defray the charges that would ensue, they agreed to stent themselves at the rate of 10s. Scots on each £100 of valued rent; a scale of rating which continued in force for many years thereafter. The Commissioners appear to have approved of persons in each parish as "overseers," to look after the roads; but something more definite was needed; and in 1721 Alexander Jaffray of Kingswells was appointed " General Surveyor of all the highways, causeways, and bridges within the countie, who is to ryde and run the same, and make report what bridges or causeways may be necessary to be built or repaired within the county." His salary was 200 merks, with " half-a-crown of ryding charges for each day he has served, or shall serve the shire, anent the reparation of the said highways." The expenditure for riding charges was afterwards limited to £3 sterling a-year. It was the Surveyor's duty in reporting on the bridges and causeways, to state the cases which "could not be sufficiently wrought by the labouring men in the respective parishes," and where consequently the services of masons and other artificers were required.*

---

* For statement relative to Early Aberdeenshire Roads, Post Towns, &c., see Appendix (2).

This state of matters, substantially, continued for a number of years with a moderate amount of success.

A description that would apply to the state of the country a very little before the date at which Duke William of Cumberland passed through Aberdeen and Banffshire, to fight the rebels at Culloden, is to this effect—" There was no road in the county of Aberdeen on which wheels of any kind could be dragged; weighty burdens of every kind were of course carried on horseback." And when the county gentlemen had begun to form roads in the different districts, their engineering and constructive skill was not of the highest, any more than the labour they could command was efficient or heartily given. The Commissioners of Supply were empowered by statute (1719), to call upon every householder to give six days' work in the year toward the making and maintenance of the roads. And when they had decided to exact the "statute labour" more rigorously, which they did soon after road reform had been taken up as a practical question, they would employ the precentor to read out a notice on Sunday from the "lateran" immediately before the benediction; or engage the bellman to utter a "scry" as the kirk "scailt," whereby the people were asked to "take notice" that their services were needed at such a place on such a day, to work under orders of this or the other J.P. at road-making. But the people did not see why the roads that were good enough for their fathers should not be good enough for them; and they hated and scamped the statute labour, so that the man's six days frequently came to yield little more than one good day's work; a circumstance which ultimately led to the involuntary labour being generally "commuted," for a modified money payment. In commuting, they reckoned the man's labour at 3d. a-day. Thus, his six days' statutory work would amount to eighteenpence. And that was the sum at which they ordinarily let him off. As ninepence was paid for a road labourer with some "can" in him, and a little heart to the business, two days' work was thus secured; so that the sum exacted would seem to have been fairly equivalent to the services that had been given.

How averse the people were to performing their statute labour, and how little alive to the importance of good roads, is curiously illustrated by such facts as that, while warrant was granted to "poynd deficients conform to law," at least as early as 1739 no amendment seems to have taken place in their conduct up to 1755, when it was agreed that each Aberdeenshire parish should repair its own roads "as ane expedient to try if the roads will be repaired without commuting the labourer's money, and charge each man in each parish a sixpence in place of the labour they are obliged to give by law." The schoolmasters were instructed to make out lists of all the persons in their parishes liable to statute labour (nearly all the male population between fifteen and seventy years of age, except the ministers and themselves). The precentors were "ordered" not only to announce the statute labour days from the "lateran," but to certify the County Clerk where no application had been made to them on the subject, failing which, they would be "prosecuted forthwith as contemners of the law." The ministers were "entreated to prompt all concerned to forward so good a work that they may be the agreeable instruments of preventing the disagreeable necessity of imposing or incurring the several penalties."

The highways made by statute labour were of this sort—" though the principal roads have been in general lined out so as to mark their direction, and some stones and other obstructions removed out of the way and bogs filled up, yet the roads still continue to be in such a miserable state that unless it be for a few months in summer it is impossible to drive a carriage upon them with more than half an ordinary load." " What has contributed to this evil," we are again told, "is that when the roads began to be formed gentlemen were not sufficiently attentive to carry them in the most proper direction; they generally followed as nearly as they could the old course of the road; and as bogs had been originally the most dreaded obstructions, to avoid these, the roads had been in general carried along the high grounds where they could be come at; so that in many cases they were carried a considerable way about to shun a vale and get up a hill. After wheels began to be employed, it was found that the pulls going uphill were very inconvenient, to avoid which it has been necessary, in many instances, to abandon a road that had been smoothed at a considerable expense, and to make a new one in a more proper direction."

This description applies to the Aberdeenshire roads of the second half of the eighteenth century. These roads which were simply narrow, unmetalled tracks, with ditches cut along the sides, the hollows filled, and large stones removed, but rarely causewayed, speedily became a muddy slough when the weather was wet. And as early as 1741 we find the recommendation to try a layer of "small stones and chingle" (a rough approach to macadamising) "in time coming" on some of the roads. Six inches depth of this had to be applied, and the fact duly certified before "the usual allowance" would be made to those who were charged with the maintenance of the road.

Directly after the Rebellion of 1745 Government roads and bridges for wheeled vehicles began to be systematically engineered and constructed, the roads having a hard bottom of stones. The first two lines of modern road across the Eastern Grampians were made by the military. These are the road from Brechin by Fettercairn, the Cairn o' Mount, and Potarch Bridge, to Alford, Clatt, and Huntly, made about 1746; and the road (named after General Wade) from the Spital of Glenshee, by Castleton of Braemar, Crathie, Gairnshiel, Corgarff, and Tomintoul, to the Spey near Grantown, finished in 1754. Such roads as these, made by soldiers, had a sort of special recognition as the King's Highways.

The ordinary roads continued still to be of a very primitive sort. In June, 1751, at the Aberdeen County Meeting, "Meldrum" produced a letter "from my lady Dowager of Forbes, representing that the public road 'twixt Inverury and Castle Forbes is quite impassible in sevrall parts thereof, particularly that part 'twixt Pittodery's dykes and Overhall, which is dangerous to pass, especially with wheel carriages: and that lately her ladyship's chaise had stuck there and broke the graith : and therefore craving the commissioners to allow her a share of the highway money for helping the road, and power to call out the country people to give their assistance : which being considered, the meeting thought the request of my lady Forbes just and reasonable," and ordered accordingly. In 1756, an Act was passed by the Aberdeenshire Commissioners for making all public highways "20 foot in breadth, and where broader they are to be kept so." Several counties, it is said, had resolved that the roads should be at least twenty feet in width "over and above the ditches on either side," which were to be five feet. Many of the roads and highways in this shire, it is added, "are represented as being very narrow, and will not permit wheel carriages to pass by one another, or even loaded horses with curracks and creels." The roads were directed to be raised in the middle so as water might run off them, or otherwise they would be reported to the Lords of Justiciary "as disagreeable to law, and the parishes they belonged to would have to make them over again." Tenants who had arable land adjacent to public roads, were enjoined to make "head rigs next to the highway," and to cease the abuse that prevailed of ploughing across the roads.

The date of the oldest Scotch Turnpike Act is 1750,

but it was not till close on the end of the century that the system came north of the Dee.

In October 1769, the question of turnpikes came up for the first time at the Aberdeen County Meeting, in consequence of a scheme being "presently in agitation among gentlemen of the neighbouring county of Kincardine, for an application to Parliament to have turnpike roads in that county." The meeting declared "they were not presently ripe to give their opinion upon the expediency and consequences of the plan proposed." Before the year was out, however, they unanimously resolved to oppose the introduction of turnpikes into Kincardine county, unless the road 'twixt the Bridge of Dee and Stonehaven were kept free of tolls: the town of Aberdeen which had been equally moved on the subject, having made offer to maintain the road in question by calling out the statute labour. This question of turnpikes was the subject of much discussion a quarter of a century later, a draft Turnpike and Commutation Road Bill being at last ordered to be printed in 1794. This Bill, which provided for the levying of a money payment in lieu of statute labour became an Act of Parliament in 1795. The turnpike system came into operation in Aberdeenshire three years after, by the construction of the Deeside Turnpike, in 1798. This was followed by the Ellon and Peterhead turnpike in 1799. Most of the other roads of this class in the county were made during the first twenty-four years of the present century.

The current ideas on the subject of roads when improvement in that direction began, were somewhat conflicting. The minister of a West Highland parish says, a consequence of the formation of General Wade's Highland Roads and Bridges, was, "that the mind expanded by degrees to embrace within its grasp people of other denominations, and to weaken that prejudice which it conceived in favour of an individual and a particular clan." But then the cost of forming and maintaining these did not come so directly home to the community. With roads of the turnpike and "commutation" class it was different. In some quarters it was averred that nobody entertained a doubt of the advantage of a turnpike "since, at least, three times as much weight can be drawn in a carriage as was sufficient to load it before they were made." Still the engineering of those who lined them out, was not always perfect; even the turnpikes were too often "conducted over the summit of every eminence in their course, when with a little judgment and attention a direction might have been found equally near and incomparably more easy and convenient." And some could boast that "there are no turnpikes in these parts, and none are wanted;" others maintained that it was a mistake to commute the statute labour into a money payment. If they had divided the districts properly, and made each small community make and mend their own particular roads, they argued, it would have brought the matter so closely home to their practical feelings that, in place of slothful and slovenly labour, they would have been incited to give something more than measure, seeing themselves and no other would have the main if not the exclusive benefit of it. The experience of the county of Aberdeen, under the experiment of 1755, would, however, seem to teach a contrary lesson.

CHAPTER XIII.

IMPROVED LOCOMOTION—THE EARLY MAILS AND POST-BOYS—THE EDINBURGH FLY—SCORGIE'S CARAVAN—THE ABERDEENSHIRE CANAL.

ON the 8th day of May, 1765, when the Magistrates of Aberdeen went forth in state to meet the Justiciary Lords coming to the town on circuit, they, for the first time, rode in chaises in place of riding on horseback, as they had always been wont to do before. In the previous year a lady had managed to ride in a chaise from Aberdeen to Finzean, over a very indifferent road; and the fact was reckoned sufficiently notable to be recorded in her diary. In going over the Cairn o' Mount she took to horseback, and passed along what she describes as a well-made road. Up to the close of the eighteenth century, riding on horseback was the ordinary mode of performing a journey, a lady, when she travelled, frequently sitting behind a gentleman on the same horse. And the Aberdeen shopkeepers would talk of being treated by the "English riders," which simply meant the equestrian bagmen, who visited them periodically in the way of business.

Up to about the middle of the eighteenth century, the mail occupied three days in its journey from Edinburgh to Aberdeen. It came through Fife, crossing the ferries on the Forth and Tay; the messenger passing his first night out at Dundee, and his second at Montrose. About 1750 an improved system was adopted, post-boys being provided to carry the mails stage by stage on fresh horses, to all the principal towns of Scotland, while foot-runners went on the less important routes. In October, 1755, a regular post was established thrice a week between Aberdeen and Inverness, the time consumed in the journey by the post-boys being twenty-four hours. Eight or ten years later the London mail reached Aberdeen on the sixth day after leaving the metropolis.

The establishment of public conveyances for passengers was a separate matter from the carriage of the mails. It was not till 1758, when the population of Glasgow had risen to about thirty-five thousand, that a conveyance drawn by four horses, and accomplishing the journey in twelve hours, including stoppage for dinner, was successfully established between that city and Edinburgh. There was no other stage coach on that important line of road for thirty years thereafter, nor did any acceleration in speed take place during that time.

At their April meeting of 1789, the Aberdeen county gentlemen had before them a letter from the Post Office, relative to " putting the public roads and bridges thereon, by which the mail coach is to pass, in a proper state of repair." With a view to forward the matter as much as lay in their power, they appointed their Clerk to transmit a copy of the letter to the districts of Aberdeen, Garioch, and Turriff, with an earnest recommendation to attend to the contents of it, and " apply the whole statute labour within their bounds, for this year, towards repairing the public roads through which the mail coach is to pass ; and also to cause erect mile stones on the public road betwixt Aberdeen and Banff." The equestrian posts went along by Oldmeldrum to Banff. Foot-runners carried the bags from Oldmeldrum to Old Rain, and Huntly, and from Fochabers to Keith. At this time it was calculated that there would be 17,912 men in the county liable for statute labour, and 1000 horses and carts that might be called out.

The business of facilitating mail arrangements was not quickly disposed of, for in 1794 the county had represented to it the great inconvenience suffered over all the north of Scotland by detention of the north mail at Edinburgh "for near ten hours," with the result of its arriving at Aberdeen at night. The demand made on behalf of town and county was, that the mails be sent on from Edinburgh "within three hours of arrival there." Two years after, the complaint still was that all the north mails lay at Edinburgh from five or six in the morning till one or two in the afternoon —a delay equal to two and a-half days in the week, or "a space of time equal to four months and ten days in the year" during which the mails "lay dormant" at Edinburgh. In October, 1796, it was intimated that the Postmaster-General had agreed to run a mail coach from Edinburgh to Montrose "on and from 5th April next," and that the coach "would be forwarded to Aberdeen how soon the turnpike road was completed from Montrose." It does not appear that this promise was carried out so fully as had been expected, for in May, 1797, there was a proposal for the ill-used northern counties to unite in an application to Parliament on the subject. But at last, in July 1798, a mail coach, drawn by four horses, commenced to run through between Edinburgh and Aberdeen, performing the journey in about twenty-one hours. The time required previously by the post-boys was thirty-five or thirty-six hours.

The "Aberdeen and Edinburgh Fly" and the "Strathmore Diligence" were two of the earliest stage conveyances southward from Aberdeen, and which supplied the wants of the travelling public in the latter years of the last and first years of the present century—the smartly equipped "Defiance" came later. The very full particulars printed on the ticket of each passenger by the Fly may be given. They are taken from a ticket endorsed on the reverse side,

"A gentleman, to Edinburgh. Monday, 12th Nov., 1781. Paid, £2 0s. 0d. A. G., Clerk":—

> THE ABERDEEN AND EDINBURGH FLY, BY STONEHAVEN, LAURENCEKIRK, BRECHIN, &c.
>
> SETS out from Mr. SMITH's NEW INN, Aberdeen, every Monday, Wednesday, and Friday, at 4 o'clock in the morning: arrives at Edinburgh next day to dinner; and from Mr. ROBERTSON's BLACK BULL INN, Edinburgh, every Tuesday, Thursday, and Saturday, at 9 o'clock in the morning; arrives at Aberdeen next evening. The passengers both ways ly at Mr. JOHN CAMPBELL's, Innkeeper, Perth, the first night, from whence the above Fly sets out every Tuesday, Thursday, and Saturday, at 5 o'clock in the morning, and arrives at Edinburgh same day to dinner; and for Aberdeen every Monday, Wednesday, and Friday, same hour, and arrives at night.
>
> Tickets between Edinburgh and Perth 11s.; ditto between Perth and Aberdeen, 29s.;—uptakes on the road to pay 4d. *per* mile, each allowed 14 lb. of luggage; all above to pay 2d. halfpenny *per* lb. for the whole distance, or in proportion to the miles they go.
>
> Passengers at Edinburgh for Aberdeen must apply before 12 o'clock the preceeding days of the Fly's setting out, as, after that hour, seats will be given out to Perth, &c. if applied for.
>
> Tickets for Edinburgh must be taken out at Aberdeen, before 3 in the Afternoon, of the day before the setting out of the Fly, as after that time, tickets will be given out for any intermediate distance.
>
> Good convenience for boxes, parcels, &c. which will be regularly entered, and delivered on arrival. Carriage of goods the whole distance, 2d. halfpenny per lb.; small parcels [7 lb. or under], to pay 1s. 6d. each. The proprietors will not be accountable for valuable papers, cash, jewels, or plate, and those that send goods must observe to pack them sufficient to undergo the friction of the carriage, otherwise they cannot answer for damages.
>
> N. B. The Flies for Newcastle and London set out from the Black Bull every day, as usual, and from the George and Blue Boar, Holburn, London, for Edinburgh; likewise a Diligence for Glasgow, &c. and from Mr. Dunbar's, innkeeper, Glasgow, every day, for Edinburgh.
>
> §§§ It is intreated of the passengers not to allow the Drivers to take up foot-travellers between stages.

The Strathmore Diligence ran 'twixt Aberdeen and Perth every week day. One prominent advantage of travelling by it, too, was that passengers for Edinburgh and Glasgow had "the benefit of a night's rest at Perth," and were "forwarded next morning by coaches" which left that place daily for the two cities named.

The first serious effort to establish a public conveyance to northward of Aberdeen seems to have been made soon after the construction of the Inverurie turnpike, by an enterprising citizen named Alexander Scorgie. Post horses and post chaises had hitherto been the recognised means of locomotion on long journeys. The plodding craftsman of the hamlet, smith, or tailor—or the pack merchant—did not boggle at a tramp of twenty to thirty miles on foot to "the toon" when necessary; and for "gentlemen" who could afford to travel in a different style, country innkeepers had begun to let it be known that they could "accommodate," in more or less, those of them who might be disposed to make their hostelries a stage, and who happened to need horses or "a steady driver." Mr. Scorgie's idea was a bolder one. He started a passenger "Caravan" to travel on stated days 'twixt George Street, Aberdeen, and the house of John Norris, tailor, West Wynd, Huntly. The Caravan was a covered conveyance. In its original form it stood on two wheels, and was drawn by one horse. The covering was of painted canvas; and four passengers might find accommodation inside, their faces looking forward. Outside, the driver sat on a flat board at one side in front, with accommodation for a passenger on the opposite end of the board.

In September, 1807, after he had run to and from Huntly for a while, successfully it would seem, Mr. Scorgie announced that "for the more general convenience of the public," he found it necessary to extend his journey as far as Keith; and he would go thither accordingly from Aberdeen every Monday, Wednesday, and Friday, returning on the intervening days. At Keith, saddle horses and gigs were provided for the conveyance of passengers going to Fochabers, Elgin, and Forres, "where places may be taken for Scorgie's Caravan going to Aberdeen." The public are further informed that, in his anxiety to give every satisfaction, Mr. Scorgie had "an entire new and commodious Caravan in preparation," which, adopting his own description, was "upon an improved principle calculated for greater ease to the passengers than is to be found in any other such vehicle." And he flatters himself that the new Caravan would "prove little inferior to a post chaise for convenience and pleasant riding—being adorned in the front and sides with full glass windows, and elegantly padded in the inside; and full room for six inside passengers and two outside." In short, "no expense" had been spared to render the improved Caravan such as to merit the approbation of those who might honour its proprietor with their favours. In closing his announcement, Mr. Scorgie assures "ladies and gentlemen wishing to send youth of either sex" to any of the places visited by the Caravan, that they might "depend upon his most tender care and attention in conveying them in safety to the places directed."

This improved Caravan could boast of four wheels, and was drawn by two horses driven tandem. It was specified to give full room inside for six passengers, but would accommodate eight at a pinch. In addition to being padded inside, the Caravan was done up outside in bold black and yellow colours, with regular "dicky" and space for a passenger on the box seat. The "insides" gained admittance to their seats by a door behind; and when, as would occasionally happen, the proprietor-driver—a rather fussy little man, as the rustics deemed him, with a cap and big "peak" to protect him in all weathers—had no passengers, or but few, he too would take his seat inside, and contrive to steer his team through an opening in front. The pace of the vehicle was a slow trot, hardly exceeding five miles an hour on an average. But the roads were none of the best; and in the earlier days of the Caravan, at any rate, the hours of arrival and departure were by no means rigidly adhered to. For in addition to waiting any reasonable space of time at starting for an expected "fare," Mr. Scorgie, on being apprised that a possible passenger, willing to pay the hire, might be got by diverging a few miles from his wonted route, did not scruple to make the necessary *detour*, correspondingly lengthening both the journey and the time occupied by it.

Whether, and how far, the increased exertions of the proprietor of the only original Caravan in providing an improved service, may have been stimulated by threatened opposition would be a curious inquiry. Only a week after the announcement of Scorgie's extended operations, Alexander George, a "chaise letter" in Huntly, and lessee it is believed of the Gordon Arms Inn there, announced that he, too, had commenced running a caravan between Aberdeen and Huntly. He also ran on alternate days, but so as the caravans must have crossed, in place of maintaining a side by side competition. The Huntly chaise letter stated that his conveyance was "fitted up in such a manner as to afford every comfort and convenience to passengers, and inferior to no vehicle of the kind travelling in this part of the country;" and he charged the moderate fare of "seven shillings the whole way, and any intermediate distance in proportion."

The rival Caravan men had been justly regarded as postal celebrities; and the name of each lived up to probably quite the average "immortality" secured to men whose deeds have made them locally famous. The tradition even yet remains of how the Marquis of Huntly, afterwards "Duke George" (of Gordon), wanting to reach Pitmachie on a day of smart snowstorm, would trust to nobody but Alexander George to post him through the wild and dreary Glens of Foudland. George acted post-boy to his Grace accordingly; and on the return journey, having stopped at Bainshole, a small hostelry in the Glens, for refreshment, the Duke was surprised to find a pair of fresh horses turned out, wherewith to resume his journey without loss of time. "Please your lordship, this is my stick o' help," said the enterprising chaise letter in response to the Duke's admiring exclamation at witnessing arrangements so much in advance of the period. The story comes to us also from living lips, of how on a very stormy day, when Scorgie had reached Pitmachie, long a well known coaching stage, some one put to him the question, "Foo 'll ye win through the Glens in sic a nicht?" The proprietor of the Caravan showed his mettle in the reply, "I'll gae throu in coorse." And the saying became crystallised into a local "byeword"—"I'll dee't in coorse; as Carrie gaed throu the Glens."

It was not till 1811 that regular mail coaches were established between Aberdeen and Inverness.

In the month of June, 1805, when the Inverurie turnpike had been in use five years, an alternative medium of communication between Aberdeen and that royal burgh was established by the opening of the Aberdeenshire Canal, which, at the time of its construction, was reckoned rather a stupendous work.* On the opening day the committee of management "embarked" at the Inverurie bason (named Port-Elphinstone in honour of a leading promoter) in a barge "handsomely decorated." They carried a gun at the prow of the barge to signal their approach to the delighted crowds who had assembled at different points to witness the accomplished triumph of inland navigation. And their gaily decked vessel, "The Countess of Kintore," with its living freight, having completed the voyage of fifteen miles in seven and a half hours, was, amid general jubilation, safely moored at the bason at Aberdeen Quay. Two miles an hour or thereby might do for heavy goods; but it was clear that a speed considerably less than the normal walking pace was inadequate for passenger traffic; and thus, in the summer of 1807, we find a passage boat "covered and neatly fitted up for the purpose of conveying passengers and

---

* For statement relative to Aberdeenshire Canal, see Appendix (3).

light goods" set agoing. It returned to Aberdeen the same day as it left, but did not at first ply every day. The fare was two shillings to Inverurie, and twopence per mile for intermediate distances.

CHAPTER XIV.

EARLY AGRICULTURAL IMPROVERS—SIR ARCHIBALD GRANT OF MONYMUSK—IMPROVERS IN THE MEARNS—BARCLAY OF URY.

ALTHOUGH the Society of Improvers in the Knowledge of Agriculture had, as already stated, been formed in 1723, and individuals among the proprietary class had soon after that date made creditable efforts towards improvement in farming, it was not till fully the middle of the century that any movement of much consequence took place in that direction in any of the north-eastern counties of Scotland; nor, indeed, over a wider area. From the Union downward, to 1745, Scotland "experienced a state of extraordinary langour and debility. Her trade was inconsiderable, her agriculture in the most wretched state of neglect, and her manufactures nothing. Her people were oppressed, abject, and dispirited; her nobles poor, proud, and haughty, even to a proverb, and there seemed to be no hope of ever seeing a spirit of active industry excited in this nation." Dr. Anderson, whose words these are, seems to think that the abolition of heritable jurisdictions, after the date of the last Rebellion, removed the main obstacle to improvement.

The first experiment in Scotland in cultivating potatoes in the field was made at Kilsyth, in 1739. An entire half acre was planted, and many persons came from great distances to see the extraordinary novelty. But it was not till about 1760 that the potato was generally cultivated, even in gardens; and, for twenty years thereafter, it was not greatly in use as an article of food in the North of Scotland. The turnip, which had received earlier attention in Norfolk, seems to have been introduced into Aberdeenshire about the year 1750. One of the Old Statistical writers says, " Mr. Burnett of Kemnay is said to have been the first farmer in the county of Aberdeen who raised turnips in the fields ;" but he gives no date. The first time turnips were seen in Kincardineshire was about 1754 ; and ten years thereafter, in 1764, they were still so great a rarity—half an acre being deemed a large plot—that they were sold, by the few who grew them in small quantities, at the rate of a penny the stone weight as kitchen vegetables.

Imported grass seeds had been sown in but very few cases earlier than 1750. It was only about that date that they began to be kept for sale in a few shops in Aberdeen. Previously hay had been little known to the farmer, and, where known at all, chiefly in the form of indigenous meadow grass, dried more or less skilfully, and not too succulent at its best. The stall food of the poor pot-bellied " garrons " (horses) consisted, to no inconsiderable extent, of dried thistles— a plant mistakenly understood to be the special prerogative of the ass !

The name of Sir Archibald Grant of Monymusk, in Aberdeenshire, has been already mentioned. In all schemes of improvement he was prominent, and one special part of his operations was planting wood. Dr. Anderson says Sir Archibald assured him " that he alone had planted during his own lifetime upwards of 48,000,000 of trees, and he lived several years after that, and sent me word about two months after I saw him that he had in that time planted 200,000 more." Dr. Anderson expresses his belief that "no other man ever existed on the globe who had planted so many trees." The Earl of Fife and General Gordon of Fyvie planted largely, General Gordon as many as 3,000,000 trees in a single enclosure. James Farquharson of Invercauld, in the years from 1750 to 1806, is said to have planted 16,000,000 firs and 2,000,000 larches on his property in Braemar, through which he constructed more than twenty miles of roads. Toward the close of the eighteenth century, the cultivation of timber trees seems to have become an object of very general attention, as testified by the statement (in 1794) of the writer just cited, that "there is scarcely a private gentleman in Aberdeenshire who owns an estate of £500 or £600 a year who has not planted many hundred thousand trees."

The Earl of Findlater, who, for several years before his death in 1776, resided constantly at Cullen House, was the first to attempt improvements in agriculture and manufactures in Banffshire. He brought an overseer from England, and cultivated a farm near Banff in a way then quite new to the district. He introduced turnip husbandry, and granted long leases to his tenants on condition that they should enclose the lands within a certain period, sow grass seeds, and adopt summer fallowing, to a certain extent, within the first five years of their final occupancy. As early as 1752 he established a bleachfield at Deskford; and at a later period a manufactory of linen and damask cloth at Cullen, both of which enterprises fell into decay when household spinning ceased.

Mr. George Robertson, in his General View of the Agriculture of Kincardineshire (1807) states that about the year 1760 "there arose in this county a constellation of cultivators, which dispelling the mist that till then obscured the horizon of agricultural science, threw out all at once such a splendid light over the labours of husbandry as has not been exceeded, and perhaps hardly equalled even, to the present day." The detailed statements given by Mr. Robertson bear out his eloquent figure very well. And one phase of the new movement here too seems to have been " a strong bias for planting," inasmuch as during the last quarter of the century, probably 10,000 acres, previously bare and bleak enough, had been planted in forest trees.

In the case of a great many proprietors and tenants, too, in the Mearns, the spirit of general improvement seems to have moved strongly. Beginning at the north side we are told, for example, that there was not a more "haggard or uncultivated spot" in the whole country than the estate of Glassel. There were not over 30 acres of it "into which a plough could have entered." In the course of some years, 150 Scots acres had been improved, the enormous quantities of stones taken off the surface serving to form "consumption" dykes, from 12 to 16 feet thick, and many hundred yards in length. The remaining 400 acres of unreclaimed land were planted, and all this was carried out by the proprietor, Mr. Baxter, sending instructions personally down from London. The estate of Durris was held on lease by Mr. John Innes, Sheriff Substitute, who carried out very extensive improvements towards the close of the century. He made, at his own cost, a road "equal to any turnpike," running through the property from east to west, seven miles in length, besides promoting formation of the turnpike to Stonehaven and making other necessary roads. He erected a number of improved farm-steadings and cottages, and reclaimed at great cost 451 Scots acres, sub-dividing and fencing it, besides enclosing other 2500 acres. He planted 740 acres of muir ground, and built about 50 miles of stone dykes; and all this in seven years, the result being to increase the rental from £1000 to £2500, with the prospect of its soon reaching £3000. Then we have such instances as that of Alexander Walker, tenant of the farm of Auquhiries, who not only laid out and cultivated his farm in a style far in advance of his time, but planted forest trees on the barren knolls and waste corners to such an extent, that in

1796, when the lease expired, "the value of the wood which was then paid to his heirs amounted to £500."

Mr. Silver of Netherley, an old West India planter, who died in 1791 at the age of eighty-two, trenched and drained 150 Scots acres, some of it at a cost of £50 an acre. He imported lime for manure to the reclaimed land, which for some years, for lack of roads and wheeled vehicles, was brought six miles from Stonehaven "in sacks and creels on horses' backs." Mr. Graham of Morphie, was the first to introduce "broad clover," which he cultivated with success, the result being "a vast acquisition to the night food of the horses, in a country where they had been accustomed to be fed with thistles only, from the corn fields, or with the coarsest of aquatic herbage from the different swamps." He cultivated turnips too in drills as early as 1760, and had both very superior cattle and horses; some of his oxen weighing 80 and even 90 stones, while before 1775 he refused £80 for a pair of horses. And the beautiful property of the Burn is described as "an estate that may be almost literally said to have been a creation by the late Lord Adam Gordon," who built "The Burn House" in 1791.

Probably the most remarkable improvers in the Mearns were the Barclays of Ury. Mr. Barclay, who succeeded to the estates in 1760, and who was not indeed the first, any more than he was the last, improver of the name, comes chiefly under our notice.* At the time that he succeeded to the estate it consisted largely of marsh and unreclaimed moorland. "The part cultivated was badly laid out in small farms, very insufficiently tilled. The mansion was but scantily sheltered with wood, while there was not a single tree

---

* The title of "Father of the Shorthorns" was wont to be applied to the last Barclay of Ury by his brother farmers in the north, who possibly were not aware that their "forbears" had dubbed the previous Barclay "the Father of Farming."

on any other part of the estate." To facilitate his operations, Mr. Barclay took a number of the farms into his own hands as he could get them, and "in the course of about thirty years improved most thoroughly 900 acres of arable land," 300 of which had been altogether marsh or heath; and he planted from 900 to 1000 acres with wood. The cost of these improvements must have been very great, as much as £40 an acre being laid out on some fields in trenching, draining, removing stones, and other operations. And it is expressly stated that his outlay for lime-shells alone exceeded £6000.

Mr. Barclay was an athletic man, and come of an athletic race. His predecessor, David Barclay, of Mathers, who had been an officer under Gustavus Adolphus, afterwards became a convert to Quakerism. On retiring to his estate, he wished to have his land well cultivated—a point that gave him some trouble, owing to the prejudices of the peasantry. And it is related of him, that, finding a certain ploughman obstinately disobedient to his instructions, on one occasion he addressed him thus:—"Thou knowest, friend, that I feed and pay thee to do my work in a proper manner, but thou art wise in thine own eyes, and regardest not the admonitions of thy employer. I have hitherto spoken to thee in a style thou understandest not; for verily thou art of a perverse spirit. I wish to correct thy errors for my own sake and for thine; and therefore *thus* tell thee," (coming over his head with a blow which brought him to the ground). "Though the weapon was carnal," adds the narrator of the story, "this was the demonstration of power, and had the desired effect; the ploughman became tractable and quiet as a lamb." The last century Barclay of whom we have been speaking adhered to the family belief in this respect. Of him Mr. Robertson says, that while employing "only the people of the country that were bred on his own lands or in the vicinity" (he had himself acquired his agricultural knowledge in Norfolk), "his discipline was severe, but it was very correct. He would admit of no slovenly practice—no slighting of the work. Nor did he require anything of his people, but what he could do himself, for while he delivered out his directions in the most clear and distinct manner, he could with his own hand show them the true mode of peformance. He could even enforce his authority with something more effective than verbal injunctions ; for it is said that the clownish obstinacy of his people was not unfrequently corrected by manual discipline. I have, indeed, met with different people that confess (and even in some measure glory in it) that they had the knowledge of their work beat into them by Mr. Barclay. This strict government had the happiest consequences, for not a little of the general dexterity in the Kincardineshire labourers is still to be traced to the original system of their education, established by Mr. Barclay of Ury. To have been in the service of Mr. Barclay always was, and still is, a great recommendation to any servant."

Sir William Nicolson of Glenbervie was the first person in the Mearns who raised hay from sown grass, about the year 1730, the seeds he used being the best he could select amongst the natural meadow hay. These he sowed among oats of the third or fourth crop from ley ; and the result was so far superior to the ordinary mode of allowing the soil to replenish itself with wild herbage as to excite the astonishment of his neighbours. For in the Mearns, as elsewhere, the only hay obtained up to that time had been from the natural grasses that grew in the swamps and marshy spots to be found on almost every farm. It was not till about 1760 indeed that clover came to be much known in this country; and it was ten years later still before sown grasses began to be commonly cultivated.

CHAPTER XV.

CHARLES HACKET OF INVERAMSAY—A LOCAL SCENE IN THE FORTY-FIVE—HACKET AS AN IMPROVER.

DURING the closing days of September 1745 the good town of Aberdeen was put in a sad stir by reason of a certain irruption then made. Prince Charles Stewart had landed on the west coast, had advanced to Edinburgh, had fought and won the battle of Prestonpans. And now, on the 25th day of the month named, the very day, as it fell out, of the Town Council election, when, according to use and wont, the old Council had elected the new, and they had not yet got the length of electing the Provost, John Hamilton, in Strathbogie, entered the town in a hostile manner, "drums beating and colours flying," with "a band of armed men, both horse and foot," at his back. The rebel forces were paraded at the Market Place and Cross. Meanwhile the valiant councillors had promptly taken to flight, and John Hamilton had it all his own way. He sent in quest of "James Morrison, Esq., present Provost," and his messengers not finding that gentleman at home, a second party was sent with orders to burn his house if he did not appear. What effect this threat may have had is not apparent; but the Provost was at last found, and carried down prisoner to the town-house. They next set him up upon the Cross in the company of a couple of Baillies and certain of the councillors, where he had to listen to a disloyal Sheriff-substitute reading the Pretender's manifestoes. "Thereafter they caused wine to be brought to the Cross, where they openly and avowedly drank the Pretender's health, and several other treasonable and rebellious healths." They even " endeavoured, by force, to make the said Provost drink their healths," " which he refusing, they poured the wine down his breast."

After John Hamilton came Lord Lewis Gordon, who, by and by, in his assumed title of Governor of Aberdeen, issued an order, in Prince Charlie's name, for the collection of the King's cess. In the Diary of Rev. John Bisset, one of the ministers of St. Nicholas, under date February 3, 1746, is this entry :—" This day the drum went warning all yet deficient in paying their cess, in the name of Lord Lewis Gordon to repair with payment to the quarters of one Hacket, empowered to gather it up, under the pain of military execution." The Town's Collector, Mr. Dirom, being, it would seem, of loyal temper, and somewhat advanced in years, excused himself on the score of physical frailty, but recommended his clerk, Charles Hacket, as a person likely to be found suitable for the business. Charlie Hacket was an active young fellow, and being a red hot Jacobite to boot, he collected the cess accordingly with all due zeal, as indicated by the Rev. John Bisset, which served to bring him into trouble by and by, when Culloden had been fought and the Pretender's hopes shattered for ever. In those days Charlie Hacket, to use his own phrase, got familiar with the practice of "sleepin' in his beets." He skulked about where he best might, his hiding place for a while being, it was said, at the further side of the meal-girnal belonging to a Garioch laird of like leanings with himself, but uncommitted by any overt act.

Better times came, however, and Charlie Hacket having married Miss Smith, heiress of the pleasant estate of Inveramsay (anciently Poolwall) in the Garioch, became life-renter of that property, and by and by got to be well known as a zealous and successful agricultural improver.* And it is in this phase of his character that we have to look at him.

That Laird Hacket of Inveramsay was decidedly in advance of his time in his general notions of agriculture, the traditions of the place, and even the outward aspect of the home farm which he cultivated, testified long after his day. He had been at pains to lay out the land in well-arranged fields, which he duly enclosed with fences, planting rows of ash and other hardwood trees, where he thought it suitable and necessary for shelter or ornament. And the more elderly natives of the generation following that to which he belonged had ever so many stories about Laird Hacket. He was a Jacobite, as has been said, as well as an ardent farmer, possessing in full measure the Jacobite habit of swearing; and so there came the long-lived local bye-word—"Like Laird Hacket: that bann't a' the ouk an del't dockens on Sunday." He had a portrait of the Pretender over the fire-place in his sitting room, which he would gaze upon and apostrophise, not always with perfect placidity, when he thought of his own sufferings as a Royalist. Yet when he went to chapel, being a faithful adherent of the Episcopal faith, as prayer for the reigning sovereign was offered up, his response would be an audible groan in place of the orthodox Amen. At times, it is said, his feelings found vent in even a more emphatic form of expression.

Let us sketch the personal appearance of this last

---

* Among the local rebels taken prisoner in December, 1745, was Mr. Smith, Junior, of Inveramsay; and in the list of excepted persons against whom an *ignoramus* verdict was returned in 1748 was David Smith of Inveramsay.

The obituary notice of Mr. John Smith, Senior, which appeared on October 30, 1750, ran thus:—"Last week, died at Inveramsay, aged near 100, John Smith of Inveramsay; a gentleman who thro' the various scenes of a long life, in all its different stations, had the deserved character of an upright, honest man." His decease allowed Hacket to succeed to the life-rent of the estate.

century laird. A small, compactly-built man, with brownish-coloured coat, and worsted knee breeches, knitted—as were also the stockings that encased his sturdy and somewhat "bowed" lower limbs—by his own wife. On his head, when in the sort of undress that served for every-day home use, he wore a worsted nightcap, or Kilmarnock cowl, underneath which glowed his reddish visage and sharp twinkling eyes. Such was the man, who, "docken" spade in hand, strode about commanding everybody right and left, and astonishing his jog-trot neighbours by the novelty of his proceedings as an agriculturist.

He sowed turnips first about 1750, and in those days people came from the next parish, when harvest was over, to buy them by the pound and stone weight from his farm grieve, to be used as a dainty dish at the "clyack" supper and other fit occasions. He sowed at first broadcast, a practice which, although given up earlier in some localities, prevailed pretty commonly in Aberdeenshire down to the close of the century, and even a little later. And he believed in the broadcast method for the time, though not impervious to argument on the subject. When drilling began to be advocated, Hacket saw fit to forego the old practice for a season in favour of it. The crop disappointed his expectations, however, and in hot ire he exclaimed, "Deil drill me aff o' the earth if ever I drill again." Yet he did drill again, not once but frequently, having seen reason to change his opinion, while the arch enemy took no immediate advantage of his rash utterance.

Hacket's tenants, as was common in those days, were bound to give certain personal services to their landlord; and these services included a day at turnip hoeing. In order to compel the workers to keep their eyes sufficiently near the ground to admit of the plants being clearly seen, the regulation length of the hoe handle was fixed at two feet and a half; and when the laird saw a hoer standing too erect to suit his ideas, he would march up to him and demand his implement to have the handle curtailed. Certain sturdy fellows, who claimed the right to use the form of handle that was satisfactory to themselves, promptly resisted any such interference, at which the laird would explode in great wrath. He had no help but submit, however, for, with all his energy and vehemence, he possessed not the physical strength of such men as Barclay of Ury, and therefore was not in a position to follow his method of training—In those days they one and all believed in the maxim, "Kiss a carle an' clap a carle, that's the way to tine a carle. Knock a carle an' ding a carle, that's the way to win a carle."

But it was not in independent turnip hoers alone that Laird Hacket encountered the "stalk o' carl hemp." It was told how, on a "forcy" leading day in harvest, he had gone to the stackyard, where a "rick" was in process of building. It was well on toward the "easin'," when Saunders, his grieve, who was a-top of it, for some reason good and sufficient to him, desired the "forker" to slacken his hand. The laird, who, in his own impetuous way, had been urging all speed for fear of broken weather, peremptorily ordered the man to go on. He was obeyed, and the sheaves were pitched up with redoubled force. By and bye there was an ominous growl of remonstrance from the top of the stack, which had no result but a renewal of the laird's order with increased emphasis; next there appeared over the edge of the sheaves a pair of very sturdy legs, the owner of which evidently meditated a sudden descent to *terra firma*, whatever else. No further hint was waited for. With a just appreciation of Saunders's temper when roused, the "cornyard" was forthwith cleared of human occupants—the laird, who led in flight, followed by the forker, losing his stick as he doubled through between the bars of the "yett," and staying not for an instant to pick it up again.

One operation in improved husbandry, which was disliked and despised by the natives, was that of enclosing. Of old time cattle had roved hither and thither much at their will, and the idea that they should be restricted in so doing was reckoned very intolerable. Improvers generally had a good deal to do in contending against this feeling which, in some cases, led to fences being wilfully thrown down, and newly planted trees pulled up. And as Hacket's temper was none of the calmest, he was apt to get greatly irritated at the idea of any thing in the nature of a trespass upon his lands. On one occasion he had observed the cattle belonging to the miller on the neighbouring estate straying over a fine haugh upon the lands of Inveramsay, and he set off in hot haste to impound them for the damage done. Not so fast, however. The miller's herd had probably been taking a quiet snooze by the dykeside when his charge strayed over the burn, but by the time Laird Hacket had reached the lower end of the haugh, he was wide awake, as the laird speedily found. For he had scarcely begun to move off the beasts, which he was prepared to treat as his lawful captives, when the herd, a stout, half-grown fellow, as herds in those days were, came scouring along with an armful of stones, with which he forthwith commenced a vigorous assault on the enemy, who was glad to make "his feet his freens," as he had done after Culloden; ingloriously quitting his prey, and returning homeward even more quickly than he had come, while the incensed herd followed him a good way along the brae with a furious fusilade of stones.

At another time, when passing near the outskirts of his property, Mr. Hacket met Saunders Nicol quietly driving home some half-dozen sheep which had evidently been straying on the laird's land, where they had been feeding for half the day, or, it might be, nearer the whole of it. Hacket flared up at the idea of such a trespass on his "bounds," and, in the parley that ensued, lifted his stick, with the exclamation, "I'll hazel ye, sir!" uttered in his fiercest tones. "An' ye hazel me the nicht, ye maybe winna hazel anither the morn!" answered Saunders, coolly jogging on with his ewes, and leaving the laird, who, no doubt wisely, deemed discretion the better part of valour, to digest his wrath at leisure.

Such was this improving Garioch laird, and such the relations in which he stood toward those amongst whom he lived. But with all his oddities, Hacket, as an improver, achieved good results himself, and gave a distinct impetus to agriculture in his locality. The writer of the Old Statistical Account of the Parish of Chapel of Garioch, in which Inveramsay is situated, while crediting him with having first introduced "the culture of turnips and sown grass" in that parish, adds, that his example in farming had been followed by many in the neighbourhood. "The crop of one field upon the Mains of Inveramsay, which before Mr. Hacket's improvements was sold for 30s., is now," he says, "reckoned worth £60 sterling; and the rest of the farm is improved in the same proportion." He retained his reputation as a capable business man throughout, and one of the records we find of him is in the famine year 1783.* The kirk-session had met to consider the necessities of the parish on account of the dearth, and having resolved to purchase a quantity of peasemeal,

---

* There are one or two later entries. In 1790 the mortcloth is required for Mrs. Hacket. In 1792 a certain female appears before the session, and a letter is read from Charles Hacket acknowledging himself the father of her illegitimate child. He offers to pay what fine they thought right to inflict, if they would allow the case to be dismissed "sessionally"—that is, without any public appearance before the congregation. £3 being paid "to the poor," the case is dismissed accordingly. We must not forget that Hacket, who thus negotiated with the Presbyterian Kirk-session, was himself a staunch Episcopalian.

they entrusted to him the duty of negotiating for the same—a duty he seems, from the session minute, to have discharged both well and promptly, his " activity" in the matter being specially mentioned.

CHAPTER XVI.

AN AGRICULTURAL TOUR—SURVEY OF ANNEXED ESTATES BY ANDREW WIGHT—THE SURVEYOR'S OPINION OF IMPROVEMENTS IN ABERDEENSHIRE—DR. JAS. ANDERSON—A LADY IMPROVER—POVERTY OF TENANTS—INNS OF THE PERIOD.

IN the year 1773 the Commissioners on the Annexed Estates in Scotland gave a commission to Mr. Andrew Wight, farmer at Ormiston, in East Lothian, to visit and report upon the condition of the estates put under their management. The Commissioners regarded the chief motive of their appointment as being " to civilise the people of those estates, and, by kind treatment, to make them good subjects." Having, as they believed, fully accomplished that object, they were disposed to attempt a " farther reformation, viz., to lead on gradually the tenants to improve their husbandry, which has hitherto been at a very low ebb." Hence the determination to send out a competent Surveyor, with detailed instructions concerning the points on which he was to report. East Lothian was then the headquarters of advanced agriculture, and in their choice of Mr. Wight, the Commissioners seem to have been fortunate in securing the services of a man of a naturally shrewd and observant cast of mind, and who was fully abreast of the agricultural intelligence of his time. So well were the Commissioners pleased with his two first surveys, which were confined to the annexed estates, that, in the interest of agricultural improvement generally, they gave him a wider commission, under which he visited different parts of Scotland, from the Border counties to the extreme north, and including parts of the counties of Aberdeen, Kincardine, Banff, Moray, and on to Sutherland and Caithness; his labours extending at intervals over ten or eleven years.

The Commissioners felt the time to be fortunately critical for such a survey—" While the bulk of our farmers are creeping in the beaten path of miserable husbandry, without knowing better, or even wishing to know better, several men of genius, shaking off the fetters of custom, have traced out new paths for themselves, and have been successful, even beyond expectation. But their success has hitherto produced few imitators: so far from it, that among their slovenly neighbours they are reckoned giddy-headed projectors." A comparison of the new mode of agriculture with the old could not fail, it was thought, to incite the old school farmers to follow the example of the improvers; especially in view of the great profits made by them; for, "if this motive prevail not, it is not easy to say what can prevail." "Fifty years ago a survey of this kind would have been of no avail; because our practice, cramped by custom, was the same everywhere; and there was nothing to be learned. Fifty years hence the knowledge and practice of husbandry will probably be spread everywhere, and nothing will remain to be learned." The Commissioners reasoned soundly concerning the expediency of their course; and as we have already seen, they were not altogether singular in their mistaken anticipation of the time when "nothing will remain to be learned" in agriculture.

We shall not follow Mr. Wight in his agricultural details; nor indeed follow him closely at all; but simply endeavour to obtain from him a few glimpses of the rural life of the time as it presented itself to the eye of an intelligent stranger. On his third survey, he visited the county of Kincardine, of which he says —" I am sorry to observe that agriculture in this county makes little figure, except among a few patriotic gentlemen." Various of the more prominent of these he had visited, but time did not admit of his coming on to Aberdeen. And a considerable while after he records, at second-hand, a particular impression concerning the husbandry of three local counties, viz., the observation that had been made by a gentleman, when travelling through Angus, Mearns, and Aberdeenshire — "Many enclosures he saw fenced with dry stones, some new, some decayed, and some tumbling down; but not a gap made up, nor the slightest reparation on any of them. This surprised him. To be at the expense of building fences, and yet never to think of keeping them in repair, appeared unaccountable. But at last he discovered the cause; for, upon looking back he remembered that in every one of these enclosures there was corn as well as grass." In point of fact, "inclosing," as known to the farmers of the time, was simply a delusion and a snare. It did not partition off the pastures from the cereal and other crops, and consequently herding was just as much needed as if no enclosures existed.

Aberdeenshire was visited in the autumn of 1779; and the natural advantages in respect of recently-made roads and harbours for export and import of commodities are remarked upon, together with the recent "amazing" increase of manufactures, trade, and population. In the towns of New and Old Aberdeen, and various suburbs 'twixt the bridges over the rivers Dee and Don, there was good warrant for saying there were at least twenty-five thousand people, old and young. A few particulars concerning the trade of the town are given, and the Surveyor, who elsewhere indicates his lack of confidence in the villainous raw whisky of the time, takes delight in mentioning "a considerable brewery for making porter, erected chiefly with a patriotic view. This brewery was erected to give vent to their own bere and barley, and to save great sums remitted annually to London for porter. This brewery meets with great encouragement, and it is the great boast of the citizens that they can now rejoice over their own porter, instead of bringing it from London." So much for Aberdeen porter and patriotism a hundred years ago.

The social state of the inhabitants, urban and rural, is statistically given in a few compendious sentences —" The inhabitants are sober and industrious; and the following particulars will show that wages and provisions are moderate :—The wages paid to labourers in remote parts are from 5d. to 7d. per day ; at Aberdeen, 9d. in winter and 12d. in summer. The women are so well employed in knitting stockings as scarce to undertake field work, even at 6d. Beef gives 2½d. a-pound, and mutton 3d.—Dutch weight. In the spring, beef and mutton rise to 3½d., 4d., and 4½d. per lb., there being little or no early grass in the county. A pound of butter, of 28 oz., can be had for 7d., and cheese, poultry, and meal in proportion. They have indeed no coal but what is imported. Peats they have in plenty ; but they are too remote from many places to be a cheap firing."

About this date the more prominent citizens seem to have taken strongly to farming. Even the skilful East-Lothian Surveyor declares that " there is perhaps no place in the world where a spirit for husbandry has made such a figure as about Aberdeen. A corner between the rivers Dee and Don has for many years been cultivated in the most skilful manner by a mixture of the garden and field crops, one year cabbage, next year barley; one year turnip or potatoes, next year oats, and so alternately, a mode of cropping unknown anywhere else in Scotland." Outside this corner a dry, barren, stony muir prevailed. To think of profitable improvement of the same might appear in vain. But "men of all ranks here are struck with the enthusiasm of farming," and citizens, who had amassed a little cash otherwise, were prone to bestow it in the pursuit of husbandry for its own sake, or, perhaps, in the desire to have country villas; and thus they attacked the stubborn glebe regardless of expenditures as high as from £20 to £25 an acre (quite equal to double the amount now), the result, in 1779, being that the reclaimed lands, "to the distance of three or four miles, carry as rich crops as are to be seen anywhere in Britain." Adam Duff, the late Provost, had feued 150 acres, as stony and barren as any in the neighbourhood, at 3s. per acre of feu-duty, and at a cost of £25 an acre, converted it into excellent arable land. Mr. Angus, late bookseller, and Mr. Mossman, advocate, are also mentioned as skilful and successful improvers of the barren, stony waste; and the estate of "Robslaw," which within not many years had risen in rental from £100 to £600, is referred to in evidence of the growing taste for suburban possessions. Generally—"Were a traveller in his wanderings to come upon any farmer in the neigbourhood of Aberdeen commencing his improvements upon this stony barren muir, he would, without the least hesitation, pronounce the poor man to be crazy. Anyone would think so with respect to the first improver; but now the certainty of success makes it a rational system for gain, and spreads the improvement of that muir wider and wider every day. At present, as far as one can cast his eye round Aberdeen, there is not a vestige of the muir remaining."

Passing out by Grandholm, Mr. Wight finds Mr. Paton engaged in reclaiming a muir of great extent, and little better than that about Aberdeen, except that the stones upon it are less numerous. He is at work with a strong plough, which makes a furrow from fourteen to eighteen inches deep, and is drawn by "no fewer than ten good oxen." Mr. Paton's apology for such a number, "is, not that they are absolutely necessary for so deep a furrow, but that they relieve one another, by taking up the draught by turns." The Surveyor ridicules this idea, and avers that, but for the prepossession of custom, Mr. Paton would not be capable of reasoning that way. " To leave oxen to pull or not, according to their own discretion, would be a very imperfect way of relieving one another. I have often seen ten oxen in a plough, in the counties of Aberdeen and Banff; but I never once saw them pulling all together. One or other of them are seen hanging on the yoke, keeping back the draught instead of advancing it." The improvements carried on at Udny, by Mr. Udny, attract prominent notice. The land around Udny House had originally been even rougher than that round the town of Aberdeen; yet now, at great expense, and " with unremitting perseverance," it was so improved, that no vestige remained of what it had originally been; nothing was to be seen but neat enclosures, thriving hedges, and commodious offices; presenting such a picture as made the traveller loath to prosecute his further journey over the many barren, out-lying acres. A favourable rotation of cropping had been established; Mr. Udny was "famous for a breed of horses, full blood, on both sides." Mr. Wight admired his "English bull, Shorthorn," and declared his cows, some of which were from England, some from Berwickshire, and some the very best of his own country breed, to be good.

At this point the Surveyor was destined to encounter a keen disappointment. It was common for spirited improvers of the landlord class—and the improvers of the time were generally of that class—to bring men from the Lothians as overseers or chief ploughmen; and they not unfrequently helped them to settle ultimately in farms of their own. Mr. Udny went a step farther. In his zeal for agricultural improvement he had prevailed upon Mr. James Anderson, "a young gentleman of a good stock, and addicted to husbandry," to leave his home at Hermiston, near Edinburgh, and settle upon the farm of Monkshill, formed out of several smaller farms, and extending to 1130 acres. He gave him a lease of 63 years, with power to assign or sublet; the rent, running from 1s. 7d. to 2s. 4d. per acre, to increase progressively after ten years, until it doubled. "I hastened there, greedy to receive instruction from a gentleman who makes a figure by his publications; but I was much disappointed in finding neither him nor his overseer at home. All I saw was a field of turnip, one of oats, and one of barley, all in good order." So writes the tourist Surveyor.

Concerning the famous tenant of Monkshill, it may here be said that he was a man of liberal education; he had studied chemistry at Edinburgh, under Dr. Cullen, and, in 1780, received the degree of LL.D., at Aberdeen. Twelve years before he had married Miss Seton, of Mounie, by whom he had thirteen children. He was a contributor to the first edition of the *Encyclopædia Britannica*, and wrote the first report on the Agriculture of Aberdeenshire, published in 1794. Ardent in temperament, independent in his style of thought, and very outspoken, he took the keenest possible interest in the agriculture and social life of the region; his ideas, to which he never hesitated to give vent in one form or another, being not unfrequently in direct conflict with the established order of things, a circumstance which seems in no way to have disturbed his equanimity, marred his good humour, or cooled his enthusiasm. He was the originator, conductor, and chief contributor to a well-known weekly publication called "The Bee," carried on for several years, and in which agricultural, scientific, and other questions were discussed; and his separate publications, which include a great variety of subjects, from the construction of Chimneys to the nature and formation of Peat Moss, form altogether a very long list. Dr. Anderson died at Westham, near London, in 1808.

Passing on from Monkshill where, as we know from other sources, the farming was of the most advanced sort, our tourist went by Ellon, where, though the soil was good, he could not admire the husbandry. At Auchmacoy the improving proprietor had taken to fencing by means of hedges and ditches, in lieu of earth dykes, which were destroyed by the horned cattle thrusting their horns into them and tossing the material about; and it is a rather curious circumstance that, though horned cattle are mentioned repeatedly afterwards, not a single allusion is made to the black polled breed, of which Buchan is said to be the native region.

But, by universal consent, the person who took the first place for knowledge of farming in Buchan was a lady—Miss Fraser of Inverallochy—who had the entire management of the farm of Knockhall, leased from Mr. Udny, by her brother resident in London. This farm was all fenced with stone dykes and thorn hedges, with intervening strips of plantation. The stone fences are declared to be "incomparably good," while the highly-cultivated state of every field discovered "not only industry, but a superior genius. Drilled turnip, bear with grass seeds, thriving exceedingly, fine pasturage, the best sort of cows and young steers, in short, everything in perfection. I met a wain, deeply loaded with sea-shells, drawn by four fine bullocks. They were trained to draw in harness, and I was charmed to see them take all the turns of the road like the best-trained horses. In short, this lady is a miracle for farming. Her genius must be uncommon to excel so eminently in a vocation that Nature seems to have confined to the male sex." This opinion is fairly borne out by a written statement obtained from Miss Fraser, in which she discusses various practical points with much shrewdness and intelligence, urging in particular the economy effected by using oxen for draught purposes in place of horses, alike in the plough and for farm carriages. They did the work, at least as well, and in the end were fit for the butcher's purpose, which horses were not.

Farther on, toward the Fraserburgh coast, a picture of the poverty prevailing among a considerable part of the smaller tenants is given. "Their poverty, their weak horses, and small ill-constructed carts" are spoken of; "their mean crops," it is said, "yield little fodder; their horses, cows, and winterers are starved." "I have met many samples of the picture I have drawn. I have seen a long train of small carts, the bottom and sides done with spars for lightness, with ropes twisted about the spars for holding in peats or shells, as much as a feeble horse is able to drag along, and a man for every cart. Reflecting on the burdens of sand carried by women on their backs to Edinburgh, three or four miles, I am certain that the load of the cart was less than what was carried by a woman."

Coming to the pith of our Surveyor's general remarks, we find it stated of Aberdeenshire, as a whole, that —"This county is populous, and is turning more so daily. The people are sober and industrious, at the same time sufficiently docile. Wages for men servants are moderate; for women they are much higher than in the Lothians, owing to the extensive manufactory of stockings at Aberdeen, which has taught all of them to knit; and so industrious they are, that, in travelling the high road, they knit as busily as at home. The horned cattle, in general, are of a good kind, but ill managed. . . . The poverty of the pasture here is the bane of improvement, as likewise the number of cattle that are kept. . . . The native breed of sheep is diminutive, and no wonder; for the custom is to tether them; and yet I could observe no grass till I alighted and put on my spectacles." And then he condemns the general practice of tethering horses. And not without cause, as other authorities inform us that the poor animals were frequently kept upon the bare roadside on the miserable "foggage," their stall feeding being chiefly thistles gathered amongst the growing corn.

Not dissimilar in their general scope are Mr. Wight's observations upon the agriculture of Banffshire and the adjoining counties. Concerning the town of Banff he tells us that it possessed an extensive manufacture of thread for stockings, and that the thread manufactured was sent to Nottingham from Banff in waggons, and even then could be afforded at a cheaper rate than the thread made in Nottingham. The yearly returns, at first but small, had risen, it is said, to between forty and fifty thousand pounds sterling. The yarns, chiefly made from Dutch flax, and which gave employment in spinning to upwards of four thousand women in all, in Banff, Elgin, Forres, and intervening towns, amounted to about 150,000 spindles annually.

Mr. Wight does not appear to have considered it within his remit to offer remarks in detail upon the state of the roads, a circumstance rather to be regretted; and accounted for perhaps by the fact that he seems to have journeyed on horseback in place of attempting to drive in a wheeled conveyance. Once and again he adverts to the want of sufficient accommodation, or sufficient attendance at the inns where he had to put up. At Fochabers, where, after two hours waiting, he was at last supplied with "a half-boiled dish of hodge-podge," his candour compels him to mention the circumstance, "for the sake of travellers, that they may not be detained by the stupidity of a landlady and daughters, whose sole care seemed to be adorning and dressing their own persons in place of attending to dressing of victuals for the accommodation of travellers." And of Inverurie it is recorded that "although the town is one of the royal burghs in Scotland, yet the best public-house in it has but one decent room, and that on the ground floor, which serves for dining-room and bed chamber too. The traveller would feel himself well put up with the master and mistress of the inn, provided the house were but decently fitted up for accommodating travellers, when the number is more than one."

CHAPTER XVII.

DOMESTIC LIFE AND SOCIAL HABITS—DRESS—FOOD—
DRINK AND DRINKING CUSTOMS.

UNDER the date of October, 1730, the compiler of the Domestic Annals says:—"We are now arrived at a time which seems to mark very decidedly a transition in Scotland from poverty to growing wealth, from the Puritanic manners of the seventeenth century to the semi-licence and ease of the eighteenth, and consequently from restricted to expanded views." This statement is no doubt true in a general sense, though one rather hesitates to accept without considerable abatement Mr. Chambers's averments concerning the severe theological creed and dismally morose habits of "all respectable persons" in Scotland previous to 1730. There is some temptation even to say that there must have been a dash of conscious if not intentional caricature in the picture given—" Amongst the upper classes, the head of the family," we are told, "was for the most part an awful personage, who sat in a special chair by the fireside, and at the head of the table, with his hat on; often served at meals with special dishes, which no one else, not even guests, partook of. In all the arrangements of the house his convenience and tastes were primarily studied. His children approached him with fear, and never spoke with any freedom before him. At meals the lady of the house helped everyone as she herself might choose. The dishes were at once ill-cooked and ill-served. It was thought unmeet for man that he should be nice about food. Nicety and love of rich feeding were understood to be hateful peculiarities of the English, and unworthy of the people who had been so much more favoured by God in a knowledge of matters of higher concern. There was, nevertheless," it is added, "a great amount of hospitality." How the virtue of hospitality could possibly be exercised under the depressing influence of such morose and gloomy hosts is not quiet apparent. And, despite any reliable evidence yet produced to the contrary, we are convinced that Puritanic theology, even where it was most generally influential, was never in our history effective in suppressing the features of humanity to the extent indicated, except it might be in the case of a rather limited number of fanatics; whose example would not seem to have been by any means slavishly imitated by the great body of the people.

Up to about the time mentioned the almost universal dress of middle-class gentlemen was "hodden grey;" though we are told that as early as 1731 "hoops were constantly worn" by the ladies, "four and a-half yards wide," and which "required much silk to cover them." An ungallant local writer, twenty years later, speaks of the ladies at a public ball wearing "hoops of immense deformity." The heads "were all dressed in laces from Flanders;" but though "the price of these was high, two suits would serve for life; they were not renewed but at marriage or some great event." An English gentleman who visited Scotland at the beginning of the century, states that about 1702 he found the Lowlanders "dressed much like his own countrymen, excepting that the men generally wore bonnets instead of hats, and plaids instead of cloaks; the women, too, wearing plaids when abroad or at church." Women of the humbler class generally went barefoot, "especially in summer." The children of people of the better sort, "lay and clergy," were likewise generally without shoes and stockings. This description would apply very fairly to the state of matters a hundred years later.

After the Union with England in 1707, amid a good deal of grumbling over that event, the consumption of "fleshes and wheat bread" sensibly increased with the growth of trade among the better-to-do of town populations. In the rural districts there was little improvement in that way for a long while after. And change was by no means universally welcomed when it came. It is amusing to note the vehemence with which many of the writers in the *Old Statistical Account* (A.D. 1782-94) bewail the degeneracy creeping in through extravagance in dress and luxury in respect of food, and so on. The minister of a Banffshire parish asserts that "a very great change as to diet and dress has taken place during the forty years last past." Prior to that era "neither tea kettle nor tea could be found but in two families" in his parish. "Two hats only appeared at church; a lady adorned herself with the plaid, and a gentleman was not ashamed of homespun clothing. But now most families drink tea once, many twice, a-day. The ploughman appears at church and market with his hat, linen, and good broad cloth, and it may be taken for granted that the country belles will exert themselves to outshine the country beaux." Another writer tells us that "about fifty or sixty years ago there were not above seven tea kettles, as many hand bellows, and as many watches in Forfar; now tea kettles and hand bellows are the necessary furniture of the poorest house in the parish, and almost the meanest menial servant must have his watch." A third, who is even more explicit, says :—" The dress of all the country people in the district (central Aberdeenshire) was some years ago, both for men and women, of cloth made of their own sheep wool, Kilmarnock or Dundee bonnets, and shoes of leather tanned by themselves. Then every servant lad and maid had a quey or steer, sometimes two, and a score or two of sheep, to enable them to marry and begin the world with. Now every servant lad almost must have his Sunday coat of

English broadcloth, a vest and breeches of Manchester cotton, a high-crowned hat, and watch in his pocket. The servant maids are dressed in poplins, muslins, lawns, and ribbons. And both sexes have little else than finery to enter the world with, which occasions marriage to be delayed longer than formerly, and often brings distress along with it."

Of the usual dietary of the common people during last century, a writer of the time gives a concise and comprehensive account in the interrogatory form. If one wished to know how they lived, it might, he says, be indicated thus :—" Have you got your pottage ?—that is, your breakfast. Have you got your sowens ?—*i.e.*, your dinner. Have you got your brose ?—*i.e.*, your supper." The use of tea had become pretty common in the upper ranks from about 1720. It was gradually creeping in amongst the "commonality," but was strongly denounced by many as not only extravagant, but also calculated to make the people effeminate and weakly. Even the good Lord President Forbes of Culloden had his doubts, and wished for a law to restrain people under a certain income in the use of the leaf. During 1744 there was a sort of general movement over Scotland to put it down, and towns and parishes passed resolutions to that effect. The tenants of one Ayrshire laird, whose findings were put upon record, declared, with an air of high superiority, that it was needless for them to enter into any formal bond against the use of tea, which, say they, " would be but an improper diet to qualify us for the more robust and manly parts of our business ; and therefore we shall only give our testimony against it, and leave the enjoyment of it altogether to those who can afford to be weak, indolent, and useless."

So, with only their porridge, their sowens, and their kail—(whether common greens or the not too delicate "red kail," which had latterly become the exclusive perquisite of the bovine race, and seem now to be much neglected as an article of cultivation)—supplemented at exigent times by a dish of nettletops or "mugworts," it is not to be supposed that the food of the common people was over luxurious. Their favourite drink was home-brewed ale, which they manufactured to pretty good purpose, the proportion of malt used being probably quite as liberal as is the case now in certain instances. And concurrently with lamentations over the introduction of tea, we have strong laudations of the superior virtues of home-brewed ale. One Edinburgh physician, who denounces those "baneful articles, tea and whisky," as tending to "corruption of morals and debility of constitution among the poor," says expressly that their introduction "is one bad effect of the present practice of debasing and vitiating malt liquor. Formerly," he adds, "when that liquor was the only beverage in use, excesses from it did not affect the constitution, as it contained a good deal of nourishment. But now, since it has been debased, it is entirely given up."

It sounds a little odd to us, who have been accustomed to regard whisky as specially the national liquor, to be reminded that about the close of the seventeenth century French claret was the usual drink among the gentry and well-to-do classes, and twopenny ale among the common people. While brandy and whisky were comparatively rare, claret was to be found "in every public-house of any note except in the heart of the Highlands, and sometimes even there." And great quantities of it were drunk in many of the hostelries, as also in the houses of private gentlemen. In Arniston House, the country residence of President Dundas, the annual consumpt of claret about 1750 is stated to have been sixteen hogsheads; while it was the practice of John Forbes of Culloden, "Bumper John," as he was called, "to prize off the top of each successive cask of claret, and place it in the corner of the hall to be emptied out in pail-fuls."

The drinking habits of the time were indeed of a

somewhat outrageous kind. Many hospitable gentlemen made it their practice at the social board to see all their guests, if not literally under the table, at least in a condition to require assistance to bed before breaking up for the evening. And it was wonderful how even the common people "boosed" and got glorious on their "tippeny" when what seemed fit occasion, public or private, offered.* On this question of fitness the notions that prevailed were certainly not over strict amongst any of the classes of society. Nothing, for example, strikes us as more incongruous or ill-timed than the excesses that were wont so generally to prevail in connection with the solemnities of death and the grave. In his book on "Social Life in Former Days," Captain Dunbar gives a letter from a Mr. William Forbes, excusing himself from attending a funeral at Elgin. The date is 1742, and the writer says, "I told you that I could not doe myself the honour to witness the interment of your worthy father. This is to tell you that I have been drinking this whole day with our Magistrates and Town Council (God bless them), and am just now almost unfitt for your conversation, and therefor choose to goe home rather than expose myself; which I hope you will approve off." Mr. Forbes had either been an unduly sensitive man, or the "spate" in which he had indulged with the Magistrates must have left him in a very queer state; for in his day, and even a good deal later, it was not very uncommon to find that the major part of a funeral company had got more or less tipsy before they "lifted." Instances have been known of the "bearers" staggering so badly from the effect of their libations as nearly to pull the coffin they carried in pieces; and such tales have been told as that of

---

* Captain Burt says the price of the ale he got acquainted with was twopence for a Scots pint. The liquor was disagreeable to those not used to it, the malt which was dried with peat, turf, or furze, giving it a taste of the fuel. "When the natives drink plentifully of it," he adds, "they interlace it with brandy or usky."

a funeral company at starting being unable to determine which was the proper route to the grave-yard ; or even that they would "tak road" in utter forgetfulness of the melancholy burden they should have carried with them, but did not. A story is told in connection with the death of Sir Alexander Ogilvy, Lord Forglen, one of the Judges of the Court of Session in 1727, which shows how cordial was the belief in deep draughts as an antidote to grief. Dr. Clerk, his medical man, had called on the day he died. The doctor was let in by David Reid, Lord Forglen's clerk. On his asking how his patient was, David solemnly replied, "I houp he's weel," which meant, of course, that all was over. The doctor was conducted into a room, where he was shown two dozen of wine under the table, and other doctors coming in, David made them all sit down while he told them his deceased master's last words, at same time pushing the bottle about briskly. After the company had taken a glass or two, they rose to depart, but David detained them. "No, no, gentlemen ; not so. It was the express will o' the dead that I should fill ye a' fou, and I maun fulfil the will o' the dead." All the time the tears were streaming down his cheeks. "And indeed," said the doctor afterwards in telling the story, " he did fulfil the will o' the dead, for before the end o' 't there was nae ane o' us a' able to bite his ain thoomb."

CHAPTER XVIII.

DOMESTIC INDUSTRIES AND OUT-DOOR LABOUR—THE TRADE IN PLAIDING AND FINGRAMS—SPINNING AND KNITTING—A SPINNING MISTRESS—REGULATION OF THE TRADE—SCHOOL EDUCATION—THE FARMER'S EVENING FIRESIDE—THE FLAILMAN.

In the latter part of the seventeenth century the home manufacture of plaiding, fingrams, and stockings was a very important industry. Both spinning and weaving of wool and lint were carried on, not in large factories, but as domestic employments, pursued all over the country in their own houses by those who had no other occupation, as well as by the members of the farmer's and cottar's families. In a letter of date 1680, and attributed to the Countess of Erroll of that time, it is said "the women of this country are mostly employed spinning and working of stockings and making of plaiden webs, which the Aberdeen merchants carry over the sea; and it is this which bringeth money to the commons; other ways of getting it they have not." Very similar is the language of Baillie Alexander Skene of Newtile,* writing five years later. He enumerates plaiding, fingrams, and stockings among "the natural products of our land"; and maintains that with due attention to keep the market by an honestly produced article, which condition it appears was not fulfilled latterly, the whole wool grown in Scotland could be wrought by "the commons of the nation," working at "such times as

---

* Memorials for the Government of the Royal Burghs in Scotland, 1685.

their other country work permits," at rates that defied competition by those who set up a "particular manufacture." In proof of this latter point, he relates how —in view of the large sums of money brought into the kingdom by the plaiding trade, especially through the Aberdeen merchants, who got their wool chiefly from the south of Scotland, and then sold it out in "smalls" to the country people—a "substantious merchant in Edinburgh called Mr. Barnes," conceived the idea that having the wool at first hand he could, by employing people expressly to manufacture for him, sell in the market of Holland at a greater profit than the Aberdeen merchants with their roundabout mode of manufacture. But having made "about ten sea packs of plaiding, which might be reckoned worth twenty thousand pounds," he perceived that the Aberdeen men were selling their plaiding in Holland "at as low a rate as his stood himself at home"; whereupon he "fell a wondering" as to the reason of this. Having put the case to Alexander Farquhar, an Aberdeen merchant of his acquaintance, the "substantious" Edinburgh trader was informed "that the people that wrought *their* plaiding had not by farr such entertainment as *his* servants had, and that they drank oftener clear spring water than ale; and therefore they had their plaiding much cheaper than his; whereupon he quickly gave over his manufacture." Baillie Skene adds that notwithstanding the "sober rate" at which the commons lived they were "so set at work upon the account of their advantage in the north parts of Scotland, that in former years the product of their labours hath brought into this kingdom yearly upwards of an hundreth thousand rex dollars for many years together; without this the nobility and gentry in thir parts could not get their money rents well paid." Surprisingly high prices had been given; for our present authority speaks of a certain George Pyper, who to prevent decay in the trade and stimulate improvement in the style of knitting stockings, had encouraged the country people by giving them a little money or some linen at times, so "that from five groats the pair he caused them work at such a fynness that he hath given twenty shillings sterling and upward for the pair." Mr. Pyper flourished a little after the middle of the seventeenth century, and about 1676 had as many as four hundred people spinning and knitting for him.

In a memorial to the Trustees for the Improvement of Manufactures, of date 1728, the local importance of the question is urged "as it will not be denied, but there is a greater quantity of coarse wool, commonly called tarred wool, manufactured in the shire of Aberdeen, and the manufactures thereof exported yearly from the port of Aberdeen than from all Scotland besides." There was also a considerable quantity of linen cloth made and sold yearly; and thus "the gentlemen of the county of Aberdeen, whose rents are for the most part paid by the produce of their manufactures, have a very great concern that they should be improven."

Substantially the same style of domestic industry continued throughout the eighteenth century, as is seen from the statements of various of the Old Statistical writers. The minister of Kincardine O'Neil says of his parish, "600 women are employed in spinning and knitting of woollen stockings, at which they earn from 2s. to 2s. 6d. a-week." Of the women of Strathdon we are told that "they are in general capital spinners, and they bring a great deal of money into the parish." The statist for the parish of Rayne calculates that the knitting of stockings—at which all the women and some of the boys, and old men even, of his parish were employed—yielded about £400 sterling; and, he says, if it were not for the results of the knitting "the rents of the crofts could not be paid." The minister of Glenmuick says, with some emphasis, "while I accuse the men of indolence, I should do great injustice to the women if I did [not] exempt them from the charge, by whose industry and diligence their families are in a great measure supported." Those exemplary women of Glenmuick, it appears, spun flax for the Aberdeen manufacturers, as well as made blue homespun cloth and tartan webs of their own wool, and which they sold at 2s. and 2s. 6d. an ell.

The statements of various writers show that the stocking manufacture was of much local importance all through the eighteenth century. James Rae of Whitehaven, a volunteer under the Duke of Cumberland in 1745, in his History of the Rebellion, says of Aberdeen trade, "the manufacture here is chiefly stockings, all round the adjacent country; and every morning the women bring in loads to sell about the town to merchants, who have them scoured for exportation to London, Hamburg, and Holland. They are generally all white from the makers, and knit most plainly; some are ribbed, and a great many with squares, which greatly please the Dutch. They make stockings here in common from one shilling a-pair to one guinea and a half, and some are so fine as to sell for five guineas the pair." And similarly, Mr. Francis Douglas, speaking of the rather sterile seacoast district in the north part of Kincardineshire, where one could see "numbers of poor huts and starved cattle," says, " being within a few miles of Aberdeen, the females have constant employment in knitting stockings to the manufacturers. By their unremitting labour in this branch they earn money to pay their rents." The extent of the knitting industry must have been great. Douglas says, " the manufacture was supposed to amount to from a hundred and ten to a hundred and twenty thousand pounds sterling annually; two-thirds of which are reckoned to be paid for spinning and knitting; the other third goes to pay the materials, and afford a profit to the manufacturers." The wool was still, it may be said, imported from the south; and in 1778 it was stated on credible authority, "that in the currency of a year wool shipped at the port of London for Aberdeen was insured to the value of £40,000." Few women, according to Douglas, could earn "above eighteenpence a-week by spinning and knitting stockings;" but, as we have seen, some of them did earn considerably more. He adds, that at a former time worsted stockings had been worked in the country upon very fine brass wires, which sold as high as three or four pounds sterling a-pair. A pair of these, however, was almost constant work for a woman for six months; and thus valuable chiefly "as a mark of great patience and ingenuity in the worker." These, one would be disposed to believe, must have been the stockings for which George Pyper gave his highest premium.

In domestic spinning the rock and spindle were the only available instruments during the first quarter of the century. With these a woman could produce only about three and a-half heers (each heer consisting of 240 threads or rounds of the reel) a-day. When the rock and spindle came to be superseded by the spinning-wheel, a woman could spin twelve heers a-day.

The spinning of the thread was done in the farmers' families, and the yarn was taken to the weaver to be wrought into webs. To be able to spin well was, of course, an important accomplishment; and thus in 1741, Elizabeth Thom, "spinning mistress" in Aberdeen, desires to make known her readiness to teach women to spin "with both hands." On her application, the County Clerk was authorized to sign her advertisement to that effect. Eight years thereafter, in 1749, a "further encouragement" was given to this lady, by the county gentlemen agreeing to draw the attention of the Magistrates to the spinning school, and recommending that people both in town and country should take the benefit of it. In 1751 a competition for prizes in the matter of brown linen cloth and linen yarn took place, under the auspices of Isobel Swan, a spinning mistress in Putachieside, Aberdeen.

Long before these laudable efforts had been put forth the very prosperity of the trade, apparently, through the strong export demand, had led to systematic attempts being made to deteriorate the manufacture. So early as the tenth year of Queen Anne, an Act was passed to prevent " diverse abuses and deceits " in making linen cloth, and for regulating the length, breadth, and equal sorting of the yarn. A subsequent statute of George II., applied directly to "serges, plaidings, and fingrams," and " knit stockings." What we gather from various " advertisements " issued by the Justices of Peace and Deans of Guild of Aberdeen, is, that many of the spinners and weavers contravened the statutes "by making serges and fingrams of unequal wool and yarn ; and by working the same unequally, having three or four elns of the first end of each piece considerable better than the rest of the piece ;" also that "they continued to draw and overstretch the same after they are wrought, whereby the cloth is much prejudged, and by shrinking after it is bought, the buyers become losers ;" and they made them of "unequal and irregular lengths," and too narrow in the breadth. Their perverse ingenuity had even got the length of thickening the cloth with batter, " whereby the faults and thinness of the work cannot be so well perceived." The practice with stockings had evidently been none better: and so the statute of George II., which provides under penalties that all serges and fingrams should be " of equal work and fineness from one end of the piece to the other," the narrow fingrams to be twenty-eight inches in width, and the broad thirty-eight inches ; also provided that " all stockings that shall be made in Scotland shall be wrought and made of three threads, and of one sort of wool and worsted, and of equal work and fineness throughout, free of left loops, hanging hairs, and of burnt, cutted, or mended holes, and of such shapes and sizes respectively as the patterns, which shall be marked by the several Deans of Guild of the chief burghs of the respective counties;" all according to dimensions specified in detail in the Act. Authorised stampers, whose function it was to put the official stamp on all marketable webs and bundles of stockings, were appointed for each district; but though these gentlemen had to take the oath *de fideli*, and "find bail" on their admission to office, they seem not to have been universally free from the suspicion of allowing doubtful goods to pass occasionally; and then marking the stamp so faintly that it did not show legibly, as it ought, the initial letters of the parish from whence they came. And so detection of the offenders, who were liable to a pecuniary mulct, was rendered very difficult or altogether impossible. It was even charged against them that they did not do the measuring in the manner laid down to them, and, in some cases, marked a greater number of yards on a web than it contained. Legislation, imperial and local, failed to check the prevailing evil practices effectually, till at length the Aberdeenshire manufacture of fingrams got so "insufferably bad" that the Dutch market was irrecoverably lost, the Hollanders declining to buy them at any price.

The growth of flax to furnish lint for manufacture into family linen at least, was a branch of the agriculture of the time, but not a permanent one. Flax-growing was not much known before the middle of the century, and by the end of it it was again on the decline. About 1780 to 1790 as much as 400 to 500 acres were annually occupied with this plant—generally sown in small patches—in the county of Aberdeen.* Twenty years thereafter, by the introduction of the cotton manufacture, the breadth in flax had diminished to not above 100 acres; but in Angus and Mearns the

---

* The Old Statistical writer for the parish of Cairney naively says—"The manufacture of linen has introduced a certain cleanliness all over the country. It has almost banished the itch."

plant was grown more extensively; the area in flax in the Mearns, so late as 1807, being 236 acres. The spinning of flax afforded much employment to women in the Buchan and Strathbogie districts of Aberdeenshire about 1780; and at that date a good spinner could earn sixpence, and in some cases sevenpence a-day at her wheel, which seems to have been the maximum wage ever attained at this particular industry. Between spinning and knitting worsted, and spinning flax, the time of the Aberdeenshire women may be supposed to have been pretty fully occupied. It was so as matter of fact—occupied, one may venture to think, in a very suitable fashion. And so we have a tourist at the opening of the present century recording it as what appeared surprising to him that " he did not perceive a single female employed in field labour " in Aberdeenshire; such labour being " executed by men," contrary to the practice of the southern counties, " where work of that kind was performed by girls and boys," while the men worked the horses in the summer months. Other writers tell of the barbarous way in which the women in certain regions were made to do the roughest out-door labour as occasion required. Especially was this the case in certain Highland and half-Highland parts, where the inert lord of the creation would lie on his hip and complacently look on while his wife did the most menial and fatiguing labour on the croft, even to the extent, as has been already said, of carrying the contents of the scanty dunghill a-field on her back!

But in the north-eastern section of Scotland there was little to complain of either as to fitness in the distribution of labour as between the sexes, or the amount that each was expected to accomplish. In the years of childhood a certain measure of schooling was deemed needful. With girls it hardly went beyond giving them the capability of reading in a moderate degree; not always so far. Writing was regarded more in the light of an elegant accomplishment, hardly as a thing practically useful for the female sex, and some who looked at the matter in the light of principle excused themselves from bestowing it on their daughters under the plea that "mony ane's deen ill wi' vreet." As it concerned the male sex, the school population, in the shape of sturdy well-grown boys, were simply expected to tramp up leisurely day by day during the winter months, each with his peat under his arm, to keep the school fire going, and without anything further in the way of prepared tasks than a question in the Shorter Catechism. The ordinary curriculum was not complicated with other branches, as English Grammar and Geography; as, indeed, the attainments of the dominie himself did not always admit of his handling these in any formal or exact manner. Up to at least the end of last century, the only reading books in use in the parish schools were the Bible and Shorter Catechism. The pupils read in succession the Catechism, and the Proverbs; then the rest of the Bible, and it was reckoned a great feat to read fluently those parts which were full of proper names that were difficult to pronounce. The schoolmaster rarely if ever thought of questioning his pupils on the subject matter of their lessons, or of explaining to them the meaning of what they read. Under this moderate intellectual discipline, a youth got leisure to grow to his full stature, or at any rate to reach the age of eighteen or nineteen before any heavier task was imposed upon him than that of herding the cattle of his father, or, if a cottar's son, those of some neighbouring farmer. Of course the total absence of enclosures made the occupation of cattle herd an essential and generally diffused one. We find the statement made in 1750, that the herds in the Synod of Aberdeen at that date were at least "five thousand in number."

Then when young men had got past the school and herd-boy period, the labour imposed was not very continuous or systematic. In summer, with no green crops, such as turnips, to care for, and nothing in the shape of improvement to carry out, once the "fauld dyke" had been erected, which was done by the joint labour of the tenants of the plough-gate or hamlet, there was little to do except to see to the drying and carrying home of the peats and turves for winter fuel; and that in many cases occupied a large portion of the farmer's time during summer. When shearing came, of course all were busy enough, and really hard work it was. The period of harvest was much more protracted then than now, and it was no unusual thing for the shearing to extend over six weeks or so. As was right and proper, they made harvest a time of cheerfulness and mirth; and we read of a farmer in the Mearns who, to make his "hyeucks" go on lightly and pleasantly, "kept a piper to play to them all the time of harvest, and gave him his harvest fee." It was no doubt done on the same principle that the "gaudman" was expected to whistle a voluntary, or psalm tune, to the oxen he drove in the plough, as well as to give them sharper admonition as required with his "gaud"—leading us to the origin of a pithy variation of the proverb, Much cry for little wool—" Muckle whistlin for little red lan'."

A graphic and realistic sketch of the scene about the farmer's fireside of a winter evening, when the young women of the neighbouring farm houses had met, as the custom was to meet in the several houses in turn, to pursue their knitting in friendly rivalry, while the goodwife ordered the house or "span a thread," and the men, in addition to caring for their cattle, took up such odd jobs of a light sort as could be fitly done for personal use or the benefit of the establishment, is given by a local rhymer who flourished early in the present century. He speaks presumably of his own time, but even then "the old order," had not been materially changed.* We have first the farmer plunging round

* Fruits of Time Parings, by W. Beattie, Aberdeen, 1813; republished 1873.

about byres and barn against the "endrift styth" in the growing gloamin darkness.

> For fear the poor dumb brutes sud smore,
> He staps wi' strae ilk navus bore,
>   An' ilka crevice darns.
> Syne aifter he has deen his best,
> The sheep sought hame, an' a' at rest,
> He bouns him to the house,
> An' sits him doon upo' the bink,
> An' plaits a theet, or mends a mink,
>   To sair an aifter use.

And then the scene when the "shankers" are gathered by the fireside :—

> The littleanes play at seek an' hide
>   Ahint the kists an' tables ;
> The farmer sits anent the licht,
> An' reads a piece o' Wallace Wicht,
>   Or maybe Æsop's Fables.
>
> An' little Pate sits i' the neuk,
> An' but-a-hoose dare hardly luik,
>   But haud an' snuff the fir ;
> An' fan the farmer tines the line,
> He says, "Yer light casts little shine—
>   Haud in the candle, sir !"
>
> The gaudman sits an' toasts his nose,
> Or awkwardly heel-caps his hose,
>   Or maks yoke-sticks o' rodden ;
> Auld Luckydaddy win's at brutches,
> An' granny tells them tales o' witches,
>   Until the kail be sodden.

And so on till the "brose is suppit," and they take to bed trusting to be roused betimes next morning for flail and plough by the waukrife goodman.

In autumn the "twal-owsen" plough was set agoing, when the services of the ploughman and gaudman came into active request; and about farms of considerable extent there was in addition the barnman. In winter it was his business every day and all day long to ply

" the thresher's weary flingin' tree." Here we have an outline sketch of a professional flailman or barnman. —A gaunt, sinewy fellow, six feet in height, minus coat, waist-coat, and neckerchief, with his shirt collar loose ; his towsy head bare, and barefooted too, as he shuffled to and fro in the floor and pelted away at the loosened sheaves he had strewn over it from end to end. He was paid by the boll; and when in the humour for a regular set-to, would thresh out the almost incredible quantity of six bolls in a day. We need not suppose that he was over nice in threshing clean. Quantity was his aim, and too great nicety did not tend to promote that object ; while he might justly hold, as indeed he avowed his belief, that the cattle would be "nane the waur o' a wisp wi' a fyou o' the berries on't." In the case of smaller farms the threshing was done of a winter morning by the farmer and his "man" getting up early for a " spell" at it together. Before the degenerate era of clocks and watches, which were rare in country houses down to quite the end of the eighteenth century, the proper time to get up to thresh was a matter of guess work ; and we have heard of a decent Garioch quaker who had erred on the safe side by leaving his bed about midnight and rousing his servant man. They threshed on and on, and were getting tired, and even hungry. The man had gone and looked over the barn door repeatedly for tokens of morning light; and at last he turned round with the pettish exclamation, "I've seen as muckle as it never come daylicht;" whereon the matter-of-fact quaker quietly asked, "Whaur wast thou, friend, when thou saw that ?"

CHAPTER XIX.

THE MILL AND THE MILLER—THIRLAGE—FETCHING HOME THE MILLSTONE—MULTURES—THE MILLER'S TYRANNY—SEARCH FOR A MILLWRIGHT—THE OLD SYSTEM FALLING OBSOLETE.

AMONG the "parts, pertinents, and privileges" granted under a baronial charter in the feudal times, perhaps one of the oldest adjuncts of a barony, was the mill. One mill at least, and not unfrequently several, were erected in each barony or lairdship, all the lands of the barony or lairdship being astricted or "thirled" thereto, forming the mill "sucken." The tenants were bound to have their corn ground at the mill to which they were thirled, which, in some cases, was not the nearest mill to their farms. Indeed, instances were known of a man having to pass not one, but two mills before he reached the one at which it was permissible for him to have his corn ground. But he had no choice in the matter. Each person in the sucken had to pay mill multures, and to perform certain services, such as assisting to bring home a new millstone when required, or aiding in the more frequent operation of clearing out the mill lead.

The process of fetching home the millstone must, in certain cases, have been a peculiarly formidable one. Indeed, a local "byeword," which had a sort of lingering currency, though without any very pointed application, within quite recent times, would seem to have had its origin in, and be enused as a vivid illustration of, that idea. "As gweed to ye tak a millstane oot o'

Pennan," they said, when a man had a task before him difficult enough to bid defiance to his unaided strength. Pennan, in Aberdour parish, was the site of the quarry which furnished millstones for the greater part of Aberdeenshire and Banffshire.* And in the time when there were neither properly made roads nor wheeled vehicles capable of bearing so heavy a load, it is not difficult to believe that the bringing home of a millstone from a distance of perhaps half-a-dozen miles or more, was an onerous business. The mode adopted was simply that of trundling it on its edge all the way, by the most direct route available. They got a long and stout stick, which was called "the spar," put through the eye of the millstone, and firmly wedged there. The spar projected from two to three feet on one side, and perhaps fifteen feet, or more, on the other, the long lever being used to keep the stone on its edge, the other in the way of guidance as the stone moved onward. Over the millstone was fixed a rough wooden frame. Four, or perhaps six horses, were yoked to the front of this frame, which had a steering tree attached behind, while its construction admitted of the spar turning round like the axle of the "tumbling" cart. One experienced man steered; another kept by the short end of the spar; while the general body of the suckeners managed the long end, or held on behind by ropes attached to the frame, to prevent the millstone running off on the downward gradients. Despite every precaution, it would occasionally get too much way on a declivity and overpower all concerned, creating dire confusion; or by some unhappy chance it would have its equilibrium so disturbed as to get suddenly upset on the short end of the spar, throwing the hapless suckeners, who hung grimly on at the other end hither and thither, or tilting them up in the air. These experiences were neither pleasant nor safe; and hence came the common saying, " Mony

---

* The millstone found here is a coarse sandstone, or conglomerate of the Old Red Sandstone formation.

ane's gotten an amshach at the spar." A not unfrequent source of danger, too, in connection with the mill, was found in the tendency of the indifferently set millstone to fly in pieces when grinding, maiming, or even killing the miller, if he happened to be in the way.

The mill services and the exactions made in the shape of multure and "knaveship," as part of the tax in kind was called, seem to have caused the miller to be universally detested. Of both the existing system and the men by whom it was carried on, Dr. James Anderson gives a description that is more expressive than complimentary. In speaking of the state of matters in Aberdeenshire in his own time, he says the tenants, in some cases, paid the seventeenth peck in thirlage. Then they paid " multure, or the price of grinding, which," says he, " is often the thirty-second peck. They pay also to the miller a *lick of good will*, or a bannock, which tenants have sometimes allowed to be measured ; and there are instances where another unmeasured lick has crept in. Even the seeds sifted from the bannock are sometimes paid. When all these items are added together, they amount at some mills to a twelfth or eleventh part of the whole corn carried to the mill." But even this was not all. The *cog* with which the shealing was measured was allowed to be "made or mended," according to the fancy of the multurer ; and so its size was as likely to be wrong as right ; and if wrong, the error would probably not be to the disadvantage of the miller. Then the tenant was bound to grind not only the meal to be used in his own family at the mill to which he was thirled, but also " all the other grain reared on his farm, seed only excepted ; or to pay the full multure for every ounce of it that shall be sold elsewhere or otherwise disposed of ; even horse corn and wheat which they cannot manufacture, as well as bear, are not excepted. The millers even insist for payment of the multure for the corn that might have grown on fields laid down to grass, which in the usual rotation of crops in the county ought otherwise to have been in corn." And, "besides this heavy tax," adds Dr. Anderson, "the tenants are in general obliged to clear out and repair the mill lead, which is often half-a-mile in length, and the edges of it, for the most part, serve as a road to the miller's cattle."*

Then he goes on to complain of the little trouble the miller gave himself in the way of attending to his duties. But why should the miller trouble himself about meeting the wants or wishes of his customers! They were bound to come to him; but he was not bound to put himself to inconvenience or disturb his cherished habits to please them. Neither did he. He was in a position to treat them after the manner of the churl if he was so minded; and occasionally, it seems manifest, he was. But not always, for the miller could at times be sociable as well as other people. It was told of a certain miller in the Garioch, that in doing a "melder" on one occasion, he "set on" the mill; not a very powerful one, in the matter of grinding, it would seem; and then, the alehouse being conveniently near, went away with a crony to "slocken" his drought. There they sat for some considerable time, and there the mill "hottered" away by itself. And not quite by itself either, for the worthies had left a couple of dogs about the place; and, the mill door being open, the two sagacious tykes went in, and, sitting down contentedly by the spout, licked up the meal with their tongues as fast as it was manufactured.

Of course, the farmer was expected to have his own kiln, or "killogie" as it was termed, and to dry his grain for himself before he troubled the miller about it. Dr. Anderson, in prosecution of his loud complaint, goes on to say that the millers did not give themselves the trouble to get winnowing machines "till of late" (he is writing in 1794), "that the tenants in some cases have purchased them; and, for permitting them to be turned

---

* For sample of contract between mill superior and suckeners see Appendix (4).

by the machinery of the mill, they must pay another
multure, or carry their shealing out of doors to be win-
nowed by the wind. In short," he adds, "what with
want of water at one time and want of wind at another,
I have known instances of three persons being obliged
to go to the distance of three miles to the mill three
or four times over, and be employed nearly a whole
week for the grinding of half a dozen bolls of meal."
Weary work enough, surely, but Dr. Anderson has
scarcely reached his climax even yet. After declaring
that "there is not in this island such a compleat remain of feudal despotism as in the practice respecting
mills in Aberdeenshire," he adds that "the millers, in
many cases, exercise their power with the most wanton
insolence, these men being too often supported by all
the weight of the landlord's influence, so that I have
myself seen poor farmers, by vexation and despair,
reduced to tears to supplicate what they ought to have
commanded from him."

In 1757, the season being one of scarcity, the Aberdeenshire county gentlemen appointed a committee "to
consider the state of the victual and what improvements
might be made upon corn mills and the manufacture
of grain to make it yield more and of better quality."
They had had it represented to them that John Wright,
a soldier in Captain Wood's regiment, "presently lying
in North Britain," was a man of skill and experience
in the making and improvement of the machinery of
corn mills, and would be inclined to settle in the north
country; and the committee were recommended to apply
to Lord George Beauclerk, commander of the Forces in
Scotland, to know if he would oblige them by giving
Wright his discharge, on a sufficient man being furnished as his substitute; or at least give him a long
furlough with a view to his contributing to the improvement of the mills. The facts enable us to realise
somewhat distinctly how utterly destitute of mechanical
skill the county must have been when it was deemed

an object to get hold of a stranger soldier to lead them toward improvement.

An idea of the limited power of the mills of the time may be gathered from statistics of their actual numbers within particular areas. Thus, in the large central parish of Fyvie, in Aberdeenshire, there were in the latter part of the last century thirteen corn mills, in each of which there was a "fanner turned by the machinery of the mill," enabling the work to go on in all weathers, and not leaving the winnowing dependant upon the natural currents of the air of heaven. In the neighbouring parish of Auchterless there were seven mills; while King-Edward parish boasted of ten corn mills, with two lint mills and two waulk mills.

The origin of the thirlage system was natural enough. When the quern driven by hand came to be reckoned rather behind the time, the mill, such as it was, was looked upon as "a masterpiece of machinery."* When a mill was set agoing it was deemed needful therefore that the laird and the miller should have assurance of its being supported, and their own enterprise in its establishment and working adequately rewarded. Hence were the tenants and crofters bound to cast aside their family querns, go to the public mill of their sucken, and pay the statutory multures. The abstracted multures were a fruitful source of litigation until an Act was passed in the reign of George III. (39 George III. cap. 55) authorising their conversion into money payments. Subsequent to the date of that Act the ground of complaint lay chiefly against the principle of thirlage, which in certain cases was not readily overturned.

A curious commentary on the utterly obsolete

---

* As early as 1284, the Scottish Legislature tried to supersede the quern by the water mill, the use if it being prohibited except in the case of storm or where there was a lack of mills of the new description. Querns were, however, largely used in Scotland down to the end of the last century.

character of the old molendinary system is found in the case of the mills belonging to the burgh of Aberdeen. A charter of Charles I., granted in 1638, and confirmed by a subsequent charter, sets forth that as "the said burgh is becoming a populous city, famous for humanity and renown," and as His Majesty "is sollicitous that the said burgh should daily flourish," therefore he grants "all and sundry the common mills" of the said burgh to the Magistrates and Council, "with the multures and sequels of the said mills, and of all grain growing upon all and sundry the crofts, acres, and lands of the community of our said burgh, and within the freedom and territory thereof, and of all grain pertaining and belonging to the burgesses and inhabitants of our said burgh tholing fire and water within the same." Doubtless the royal grant had been in its time a privilege worth having, and it seems to have been jealously guarded. We find, for example, that on 4th August, 1726, the Council ordained that all querns or iron hand mills "sett up" or to be sett up within the city for grinding malt or any other grain "be seized, demolished, and broken down to pieces;" the object, no doubt, being the protection of the business of the town's mills. And for very long after this the mills had no more formidable rivals than those connected with the various county lairdships, to which the tenants generally continued to be thirled during a considerable part of the first half of the present century. But it had latterly come to be the case that there was scarcely a single mill within the limits of the burgh of Aberdeen kept up in a state of complete efficiency. They had become antiquated and unfit to meet the demands of the time, while several mills that had been erected a short distance beyond the burgh boundaries were doing a thriving and profitable trade; simply because their owners saw it to be to their interest to adapt them to modern necessities. And so, a few years ago, the Burgh Corporation, notwithstanding its chartered monopoly, found that the best thing it could do was to sell the motive power of two of its mills—the water by which they were driven—to certain manufacturers; and then sell the ancient fabrics of the mills themselves, one of which had by that time stood gaunt and silent for several years for want of a tenant.

CHAPTER XX.

CRAFTSMEN — ITINERANT CRAFTSMEN AND TRADERS — COAL AND PEAT—THE SMITH—THE WRIGHT — THE TAILOR—THE PACKMAN—THE HORNER—JOCK YOUNG, AND TIB DOO.

VARIOUS facts, stated in the preceding pages, serve to show the comparatively backward condition, not only of agriculture, but of the mechanical arts as well, during the greater part of the eighteenth century. Other illustrations of a similar kind might be given. But in place of dealing with particular details of that sort, it may serve the end equally well to glance at the subject from a different point of view. Few things can be clearer than that the capability of readily forging iron, and bringing it into use for the purposes of industrial life within a community, is essential to real progress under the conditions of modern civilisation. Without that, all kinds of mechanism must remain comparatively rude, and the results achieved thereby be correspondingly inconsiderable. Now, in the business of forging iron to purpose, the aid of coal as a potent fuel has been found of the utmost consequence. And during a great part of the eighteenth century very little coal, indeed, was used in those districts of Scotland that were dependant on other parts for a supply. We get an idea of the quantity in an indirect way. At the Union in 1707, the Scottish Commissioners opposed the exaction of a duty on coal; yet till far through the century a duty of 3s. 8d. a ton continued to be levied on all coal "carried coastwise" to any part of Britain. It was only by carriage coastwise, of course, that any such heavy article as coal could be conveyed a moderate distance. Want of roads and of wheeled vehicles made long land carriages impracticable. In 1775, a House of Commons Committee had the duty entrusted to them of inquiring into the state of the fisheries on the west and northern coasts of Scotland. They seem to have entered on their remit in a comprehensive spirit, dealing with the fiscal condition generally of the districts under their notice. And the account they give of the state of the revenue in the nine northern counties, including Argyle, Inverness, and Moray, on to Shetland, could not have been encouraging in the eyes of those in charge of the Exchequer. The average yield of the taxes levied for ten years had been £5073 12s., and the cost of collection, £5167 19s., leaving a deficit on the debtor side of the Treasury account of £94 7s. In speaking of the coal duty, the Committee say—" It appears from accounts laid on your table that the whole nett duty collected on coal *over all Scotland* does not exceed £3000 a-year;" which they sensibly enough remark, " furnishes the most convincing proof to your Committee that the present duties are too high, and operate more as a prohibition on the article than as a benefit to the revenue." At 3s. 8d. a ton the net revenue from coal carried coastwise to every port of Scotland that lay outside the coal regions—probably three-fourths of the whole area at last—would represent a supply of less than 18,000 tons. As illustrating the absolutely insignificant character of this supply in the light of present-day requirements, it need only be stated that at the one port of Aberdeen the yearly import of coal "coastwise" now is much beyond 200,000 tons, while many thousand tons are imported by railway.

About the date just spoken of, the sum paid annually by the inhabitants of Aberdeen for peat as fuel was as much as £3000, frequently it was £4000; a greater sum than appears to have been realised off the coal duty from the whole of Scotland. And as dried peat probably did not cost much more per ton than the amount of the duty on that weight of coal, the yearly consumpt by town's folks must have been very considerable. In the country districts the article coal was practically unknown. About 1785, it was recorded as a thing worth making a note of that "some of the gentry burn coals in their houses." But even then coal had not come into general use with the ordinary blacksmith; and without coal the smith was not good for much. To fit up a machine of any sort where wheels and pinions and a "journal" on which they might run came into use was quite beyond him. It taxed the powers of his peat and charcoal fire and his rude "studdie" sufficiently to furnish forth the plough and plough "graith," of the style already described, and, if a moderately skilful man, to put a pair of shoes on the fore-hoofs of the farmers' horses to wear while the peats were driving, and then to be taken off and laid aside for renewed use when the like season of work came round again.*

The wright did his part without calling iron very prominently into use. He could "knit the cupples" and set up the whole roof timbers of a house, mainly,

---

* From the "Brieffe Narrative" of Gilbert Blakhal we learn incidentally that country blacksmiths could, in some cases, do the farrier's office readily enough in the middle of the seventeenth century. In the Autumn of 1641 the worthy priest, travelling with his "Mass cloathes" concealed in his valise, put up at a hostelrie on Moor of Rhynie to feed his horse; and there had his coolness and courage put to the test by the rude captain of a local company of "soldiers, all drunk as beastes," who vainly endeavoured to bully the father into telling him who he was. He passed over the hills of Cushnie, "as wyld a piece of ground as is in all Brittaine," to Deeside; when his horse, which had been stung in the breast by an adder by and bye, got so lame on the off fore-foot that he could not put it to the ground. "I did make remove the shoe of that foote at the Churche of Birs," says the Father, "to sie what did hurt his foote. The smith did not discover anything, nather in his foote or legge, and therefor set on the shoe again, and so I did sometimes lead him, and sometymes ryde upon him to Aberdeine, wher the ministers were holding their General Assembly."

or indeed wholly, by the aid of stout wooden pins driven into wimble holes. Even when slates came into use as a roofing material, they were attached to the "sarking" not by iron nails but by hardwood pins. And in the construction of a box bed, or the hanging and fixing of a door, the resort to iron was wonderfully minimised. In the case of the barn implements, including flail and thrashing floor, it could be dispensed with altogether. The ingenious business of wheelwright, in which the turning-lathe was called into use, did not necessitate resort to iron work to any noticeable extent. And the cooper or mugger, who manufactured wooden cogs, caups, and ladles, articles of very essential use in the domestic life of the time, was still less indebted to it as a material.

Apart from the smith and wright, the two other indispensable craftsmen were the shoemaker and the tailor; and of these the tailor was the most important. During summer a good part of the population did not much trouble themselves about shoes; or if they did, were content with brogues of untanned leather, fashioned by themselves. But clothing of some sort for the main part of the body was a necessity at all seasons, and a "stan' o' shapit claes" could not be had without the tailor, who pursued his craft after the peripatetic mode, travelling from house to house, and fashioning suits for the goodman and his grown up sons off the blue or grey woollen web, spun by the women of the household, and woven by the weaver driving his loom in the "midhouse" or other section of his dwelling, to the order of his customers.

A far from unimportant member of the community was the chapman, or "pack merchant," who supplied the wants of the people in so far as cloth and other articles not of home manufacture were needed. With his pack slung over his shoulder, and a big pack it often was, and his ellwand in his hand, the chapman travelled on his round day by day. He was known to his constituency, who gave him a ready welcome, and, with the due amount of deliberation and haggling, bought such things as they required. They were respectable men and industrious the chapmen, and at times succeeded, as has been already hinted, in realising surprisingly large sums of money comparatively. Here is the obituary notice of an Aberdeenshire chapman, who departed this life in January, 1751 :—" Last week died, of a short illness, William Urquhart, a well-known travelling chapman, who, without noise or hurry, without horse or packs, without fraud or dishonesty, acquired about £500 sterling, most of which was found in his pockets in bank notes and good bills at his death —a singular instance," adds the chapman's biographer, " of the good effects of sobriety and frugality.". William Urquhart's case had no doubt been a remarkable one in some particulars, though by no means without parallel in the matter of pecuniary results. The chapman, tramping away on his rounds day by day ; and attending the yearly fairs in his district to open out his pack into a " stand" for the day—the cooper and mugger taking places alongside of him with their wares—occasionally worked his way to the possession of a wellfurnished " chop i' the toon ;" and where his ambition did not lead him that way, he frequently amassed what was to him a comfortable competency. An inferior branch was the sale of chapbooks ; a species of popular literature well enough known so long ago as the time of Swift, who names among the productions of "writers of and for Grub Street" various chap books, such as "The Wise Men of Gotham," which, along with Dougal Graham's "Witty Exploits of Mr. George Buchanan, the King of Scots Fool," and much else of a similar character, found circulation through the medium of itinerants of no great standing, socially or otherwise, who perambulated the rural districts and visited fairs and markets, vending their penny chap books and halfpenny ballads, until long after the close of the eighteenth century.

A craftsman who found place somewhere between the classes who really earned their bread by the sweat of their brows and the class who were utterly given over to sorning and vagabondage, was the horner— nearly allied to the "tinkler," whose office was to " clout the cauldron." The horner supplied the community with spoons ; and the essential implement of his craft was the wooden " caums," wherein the horn —cut up and partly dressed—after being reduced to a state of greater pliability by heating, was moulded into the form of a " cutty." The horner was of course a peripatetic ; and as he tramped about, he easily carried his kit of tools and a moderate supply of horns in a rough wallet slung over his shoulder. He was not particular about his workshop. It might be in the open air, by a convenient dykeside ; or, if the weather was bad, in the barn or other outhouse belonging to some friendly person who did not begrudge him quarters for a night or two. The crafts of "tinkler" and horner were followed generation after generation by certain families of " cairds," habit and repute. One of these families, of the name of Young, furnished a noted thief and prison breaker, who, for the offence of mortally stabbing a fellow caird, ultimately terminated his career on the gallows. A younger and less notorious scion presents himself as a good type of the vagabond horner : a wandering, homeless being, alien to the comforts and hating the restraints of civilised life, ignorant and totally unlettered, yet not without a certain technical knowledge of his own, and a certain untutored mannerliness of address. Such was Jock Young, *secundus*, the horner, who flourished in the early years of the present century. Among his extra-professional accomplishments, Jock was a deft and willing dancer, and, when fit occasion offered, would foot up the Ghillie Callum or Highland Fling to his " ain sowff," for the delectation of his friends and patrons. Like every true and pure-bred caird, Jock dearly loved whisky, and when he got elevated with liquor was apt to be talkative, and a little too demonstrative perhaps. At all other times his bearing towards those among whom he was known was respectful and unobtrusive. When victuals were needed or quarters had to be asked he would lie off about the "loan" foot till his wife or other female of the party had done the necessary pleadings, and then quietly lift and go elsewhere, if need were; or retire to the barn, where his straw couch was to be for the night, not presuming to intrude himself into the farmer's dwelling unless asked. Jock's partner was Tib Doo; and as Jock loved whisky so did Tib; and through that very love, it is to be feared, came to a caird's end. It was at a favourite haunt in the Garioch. Jock had gone elsewhere temporarily; on business, no doubt; and it might be that there had been a tiff between him and Tib. Anyhow, Tib, learning that there was to be a wedding next day at Lochie's, was wondrously loth to leave. But, while she might have the barn at will, there was not a single wisp of straw for a bed. Tib would borrow a "winlin" for herself she said; and so she did; and next day, of course, saw her at the wedding, partaking freely of the "brakins" at the close of the wedding feast. Likely she had not been able, by the end, to stir further than to creep into Lochie's barn somehow and unnoticed; and there, by next morning, poor Tib Doo lay stark dead! The kindly neighbours did the last services for her as couthily and Christianly as they might. She was decently buried by the west gable of the auld "White Kirk," of which hath it not been prophesied by "true Thomas" that it shall yet fall on a Pasch Sunday! And all this was over some days ere her husband Jock came tramping round with his wallet and his horns, and wistfully asking tidings of Tib, towards whom his yearnings had begun to go forth again. On learning her fate, his grief burst forth in a way that had not been expected. Because Jock Young could drink and swear and quarrel, they had thought that the emotional feeling within the rough bosom was incapable of any other form of expression; but, when Jock had been told the site of the grave; when, as the parish choir, who had met for their weekly practising, between the gloamin' an' the light, sang—

> Guide me, oh! thou great Jehovah,
> Pilgrim through this barren land—

the poor horner was seen casting himself with wildly despairing moans and lamentations above the spot by the White Kirk, where the remains of Tib Doo lay, it was not wonderful if the more susceptible of them should start at the gleam of intense realism cast athwart the familiar words. Nor would it have been in the spirit of Christian charity either to deny to the hapless half-civilised wanderer a word of respectful sympathy; or to hold him incapable of genuine human affection, as well as some dim longing after the spiritual life.

CHAPTER XXI.

VAGRANT LIFE—FLETCHER OF SALTOUN'S OPINIONS—THE "EGIPTIANS" AND THEIR HABITS—COMMON VAGRANTS —CAIRDS—THE YOUNGS—TIBBIE CAMPBELL.

THE prevalence of vagrants of divers sorts formed a distinctive feature in the social life of the nation for a very long period. In his "Second Discourse on the Affairs of Scotland" (A.D. 1698), Andrew Fletcher of Saltoun gives a very forcible picture of the state of matters in this respect, as known to him. At the date of his writing, the occurrence of three bad harvests in succession had no doubt made things worse; yet, says Fletcher, "In all times there have been about one hundred thousand of those vagabonds who had lived without any regard or subjection either to the laws of the land or even those of God and Nature. No magistrate could ever be informed, or discover, which way one in a hundred of these wretches died, or that ever they were baptized. Many murders have been discovered among them; and they are not only a most unspeakable oppression to poor tenants—who, if they give not bread or some kind of provision to perhaps forty such villains in one day, are sure to be insulted by them—but they rob many poor people who live in houses distant from any neighbourhood. In years of plenty many thousands of them meet together in the mountains, where they feast and riot for many days; and at country weddings, markets, burials, and the like public occasions, they are to be seen—both men and women—perpetually drunk, cursing, blaspheming, and fighting together." Perhaps this sketch by the sincere and ardent patriot may be strongly enough outlined ; the numbers would certainly seem to be overstated ; but doubtless the actual reality had been sufficiently bad. Fletcher had the courage of his opinions, and he believed in thorough-going remedies. Therefore, founding upon the example of the "wise antients," such as the Greeks, he tells us he would have had all these lawless wandering people assigned in perpetual servitude to the owners of the soil and others. He did not doubt of his proposal being met " not only with all the misconstruction and obloquy, but all the disdain, fury, and outcries of which either ignorant magistrates or proud, lazy, and miserable people are capable." But they must pardon him if he told them that he regarded " not names but things." The slaves of the ancients were assured in " clothes, diet, and lodging," and by their means many useful public works were accomplished. "The original of that multitude of beggars which now oppress the world" he found to have proceeded from Churchmen, who, without warrant of Scripture, and in the teeth of Paul's injunction, that in whatever condition of life a man was called to the Christian faith he was to remain content, even if a slave, had recommended nothing more strongly to masters, in order to the salvation of their souls, than freeing those of their slaves who would embrace the Christian faith ; a course which soon led to many disorders in the East, and ultimately to that " great mischief, under which, to the undoing of the poor, all the nations of Europe have ever since groaned." Why, then, not adopt the remedy that would both better the vagabonds of the country socially themselves, and render them productive industrially in the interest of the general community ? Those vagrant tribes lived a life as miserable as it could well be for themselves; and they were the responsible agents of " such outrageous disorders that it were better for the nation," says Fletcher, " they were sold to the gallies or West Indies than that they should continue any longer to be a burden and a curse upon us." He further hints that, "for example and terror, three or four hundred of the most notorious of those villains whom we call jockies might be presented by the Government to the State of Venice, to serve in the gallies against the common enemy of Christendom." A robust style of treatment truly; yet in Fletcher's scheme there was after all a germ of the remedial idea; and as much could hardly be said of the prevailing notions among the local Magistrates of the time, which extended no further than simply to have sturdy beggars, "both old and young, men and women," and such like people warned off their respective territories, "under pain of scourging."

For a full century after Fletcher's time, vagrancy, if somewhat mitigated in character, was not greatly reduced in respect of numbers; and the scene described as taking place in Poosie Nancy's continued to be enacted, with variations, in many a similar howff :—

>Ae nicht at e'en a merry core
>O' randie gangrel bodies
>In Poosie Nancy's held the splore,
>To drink their orra duddies.
>Wi' quaffin', an' laughin',
>They rantit an' they sang;
>Wi' jumpin', an' thumpin',
>The vera girdle rang.

The "Process against the Egiptians," tried and condemned to death at Banff, in 1700, affords certain authentic glimpses of the style of life described by Fletcher. Of the four accused persons who all were sent to the gibbet, one has obtained a certain kind of immortality, James M'Pherson, said to have been the son of a highland gentleman by a gipsy mother, who is traditionally credited with his share of the ideal freebooter's chivalrous generosity, as also a measure of skill in handling the violin; and thus we are told—

>He played a spring an' danced it roun'
>Aneth the gallows tree;

winding up by breaking the fiddle over his knee because none of the bystanders would accept as a gift the instrument for which its owner had no further use. The charges found relevant against the gang of whom M'Pherson was one, were those of being "knowne habit and repute to be Egiptians and wagabonds, and keeping the mercats in their ordinarie manner of thieving and purse cutting, or guilty of the crimes of thift, masterfull bangstrie and oppressione." The depositions of the witnesses serve to inform us that the "Egiptians" (gipsies), were wont to appear in the country markets, notably St. Rufus Fair, Keith, to the number, occasionally, of six or eight together, armed, to the terror of his Majesty's peaceably disposed lieges, assaulting such as they chose, and setting on their women, who spoke an unknown tongue for the occasion to cut purses; that at other times they would get temporary housing on some doubtful form of tenancy, stealing "kail" and "peats" from the neighbours quite freely, and almost openly; while occasionally a sheep would disappear, the theft of which they would deny, but rather than have too strict inquisition made, especially if backed by adequate powers, would agree to pay the price of it; and that a more common mode of finding quarters was to take possession, without leave asked or given, of somebody's kiln-barn, and then refuse to be dispossessed until it suited them to remove. While thus located, they "some tymes stayed a fourtnight or even a month," threatening reprisals on such as chose to meddle with them; and if they needed a "fire weshel," or such like, for use, they would take it at their own hand. They also not unfrequently extorted considerable sums of money in the most barefaced fashion. The charge of one witness against M'Pherson was, that he "came into his house and spilt his ale, and stobbed the bed seeking the deponent," he being forced to flee for safety and obtain a purchased protection from my lord Seafield. From another we have the information that M'Pherson was "one night" at his house along with others of his class, and "drank with the rest, and danced all night;" a sufficiently characteristic glimpse of gipsy life on its social side.

Various writers near the close of the eighteenth century describe Scotland as sadly over-run by vagrants, including, in some cases, Irish people, who, it seems, came over under pretence of visiting their relatives; "a duty," says one narrator caustically, "to which, it must be allowed, they are particularly attentive." The Old Statistical writer for the parish of Kinnettles, in Forfarshire, speaks thus of his locality:—"We have bands of sturdy beggars, male and female—or, as they are usually called, tinkers—whose insolence, idleness, and dishonesty are an affront to the police of our country. These persons are ready for prey of all kinds: everything that can supply them with provisions or bring them money is their spoil, if it can be obtained with any appearance of safety. They file off in small parties, and have their places of rendezvous, where they choose to billet themselves for at least one day; nor do they fail generally to make good their quarters, as the farmer is afraid to refuse to answer their demands, or to complain of the oppression under which he labours."

It had been a practice of long standing for the Aberdeen Baillies to have evil-doers, including notour vagrants, "banischit the toun;" and they had occasionally the distinction of an official drumming out as far as the Bow Brig.* "Their honours the Baillies were always humane enough," says a local chronicler, "to send their vagrants all south, and for which compliment the authorities in the south no doubt considered

---

* The Bow Brig spanned the Denburn at Aberdeen between the Green and Windmillbrae, about the precise point where there is now a latticed iron foot bridge over the line of the Great North Railway. The Brig was at the southwest side of the town: the spot it occupied is now, as near as may be, in the centre of the extended city.

themselves particularly obliged to their brethren in Aberdeen." On this particular point, another Forfarshire minister (Rescobie) gives a statement of fact and an opinion :—" Perth," he says, " usually furnishes out a pretty large quota; but there is no place sends forth such legions of these itinerants as Aberdeen, meaning the county as well as the town of that name. The county is extensive, fertile, and populous; the town commercial and opulent. What harm would there be in giving Aberdeen a hint that it would be both creditable and recommendable in them to take measures, as they ought, to provide for their own poor at home, rather than set them off, like a flight of locusts, to prey upon their neighbours, who are under no local obligation to receive or relieve them." But if Aberdeen and Aberdeenshire sent off hordes of vagrants to the annoyance of other places, a sufficiency of the same class were still left at home apparently. The Old Statist for Peterculter parish, for example, says :—" This country is often infested with vagrants of various descriptions, who by threats or otherwise, compel people to give them money and the best *vivres* their houses afford. They likewise pick up poultry, apparel, and what they can lay hold of. Their exactions are oppressive, their numbers often formidable, and it hurts the feelings of the humane to see so many young people trained up to the same pernicious courses."

The vagrant class embraced two distinct sections. There was the mere beggar, of the higher or lower degree, and there was the thorough-paced " caird." The male caird, to the extent of his industrial inclination, assumed the profession of " tinkler" horner, or such like, as already indicated, leaving the details of ordinary foraging largely to his female companions. And then in the business of "sorning," pure and simple, there were degrees. Apart from the privileged bede, or blue gown men, known to certain localities in Scotland, there was a more generally diffused class of beggars, with a remnant of respectability more or less, about them, carrying multitudinous meal pocks and other receptacles, and pretty sure of an "awmous," or night quarters where asked. Then there was the inferior herd of beggars—creatures who would whine and invoke numberless blessings on your head when they appealed to your feelings of pity, on the ground of infirmities or afflictions real or feigned, and on finding the appeal to be in vain, would turn and curse you to your face with amazing goodwill and volubility.

As a sorner, the true caird differed considerably from either of the two classes of "peer fowk." He knew he had no pretensions to the standing of the one, and he scorned to demean himself to the level of the other. The pronounced caird hardly deemed it necessary to approach you with a whine; an unshrinking and, it might be, insolent demand suited his temper better; and the remark applies not to the male caird alone. When a marriage, a funeral, or other "occasion" occurred, at which meat and drink would be supplied in quantity, the cairds seldom failed to get wind of it, and as seldom to put in appearance with the express object of sharing in the good things going. It was no easy matter to satisfy a horde of some twenty, thirty, or more of these rapacious and lawless beings in the way of either meat or drink; and not unfrequently people who wished to save themselves from the insolent and endless onsets of the whole crew, made a compact with some guiding spirit, who undertook, on being provided with so much as a general booty and something in the shape of a personal consideration, to keep the whole body in order. One of the last of the class of unmitigated Aberdeenshire cairds, of caird descent, and herself a "survival" from a past generation, was Lizzie Fraser, who died not very many years ago; a woman of masculine proportions, with a voice of such grating roughness as was well fitted to startle the listener on finding it owned by one clad in female habiliments. Lizzie had been a wife in her day too, and had for her husband Moses Young, brother of Jock Young the horner, already mentioned, and himself an old soldier,

> A son of Mars,
> Who had been in [certain] wars,

yet withal a quiet undemonstrative caird, who loved to loiter by the water-side, pursuing the contemplative man's recreation. When in the zenith of her bodily prowess, this woman, in virtue of her great muscular strength, and reckless, outrageous temper, was an acknowledged queen among her class. And if Lizzie Fraser happened to be one of the motley throng of cairds that had assembled at some festive gathering, the task of keeping order was not unfrequently entrusted to her. Of course, she expected a sufficient reward—as she would not scruple to say—for her trouble; either that, or facilities for stealing, which served the end equally well, though in a different way. And other conditions being settled to her mind, she was by no means slack in exercising her authority after a fashion to be understood, even by the least tutored caird intellect. Her method was to supply herself with a proper cudgel, and, when incipient rebellion against her sovereign rule manifested itself, she did not hesitate in applying it with a practised skill and vigour that made the offender, whether man or woman, think twice before risking a second infliction.

A female caird who preceded Lizzie in point of time, and who could boast of possessing a different and perhaps higher kind of influence, was Tibbie Campbell. She was acknowledged, amongst her tribe, not only as a ruling power, but also as a sort of high priestess and sorceress or witch. And, her "skeel" found recognition outside caird circles too. The "twal owsen" team at Mill of Carden, for example, had got some glamour cast over them. And before the ploughman and gaudman could get them "streekit" in the draught, they would run wildly, bellowing here and there, shaking the yokes off their necks, and even straining the soam itself. The thing had gone on day by day, and there seemed no remeid, till the well-to-do tenant of the farm, in his perplexity, bethought him of sending Willie Nicol, his youngest servant lad, to seek the aid of Tibbie Campbell, as a weird woman. After due inquiry, Willie found her at breakfast *al fresco* among a promiscuous group of her own people; and with some trouble he obtained an audience.

"An' fat's yer erran' here, laddie?" sharply demanded Tibbie Campbell.

Willie Nicol, as duly instructed, replied in his own phraseology that his master, Mr. Tait, sent his best respects to Mrs. Campbell, and would really take it as a great favour if she would come to Mill of Carden without loss of time, to examine the bewitched oxen, and prescribe a cure.

"Ou! Jock Tait," said the Caird Queen, with a sneering laugh; and, she added, in a figure as coarse as occurred to her at the moment, that she "kent him" when he was in a state of dependant infancy. After some farther parley and cross-questioning, the messenger was dismissed with the assurance — "I canna gae wi' ye the day, man. I'm jist gaen awa' till anither pairt to mairry a pair; but tell ye Jock Tait that if I'm as lang oot o' heyven as the morn's mornin', I'se be wi' 'im." On the morrow morning Tibbie was still an inhabitant of this world, and sufficiently sober after the marriage, to perform her promised journey to Mill of Carden. She was immediately taken to inspect the oxen, and, according to the narration of Willie Nicol, at once laid her hand upon one of them, with the exclamation—"This is the De'il amo' them a'!" And sure enough "that was the ane that aye begood the starshie!" So said Willie, and Willie in his grey old age, as in his green "youtheid," dearly loved the marvellous. It might be unkind to endeavour at this distance of time to injure Willie's credit, by suggesting that Tibbie Campbell had perhaps been shrewd enough to fix on the wildest-looking ox by the mere use of her eyesight and powers of observation ; perhaps, by leading questions had picked it out of Willie Nicol himself, or even his master, Jock Tait ; or that, perhaps, it was a mere fancy on the part of the superstitious ploughmen to believe the ox thus pointed at to be more guilty than his other brethren of the yoke. At all events, having secured confidence thus far, Tibbie would have little difficulty in getting her employer to put faith in such remedies as she might be pleased to prescribe for the glamoured oxen.

CHAPTER XXII.

POPULAR AMUSEMENTS—COCK-FIGHTING—JOHN GRUB AND HIS SCHOLARS—YULE SPORTS—FOOT-BALL—THE MONYMUSK BA'IN'—WAD SHOOTING.

It may with some truth be alleged that, as a nation, we have never exhibited a very pronounced aptitude for fitting and successful sports; yet did our forefathers devote some share of their time to amusements of a public character. One of these, that obtained a sort of recognition which we should think very queer, was cock-fighting. A certain Mr. William Machrie, of Edinburgh, claimed to have been the means of introducing this sport—which he calls an "innocent and royal recreation"—into the capital about the beginning of the century. This gentleman considered cock-fighting superior to horse-racing, and such like. The very qualities of the bird, he said, recommended him—viz., "his Spanish gait, his Florentine policy, and his Scottish valour in overcoming, and generosity in using, his vanquished adversary." The ancients, he said, called the cock "an astronomer;" and he had been "an early preacher of repentance, even convincing Peter, the first Pope, of his Holiness's fallibility." In short, cock-fighting was superior to almost any other species of sport in Mr. Machrie's estimation; and his view of the matter seems to have found a remarkable degree of acceptance, inasmuch as the sport of cock-fighting became an established pastime annually practised at Fastern's Even (Shrovetide) for the delectation of the ingenuous youth in attendance at the parish schools.

When the annual holiday of Fastern's Even was at hand, each schoolboy was encouraged to bring up a cock to have his warlike prowess tested. The schoolmaster presided at this elevating sport, in which, indeed, he had a very particular interest. For the carcases of the cocks that fell in battle, as well as those of the "fugies," or discreet birds, that acted on the maxim—

> He who fights and runs away
> May live to fight another day,

became his property. The slender revenues of the dominie were, in some cases, augmented in no inconsiderable proportion in this way. In special instances, indeed, the yearly "cock-fight dues" are stated to have been equal to a quarter's fees for the school; which, after all, did not represent a large sum, if we take the statement of a Country Schoolmaster, who ventilates the grievances of his class in 1792. He gives as particulars of income—Statutory salary, £5 11s. 1⅓d.; fees, £7; session-clerk fees and emoluments, £2; in all, £14 11s. 1⅓d.—somewhat under 11d. per day. Many schools, says this writer, were not worth so much, and at least four-fifths of the schools in the northern part of the kingdom did not much exceed the calculation he had made.

This subject of cock-fighting finds incidental treatment in an obscure little book published in 1794.* A pretty full Preface and Dedication inform us that Mr.

---

* Its title is ORATIONS ON VARIOUS SELECT SUBJECTS. By Mr. John Grub, late Schoolmaster of the parish of Wemyss, in Fifeshire, as Performed by his Scholars after the usual Examination on Harvest Vacation days, and on Shrove Tuesdays in place of cock-fighting. These orations for the use of Grammar Schools on the above days are published by Mr. Robert Wilson, of Sylvania, near Dunfermline. Edinburgh: Printed for the Editor. 1794.

John Grub, born at or near Aberdeen, and who had got a University education there, was chosen schoolmaster of Wemyss, in Fifeshire, in 1748. He lived only seven years thereafter, but, in course of that time had by his attainments and ability as a teacher, raised his school to "a very great character." One of his methods, adopted with a view to improve the minds of his pupils "in moral virtues, and to refine their manners," was to make the boys on certain days, including Shrove Tuesday, deliver short orations, which they had committed to memory, in presence of their parents. To use the words of the editor, who had himself been one of Mr. Grub's boarders, each of the elder scholars in turn "mounted the schoolmaster's desk, after making a low bow to the company, and audibly and distinctly delivered an oration from their memory, and, after another bow to the company, returned to their seats—all highly to the praise of the scholars and admiration of the company." Three orations, out of a large number on diverse subjects, are devoted expressly to the question of cock-fighting, in the way of argument and reply. The first speaker opens with a simple denunciation of cock-fighting. And though it has from "time immemorial" been "a custom to make one day in the year remarkable for the inhuman practice of bringing many of the noblest of the feathered creation to a lingering and cruel death," he ventures to make a "motion" "to have our yearly cock-fight entirely laid aside, or at least metamorphosed into some diversion more useful and entertaining to youth." The motion, he knows, will be a "little unpopular" in that part of the country, but the sport is "too bloody and cruel," and ought not to be countenanced "by public and established instructors of youth." The second speaker declares the motion to be "something more than unpopular"—it would be "pernicious if complied with;" and the three grounds on which he would encourage the yearly cock-fight are :—" 1, It is an old custom of this school and so should be observed ; 2, It raises a noble ambition in a youth when he sees his cock fight well, and so great an aversion to cowardice when his cock does not fight well, that he is ready to fight himself upon the slightest affront offered; 3, I am surprised to hear any one of our number propose anything that would hurt the income of the master." With him this weighs more than any other consideration, and must be his excuse for contradicting his "learned friend's motion." The reply is that custom can never be a good reason for perpetuating an erroneous practice. When a man's sagacity and penetration enable him to discover error, he should " make no scruple to step out of the paths of his forefathers." " As cocks are not trained at school, they have," says he, " no title to show their parts there ;" it is below " a sprightly youth" to value himself upon his cock's parts, and " as for a blockhead, though his cock were victor over twenty, he is a blockhead still." Were it in " military discipline" the boys were to be trained, one might encourage the sport, but even then the preferable mode would be to "set the boys a fighting themselves ;" and lastly, it is argued, were the Shrove Tuesday combat to be in the various parts of learning, and the boys the sole combatants, premiums could be given to the victors "in their several degrees and classes ;" tickets of admittance on that day could be bought of the master, and each pupil delivering an oration could make him " some compliment."—" This, sir," adds the orator, " in my opinion, would be a more noble and more useful diversion than the other ; and parents would pay as generously for their sons who meet with applause as formerly they did for their cocks."

Such were the sentiments of an instructor of youth who seems to have been a good half century in advance of his time on the question of cock-fighting. The general feeling of the country did not begin to revolt from the sport, on the ground of its barbarity, till long after; as indeed the tendency of feeling on questions of sport in all times is apt to lie rather the opposite way, due, no doubt, to the fact that participation more or less in the nature of the wild beast is a somewhat general attribute of humanity.

Cock-fighting continued to be a school sport in the north-east of Scotland, in some cases, well into the present century. In 1818, the boys at one of the schools in Fetteresso parish, in Kincardineshire, who still had their periodical cock-fight, looked down with a sort of contempt on the boys of another school in the same parish where the practice did not then exist. "Ye haena a cock fecht at your skweel, min," one boy would say to another in reference to this state of matters, and implying that something was wanting in the regular routine of a fully efficient and properly equipped educational institution. In the neighbouring parish of Drumlithie, cock-fights were held ten years later than the date mentioned.

With the annual cock-fight went the annual contest at foot-ball. It also took place at Fastern's Even, or, less commonly, at Yule. The author of "Tullochgorum," in his juvenile poem, "The Monymusk Ba'in',"* fixes it at the latter festival. Three entire days were abstracted from the routine of daily labour, and religiously devoted to Yule observances. The requisite "fordel strae" for the cattle had been carefully provided before-hand, so as no flail need be lifted during Yule. In a Presbyterian community there was no formal religious service of a public sort; and thus there was abundant time for the "ba'in'," or any other recreation that might find favour, "sowens" and general feasting, of course, obtaining their own share of atten-

---

* The poem in question, which is marked by a good deal of graphic force, is modelled very closely after "Christ's Kirk o' Green," the names of various of the characters, even, being imported from that poem.

tion. Of the general characteristics of the "ba'in'," a graphic summary is given by Skinner in his opening stanza :—

> Has ne'er in a' this countra been
> Sic shouderin' an' sic fa'in',
> As happen't but few ouks sinsyne
> Here at the Christmas ba'in'.
> At evenin' syne the fallows keen
> Drank till the neist day's dawin',
> Sae snell that some tint baith their een,
> An' coudna pay their lawin'
>   Till the neist day.

The heroes of the field were those who could fearlessly head the "hurry burry," grappling all and sundry, right and left, and amid the general scrimmage of "routs an' raps fae man to man" gi'ein at any rate as good as they got in the way of cuts across the shins, and "clammy-houits" over the cranium, or strokes "alang the chafts." It was a feat worth mentioning to make a man's "harnpan" ring, or lay an opposing player sprawling on his back with the suggestion of damage to some one or other of his limbs. As the struggling mass of players swayed hither and thither, now up now down, those of the feebler sort got drifted away from the vortex fairly out of wind, and perhaps not altogether scatheless in person or apparel. And clearly victory was to be hoped for quite as much from the reckless exercise of muscular strength as from agility and skill in hitting the ball, which finally, by "a weel-wil'd-wap" from Sawney's foot, is "yowff't" in o'er the park, "a space an' mair" from the Kirkyard, the recognised field for the parish ba'in', and where it has been going on all the while in the lively fashion indicated. The incidental humours of the scene are in entire harmony with the general ongoings, and few mere spectators, even, are allowed to escape without mishap more or less. The "insett dominie," a "young

13

mess John," who was "neither saint nor sinner," cannot come on the scene for a moment, till

> A brattlin' band unhappily
> Drave by him wi' a binner,
> An' heels o'er goudie coupit he,
> An' rave his guid horn penner
> In bits that day.

And when the meek parish clerk comes up the churchyard, his "claithing fu' fine" is too strong a temptation. By a special act of wickedness he is speedily "beft" over backward,

> Just whaur their feet the dubs had glaur'd,
> An' barken'd them like brine,

calling into use the services of ostensibly sympathising onlookers with their "whittles" to "scrape his hat" and otherwise make his raiment decent again.

"The Christmas Ba'in'" was written by Skinner when under seventeen years of age, which fixes its date as being about 1737. From the minuteness of the details, and the number of individual characters named, the picture given may be accepted as in the main somewhat closely realistic. The freedom and zest with which kicks and blows were given out amongst the leading players looks rather startling. But then what use to possess muscular strength, and not let it be known? The feeling on this point was very pronounced; and it sometimes found practical manifestation in what would seem unlikely modes. To determine which of two men was the stronger, was often a nice question—Here now are a couple of brawny fellows of the class and type described who have never yet been able to decide that particular point; and they have met of a winter evening in the house of their mutual friend the weaver. What better chance than settle it now? The weaver, a "sober bodie" whom either of them could have put *hors de combat* by a single blow of his fist, had no help but accept the situation.

To put him out of harm's way, and make him useful according to his capacity, he was set up on the top of the "boun' bed," with a blazing "fir" in his hand, to give light for the operations about to commence on the floor below him. And there the two set on in their fierce if unskilled wrestle, which, being equally matched, they kept up with the most unflinching determination till so completely exhausted that the unboastful weaver declared they were "like twa burs'n cocks—I cud 'a rappit their heids thegither mysel'." It was one of these two again who went to Lowrin' Fair in search of amusement; and in passing an unknown Highlandman, after deliberately surveying the stranger from head to foot, dealt the unsuspecting Celt a heavy blow on the face, a hand to hand combat instantly ensuing without a word spoken on either side. The reason given for this unusual mode of saluting a man he had never seen before, was that the Highlandman "was a gey stout-like chiel;" whose appearance gave the prospect of a good fight, wanting which Lowrin' Fair would have been dull to the Highlandman's assailant.

"Wad" shooting was another Yule sport of later origin, "the wad" being a prize of some sort laid in pledge. The pieces they shot with were in no sense arms of precision. So little of that indeed, that the man who owned, or could command the use of a rifle, became disqualified as a competitor. What good in shooting against a man who, if he took his aim well, could count on hitting within a foot or so of the bull's-eye? The sturdy, single barrelled flint-lock musket, which had seen service at Fontenoy or elsewhere in its time, and was now used for the miscellaneous discharge of pellets, from swan-shot downward, against the pests of the farm, was common enough; and quite as good for "wad sheetin'" as the lighter fowling-pieces of the rough and rusty class owned by others of the marksmen. Neither one nor the other would drive a ball so certainly to its mark as to destroy the pleasing hope of luck, or chance, doing a turn for the individual competitor over and beyond what he could expect as the result of his best skill. The prize to be shot for would be some useful article, ranging from an eight-day clock to a shoulder of beef, or a wooden plough. The marksman cast his own bullets of molten lead in a cambs, which might or might not have been made to suit the bore of his piece; in like manner he measured out the charge of powder from his horn, by rule of thumb; and, as exact results in shooting were hardly to be looked for in the circumstances, neither was perfect comfort to the shooter always secured. When he had paid his sixpence, and spread his bonnet on the top of the yard dyke before him to get a true and stable "reest," the eager competitor would lay himself along, and with all earnestness take a deliberate, and, if it might be, correct aim. Such trifles as windage and adjustment of elevation to distance troubled him not. He simply kept his eye as hopefully on the centre of the target as he could. Probably the possibility of an unusually ugly "putt" from his piece helped to excite his nervous feeling a little, but shoot he would at all risks, and gain the wad if he could. The target was only a hundred yards off, and its dimensions by no means scanty—most likely it was an old barn door with a few alternated rings of black and white paint put on about the centre; and it seemed very possible to lodge the ball somewhere amongst these rings. Crack goes the shot at last, but with a rent and unsatisfactory sound, and an unpleasant upward jerk of the muzzle of the marksman's gun! No! The bull's-eye is untouched; not even the barn door itself has been hit, as is definitely certified when the two or three lads who act as volunteer markers have run in from their posts full fifty yards off on either side—a distance that must be maintained in consideration of the wildly erratic course taken by many of the balls. Another and another shoots with pretty similar results ; and though an occasional man may grudge the dead loss of the sixpence he has paid for the right to shoot, and talk as if something must be out of joint because he has got no nearer the centre, yet they know it is all in a good cause and they will " go in " for another " chance." And, clearly enough, if the shooting were more exact or certain the thing would be over in an hour or less ; whereas they can spend a whole day upon it with no likelihood of more than one or two marksmen getting close to the bull's eye ; as in point of fact, was a common result of the Wad Sheetin', which nevertheless afforded quite as much interest and enjoyment while it lasted as does the best rifle competition of the present day ; in addition to furnishing an engrossing subject of talk in the hamlet and farmhouse in the days that went before and after the great contest.

CHAPTER XXIII.

SMUGGLING — FOREIGN CONTRABAND — LOWLAND AND HIGHLAND SMUGGLING — PHILIP KENNEDY THE SMUGGLER—MALCOLM GILLESPIE THE GAUGER.

DURING the second half of the last century, and somewhat more than the first quarter of the present one, smuggling, in various forms, prevailed extensively. In the earlier time it was confined mainly to seaboard districts. Kegs of gin from Holland and other foreign goods were landed contraband at many convenient creeks and baylets along an extended line of coast. The statement has been made, that there was scarcely a family along the coast, from Don to Spey, who were not more or less implicated in this particular system of "free trade." Some of the landed proprietors even quietly countenanced the practice, and participated in its gains; and all the more readily if their sympathies happened to lie with the Jacobites. In that case, so far from disgrace, there was actual merit in the contraband operations; it was not depriving the King of his due, but simply avoiding the exactions of an unrighteous usurper. Along the coast, from Stonehaven to Peterhead, the business of smuggling foreign goods was pursued systematically and perseveringly. On parts of the Buchan coast, it had evidently engrossed the exertions of a large part of the population. They acted under leaders, and had their own cant watchwords, *aliases* and *soubriquets;* and there was an oath of secrecy administered all round among those who took an active part. In addition to the available natural caves, artificial places of concealment, " capable of containing from sixty to two or three hundred tubs of gin," were constructed where necessary, by digging deep down into the soft earth or sand, and forming a pit with bricks or planks of wood. These pits, which were covered over to the depth of several feet, in order to be safe from the searchings of the excisemen, were exactly measured off, from some conspicuous point, so that the precise spot could be ascertained, and the pit opened, as required, even on the darkest night.

When one of the smuggling luggers had arrived off the coast, the skipper would run pretty close in shore, during daylight, and exhibit preconcerted signals to some of those on the outlook in the neighbourhood. Satisfied that his movements were understood, he then hauled off again, and stood out to sea in an indefinite sort of way. Meanwhile, the news spread for miles around. A primitive system of telegraphing, sufficiently intelligible to the initiated, had been established; as, for example, by spreading a plaid or blanket out, as if to dry, on the top of the peat stack. Messages, in cant phraseology, were sent from hamlet to hamlet, by children, if need were, there being no risk of their indiscreetly communicating what outsiders would not understand, even when they heard it. And then, by night-fall, there was a silent but rapid and watchful muster about the point where the signalling lugger was expected to approach; and, in all probability, a busy night followed at the landing, and concealment of her freight, in the safety of which all those taking part were, to a greater or less extent, directly concerned. The time when coast smuggling seems to have been carried on most extensively, was in the years between 1660 and 1680; the profits attending the successful prosecution of the business tempting many to engage in it. It was by and by seen, however, by those who had a stake in the country, and especially by the landed proprietors—even those not disinclined quietly to enjoy a drop of Hollands, duty-free—that the questionable gain effected was purchased at an enormous loss, in diverting the attention of the people from the cultivation of the land and other honest industrial pursuits, and teaching the male part of them at least dissipated and reckless habits. And, though during the last ten or fifteen years of the century coast smuggling still continued, it had got considerably discredited amongst all the more respectable classes of the community; and, under that feeling, and the increased efforts of the excise, was getting more limited in extent. With inland smuggling the case was entirely different. It was only through the increase in the duties on malt liquors, made not many years before the close of the century, that the temptation to the private manufacture of malt and distillation of whisky first occurred; and the practice, by and by, became very general, alike in the Lowlands and Highlands. Among the Lowland peasantry, male and female alike engaged in it, there being no more persistent devotees of "the worm" than some of the "sma' goodwives" who had got into the habit of "rinnin' a drap," and getting it quietly marketed as they best could. There was nothing disreputable in the practice in the public opinion of their neighbourhoods; and nothing disgraceful in being caught by the gaugers. Such a mishap might, indeed, be inconvenient; but then the awards of their honours, the Justices, were not of formidable severity. They would at times sit a whole day adjudicating cases of private malting or distillation, and, in the course of the entire sitting, impose no higher penalty than half-a-crown or so upon any one of the dozen or score of delinquents arraigned before them. It would be quite the exception where a culprit of a superior class came up, as happened at a certain Court of Justices, at which my Lord Kintore presided. Amongst the offenders cited by the Excise, was Robert Fraser, of "Folla," who was fairly entitled, as he would probably have claimed, had the title then been common, to be recognised as a gentleman-farmer. At any rate, it was Robert's weakness to wish to be considered very wealthy ; and of this some one had given the Preses of the meeting of Justices a hint. When the tenant of Folla was called for sentence, his Lordship, accordingly, with a sly insinuation, and doubtless anticipating a very different style of reply, remarked—" Mr. Fraser, I understand you are very rich ?" "Vastly so, my Lord," replied the undaunted tenant of Folla, promptly and gravely. " Well then, you are fined five pounds !" "Five pounds—My Lord, I'd rather pay fifty pounds than stand here a whole day among a parcel o' poor things !"

In the case of the Highlanders, smuggling was conducted with perhaps fully as much system and perseverance as anywhere; at anyrate, the whisky the Highlanders made seems to have had a more distinctive reputation than that made in the Lowlands. It may well be doubted if either the one whisky or the other would be much relished by connoisseurs of the present time ; certainly much of the smuggled Lowland whisky was very detestable stuff. At any rate, when the Highlander went abroad to seek a market for the results of his private distillation, it was to the Lowland towns that he came, either singly, or more commonly in a company joined together, and sharing the perils of the way in common; the string of shaggy ponies carrying the kegs of whisky, and the smugglers keeping a due outlook against being trepanned by the detested gaugers.

And while there were many amusing episodes in connection with smuggling, first and last, there was not a little rough and demoralising work, especially when a set of stout smugglers encountered an equally stout and better armed *posse* of gaugers. To outwit the commonplace gauger in the ordinary run of business was a feat to which the female, as well as the male, smuggler was frequently found adequate. And in the case of the masculine contraveners of the law, the exciseman was deemed a fit subject for rough handling as occasion offered. To tie his legs together, fasten his hands forcibly behind his back, and leave him lying helpless on the lone hillside was not deemed much out of place by any means. One of the most tragic smuggling incidents locally recorded is that of the death of Philip Kennedy, at Ward of Cruden, in 1798, the circumstances connected with which are powerfully reproduced in *Guy Mannering*. A smuggling lugger had been in process of landing her cargo, part of which was being conveyed inland at night in carts. The gaugers had, however, got notice, and three of them, fully armed, lay in wait near the Kirk of Slains. The smugglers had taken the precaution of sending several of their number on in advance to see that the way was clear. One of these who first encountered the excisemen was Kennedy, and being a man of fearless courage, as well as powerful physique, he seized and threw down two of them, calling to his companions to secure the third. But so far from doing their part, they fled, and taking shelter amongst the bushes to watch events, left him to his fate. Kennedy held on to his two prostrate foes with grim determination, when the third, with surely needless barbarity, drew his sword and cut him repeatedly about the head. The smuggler, even then, refused to relax his grasp, and was still able to keep down the two excisemen. It was moonlight, and the savage gauger who was still free, was then observed by some of the cowards lying *perdu* in the adjacent bushes, to hold his sword above his head as if to make certain that he was using the edge, when next instant, with a sweeping and relentless stroke, the smuggler's skull was laid open with a frightful gash. With the blood streaming in torrents from his wounds, the poor fellow got to his feet and staggered on to Kirkton of Slains, distant nearly a quarter of a mile, where he expired in the course of a few minutes, his last words being, " If a' had been as true as I was, the goods wud 'a been safe, an' I wudna hae been bleedin' to death." His age was but thirty-eight. The men who were the cause of his death were tried on a charge of murder, but were acquitted.

At the Aberdeen Circuit Court of Justiciary, in September, 1827, my Lords Pitmilly and Alloway tried a somewhat notorious culprit, in the person of Malcolm Gillespie, officer of excise, whom the jury found guilty of forgery, and who was sentenced to be hanged; a sentence which was duly carried out, on the ensuing 16th of November. During the period of his incarceration, Gillespie had employed part of his time in writing an account of his experiences as an excise officer, during nearly twenty-eight years. His story is marked perhaps by a little of the braggadocia spirit, but enough is known independently, to enable us to shape the story to about its proper dimensions, and obtain a reliable glimpse or two of the actual state of matters. Malcolm Gillespie, who was a native of Dunblane, and apparently of respectable parentage, had entertained the wish to serve in the army, but was disappointed in getting into active service through the declinature of his relatives to buy him a commission—a matter probably to be regretted, as the man most clearly had in him qualities that would have been of value where hard fighting was going on. After a short experience as a recruiting agent, he turned his energies in another direction by joining the Excise. Gillespie's service was at first on the coast, and latterly inland. When stationed at the fishing village of Collieston, on the Buchan coast, in 1801, he states that upwards of 1000 ankers of foreign spirits were landed in that region every month. He continued at Collieston till 1807, when, at his own request, he was appointed to Stonehaven, the inspiring motive being zeal against the contrabandists. He had broken up their trade at Collieston, and they yet flourished at Stonehaven. A five years' residence there sufficed to make him "a complete terror to these depredators," and to reduce their nefarious traffic to limited dimensions; and accordingly, in 1812, again on his own application, he was removed inland to the Skene Ride, where he might intercept the Highlanders on their way to the Aberdeen market. The experiences of Gillespie, while in this situation, where he remained up to the date of his trial, seem to have been much according to his taste. The "first engagement worthy of notice" occurred, he tells us, on a certain night, when, in the attempt to intercept a cart of whisky, single-handed, the four "notorious delinquents" in charge of it fell upon him with bludgeons, mauling him unmercifully. To prevent the possibility of his prize—which turned out to be eighty gallons of whisky—escaping him, he pulled out a loaded pistol, and wounded the horse. And he takes credit to himself for so commanding his temper as to resist the temptation to subject one or more of his assailants to similar treatment. With the assistance of people who had been alarmed by the report of the pistol, a full victory was gained, and the two principals in the assault in due course stood their trial, and received sentences of several months' imprisonment. A few similar encounters convinced Gillespie of the utility of a properly-trained dog to accompany him in his nightly excursions; and he accordingly procured one "of the bull kind;" from a famed breed. Under proper training, the dog by and by learnt to seize the Highlanders' horses "one by one," till, by tumbling them, or making them "dance about," the kegs they carried were spilt off their backs: the dog's owner and the smugglers, meanwhile, carrying on the struggle for the mastery, with bludgeons, or still more dangerous weapons. And we speedily find the dog so employed during an engagement, in which "a deal of bloodshed occurred on both sides." But indeed the dog got so perfect at his work, that when any of the horses were running past him, that had no load on their backs, he paid no attention to them; and when he seized any of them it was always by the nose, which he would never quit, " until the goods were either thrown off," or in possession of his master. The ultimate fate of this valuable animal—to the great grief of the zealous gauger—was to be killed by a shot "promiscuously" fired in a preliminary skirmish that occurred on a certain night while he stood by, muzzled, waiting his part in the play.

Gillespie had in his pay no fewer than five assistants, men who doubtless possessed qualities fitting them for his purposes, but of whose moral character even he does not seem disposed to give us any strong warranty. And in his various encounters he ordinarily had the support of more or fewer of his men. Meeting a couple of smuggling carts in the woods of Drum, with a "strong hardened desperado, named Hay," employed to go along as a protecting bully, a severe engagement ensued, during which one of the excise force got three balls lodged in his groin, by the accidental discharge of his own pistol; Hay's cheek was nearly severed from his face, by a stroke from a sabre wielded by Gillespie himself, and another smuggler got an arm broken, which terminated the fight. On another occasion, in an encounter with ten or twelve Highlanders, near Kintore, Gillespie got thrown down, with three or four fellows above him, "beating him in a most unmerciful manner." The sabre was twisted out of his hand, and, while he was still kept down, a stroke from the weapon laid open his chin to a great extent. He then discharged his pistol at the smuggler, the ball lodging in his thigh; a second shot in the shoulder was necessary to drive him off finally, and in the meantime Gillespie had saved himself from strangulation by getting another assailant's thumb diverted from his windpipe into his mouth, where he bit it so savagely and tenaciously that the smuggler, in his wild struggles to get free, greatly aided him in once more regaining his feet. One of the greatest fights recorded occurred on a January night in 1824, near Inverurie, as he lay in wait for a formidable gang of Highlanders who were coming down with a large quantity of *aqua*, which they had publicly declared their determination to accompany to Aberdeen, despite the officers of excise, of whom they were prepared to make short work. He came suddenly on the cavalcade of ten carts, with twenty-five to thirty men, while his party were scattered, and only one assistant with him. "This formidable group were very indifferent to his threats, and looked upon him with his assistant in a scornful way, and were proceeding onwards, when he immediately fired and killed a horse. The next shot he had occasion to discharge went through the shoulder of a robust delinquent, while in the very act of bringing down upon Mr. G.'s head a large bludgeon, which would undoubtedly have felled him to the ground, if the ball had not taken proper effect. The whole gang were now upon Mr. G., but by this time the rest of his party had assembled through the firing, when a terrible conflict ensued. Bloody heads, hats rolling on the road, the reports of alternate firing and other noise, resembled more the battle of Waterloo than the interception of a band of lawless desperadoes;—but in the end they were obliged to lay down their arms, and submit to the laws of their country. Mr. G. and his party were all and each of them much debilitated by severe wounds and bruises, and loss of blood; but the greater part of the smugglers were in a much worse situation. It was fortunate," adds the narrator, "that no lives were lost on this memorable occasion;" but he does not doubt that he himself would carry some of the wounds he then received to his grave.

In summing up his story, which, he says, gives but a faint outline of a few of the many severe encounters in which he had been engaged, Gillespie informs us that he had received "no less than forty-two wounds on different parts of his body, and all inflicted by these extraordinary characters." The drift of his narrative is to make out that he was triumphantly successful in his object on all occasions. But without going quite so far as to accept that view without qualification, he was, beyond doubt, a fellow governed by a determined will and a sort of coarse reckless courage; and animated by an unflagging zeal in a line of duty that accorded with his tastes. Into his character and connections otherwise we need not enquire too curiously; only there is evidence to show that the rough and dangerous, if unscrupulous, service he rendered was not unappreciated by the legitimate traders of the district. And the facts that are beyond dispute concerning the transactions in which he was engaged, and the seizures he made* illustrate, in a somewhat vivid fashion, both the extent and character of the smuggling that prevailed up to fifty years ago.

---

* For Abstract of Gillespie's Seizures, see Appendix (5).

CHAPTER XXIV.

THE PROPHET OF BETHELNIE—STATE OF MEDICAL PRACTICES—DR. ADAM DONALD—HIS HISTORY AND CLAIMS CRITICALLY VIEWED—SUPERSTITIOUS BELIEF IN WITCHES AND OCCULT SKILL.

IN the early part of the eighteenth century, as indeed was the case till near its close, the learned professions —apart always from the office of the ministry—held but dubious footing in country districts. The schoolmaster, as has been already remarked, was a person of no great consideration in point of erudition or otherwise. In the Aberdeenshire Poll Book he is never rated as a "gentleman"; and they did not deem it worth while to exact anything more of poll money from him than was paid by an ordinary cottar. Here and there—sometimes in rather out of the way places—a man qualified to act as a "notar publict" was set down; but for the matter of fifty miles along the main route northward from Aberdeen, only a single individual with the technical qualification of a doctor of medicine presents himself at that date.* Sixty years later, so meagre were the means of medical instruction that an Elgin doctor thought it worth his while to inform the people of Aberdeen that any gentleman "desirous of breeding a son to medicine," provided the lad had made sufficient progress in Latin, Greek, and Mathematics, might through his services have him initiated in Pharmacy, Chemistry, the Materia Medica, Anatomy,

---

* Mr. James Milne, doctor of medicine, Inverurie.

and Surgery, on reasonable terms, and in such a way as would "render his future studies easy and agreeable." And for lack of independently established practitioners with the requisite skill, it became a common practice with kirk-sessions to get a midwife trained for the parish at their charge.

Yet the needs of humanity are in all ages the same. And hence the emergence of men, and women too, claiming to possess a skill which, if not of the schools, nor altogether so exact or definite as a more inquisitive age would have demanded, was on the whole accepted as adequate to the varied exigencies for which it was sought. Science was not then in the ascendant; faith spread its wings unhampered by doubts about the existence of the supernatural, and critical methods had hardly yet found place. One of the most notable of this class of persons of whom I have seen any reliable record was "Doctor" Adam Donald, known as "the Prophet of Bethelnie." Adam, whose fame was widely spread during a period of some thirty years from about the middle of the century, was born in 1703, and died in 1780. Dr. James Anderson[*] published an account of the prophet ten years after his death; and he had the kindness to accompany it with a fairly well executed woodcut portrait of him. Apparently Adam knew for what purpose the picture was taken, as he desired a certain sentiment to be inscribed below it. And the woodcut enables us to know that he had been a goggle-eyed man, with a double chin, long hair, and a short neck, whose characteristic attitude seems to have been that of standing with his feet apart, his arms hanging loosely by his sides, and his hands placed back to back in front of him, the helpless look of the long crooked fingers suggesting the notion that his wrists have been at least partially dislocated. His dress is a Kilmar-

---

[*] *The Bee*, Vol. VI. 1791.

nock cap, a long square-tailed coat, with heavy flaps and spreading collar, a waistcoat of corresponding expanse, knee breeches, and shoes with buckles.

Dr. Anderson, who, it must be said, does not seem to have looked upon the prophet with any excess of respect, expressly says that Adam had "remarked with what a superstitious veneration the ignorant people around him contemplated that uncouth figure he inherited from nature, and shrewdly availed himself of this propensity for obtaining a subsistence through life." To this end he "affected an uncommon reservedness of manner; pretended to be extremely studious, spoke little, and what he said was uttered in half sentences with awkward gesticulations and an uncouth tone of voice, to excite consternation and elude detection." Rather a remorseless analysis of the elements of the prophet's influence it must be allowed.

In those days the fairies played queer antics; nor was the quiet region of Bethelnie exempt from their operations. And thus it was that when Adam Donald's mother gave birth to a fine boy the "gweed neibours" whipt the child away to Elfland, and left the poor cottar and his wife a mere changeling in his place—a sallow mis-shapen unthriven creature. How then could Adam Donald be like other bairns mentally or physically? The defects of his ill-compacted body prevented him gaining a livelihood by hard physical labour; and he thus amongst other things took to amusing himself in his earlier years with such books as chance enabled him to obtain; "and though he could scarcely read the English language, yet he carefully picked up books in all languages that fell in his way." Dr. Anderson says he had in his possession books bought at the sale of the prophet's effects after his death in French, Latin, Greek, Italian, and Spanish. "He delighted chiefly in large books that contained plates of any sort; and Gerard's large Herbal, with wooden cuts, might be said to be his constant *vade mecum*, which was displayed with much parade on the table, or the shelf, among other books of a like portly appearance, to all his visitors."

Bethelnie, erstwhile the seat of the parish church (now of Meldrum), and dowered with the legend of the pious Percock, who warded off the plague by creeping round the parish on his bare knees, and planting a tree to mark the spot where his self-sacrificing labour began and ended, was still fortunate in the possession of a church crumbling to ruin, and a picturesque and finely situated churchyard. This latter spot it was the practice of the prophet to visit all alone at suitably eerie hours. How could it be doubted that his purpose was to hold converse with departed spirits, and to be by them " informed of many things that no mortal knowledge could reach ?"

The prophetic fame of Adam Donald grew, as it needs must, in the circumstances, until people came from far and near to consult him ; and ultimately " scarcely anything was deemed beyond the reach of his knowledge." " When articles of dress or furniture were amissing he was consulted ; and his answers were so general and cautiously worded, that though they could scarcely be at all understood at the time, yet when any of the things lost were accidentally found at a future period the people were easily able to perceive that his mysterious answer plainly indicated where the goods had been if they had had the ingenuity to expound it." We must not forget that this latter sentiment is merely the personal opinion of the sceptical Dr. Anderson, speaking against

The 'sponsible voice o' a haill countra side !

In his capacity of physician—he was, of course, a skilled cow doctor as well—" Dr." Adam Donald was " chiefly consulted in cases of lingering disorders that were supposed to owe their origin to witchcraft or some supernatural agency of this sort." " In these cases he invariably prescribed the application of certain simple unguents of his own manufacture to particular parts of the body, accompanied with particular ceremonies, which he described with all the minuteness he could, employing the most learned terms he could pick up to denote the most common things, so that, not being understood, the persons who consulted him invariably concluded when the cure did not succeed, that they had failed in some essential particular; and when the cure was effected he obtained full credit." Very evidently Adam Donald had not been lacking in some of the qualities on which various others, since his day, have sought to build a reputation for skill and profundity!

From distances of ten, twenty, aye thirty miles, they came to consult him, either as necromancer or physician. Sunday brought the greatest pressure of business, and on that day duly, for many years, the prophet's house was always crowded with visitors of various sorts. His professional fees were not extravagant, never exceeding sixpence where no medicines were given, and a shilling was said to have been the highest fee he was ever known to obtain. On this scale of charges, however, he contrived to maintain himself comfortably; and on the faith of his lucrative calling, when pretty far advanced in life, " he prevailed," we are assured, " on one of the handsomest girls in that neighbourhood to marry him."

That the prophet of Bethelnie was a man of superior talent in any way, Dr. Anderson declines to admit. Despite the prudence with which he conducted his operations, his mental power seemed to be below the ordinary standard. True, he had the art of concealing his defects by never vainly attempting to display his knowledge where detection seemed probable, but his general reserve " seems to have proceeded from his want of ideas; and he was more indebted to his singular appearance than anything else for his celebrity." While he "was able to impose upon those at a distance by the appearance of much wisdom he found it more difficult to do so with regard to his own family." His wife, " whose superior judgment supplied the defects of his," from motives of prudence took care to keep the secret, but his daughter did not scruple to cheat the seer openly, mulcting him of part of his professionally earned sixpences under his very nose to buy fine clothes, and then openly laughing at him among her companions. " He never," says Dr. Anderson, " had any friend with whom he kept up a cordial intercourse ; he left no sort of writings behind him ; nor have I ever heard of a single sentence of his that was worth repeating ; unless it be the four lines of poetry which he desired the painter to put at the bottom of his picture :—

> Time doth all things devour ;
> And time doth all things waste,
> And we waste time,
> And so are we at last."

Of imitators of the prophet, or rather of practitioners, more or less renowned, of the same class, there was no great lack up to a considerably later time. The indispensable qualification was possession of a certain amount of low cunning ; and ugliness, or oddity of personal appearance, was undoubtedly an advantage. Hence the readiness with which queer-looking old women were accepted as witches, and credited with the power of performing various cantrips. Superstitious belief in the supernatural, and an easy credulity regarding physical phenomena were the common endowment of the mass of the population, so that whoever chose to attempt the *role* of warlock or " skeely man," would find the path open and easy ; and once entered thereon it might be hard to say in some cases whether the witch-doctor made most progress in deceiving others or deceiving himself. Certain it was that a good many of them came to have a῾firm, if somewhat vague and inarticulate belief in their own powers. As time went on, the business tended to get less reputable and more directly rascally, inasmuch as the progress of general enlightenment both served to show the pretensions of its professors in a more contemptible light, and forced them to resort to extended and often very palpable subterfuges in order to keep up their credit with those still willing to be duped by them. And these, beyond question, were a class wonderfully tenacious of existence. Belief in witchcraft generally, and in the existence and *can* of the fairies, held wide sway among the country population till the close of the century; and, indeed, for a good while after. The merry little folks with their green coats were the "gweed neibours," who seldom did serious harm, except when they played the sort of "plisky" performed in substituting an uncouth changeling for the infant son of the Bethelnie cottar. They would do many a good service when the humour was on them; and happy was he who, when some sturdy male fairy took a bout at thrashing in his barn floor of an early winter morning, could creep quietly up behind, and, getting hold of the flail souple, "catch the speed!" Such cantrips as an old wife converting herself into the form of a hare, and hirpling about from "toon" to "toon" at uncanny hours; or in other guises "trailin' the rape" to deprive a neighbour's cow of its milk-giving powers, transferring them to some other cow, or inanimate object even, for her own behoof, were regarded as serious contingencies, against which protection was needed. And, of course, it could be had from a class of operators who sprang into existence, partly from the necessities of the case, and partly from their own tastes and turn of mind. The more pleasing superstition, which had respect to wonder-moving tales of Elfland and its inhabitants, got gradually attenuated, and died out with the wooden plough and the small oats; the grosser and less ethereal one lingered much longer; and, indeed, in regions where primitive ideas are allowed to have some footing, the notion that certain occult powers, derived from an evil source, might be exercised on man or beast by people of sinister antecedents and reputation is hardly more than extinct even yet.

CHAPTER XXV.

THE KIRK-SESSION AND ITS DUTIES—A GHOST LAID—TIBBIE MORTIMER AND GEORDIE WATT.

THE oversight exercised by the Kirk-Session, and the extent to which it felt bound to interfere for the regulation of morals and promotion of the material interests of the parishioners, were not a little remarkable. If the Session might not still go the length of "dealing" with women of rank and position, as had been done a century earlier, worrying them effectually because they failed to appear duly at church, and were "suspect" of being "obstinate papists" and the like, they had, at any rate, little difficulty in getting an ordinary laird to submit to discipline; to pay the wonted fine for his incontinence, and probably a good round sum in addition for behoof of the poor—if on that footing he might obtain the privilege of taking his rebuke in private, and not in presence of the congregation, a concession not very infrequently made latterly. There were not wanting instances, moreover, of persons of the Episcopal persuasion coming voluntarily forward, and, for the quieting of their own consciences, presumably, entreating discipline to be exercised upon them. And while the sway of the Session received something like universal acknowledgment, the variety of things in which it intermeddled was great. Censure would be threatened, or, if need were, passed upon " dishaunters of ordinances," upon women who indulged in idle "claik" about the kirk door on Sunday, or used their tongues in vulgar and scandalous " flyting " at other seasons, and so on. Special Acts were formulated to meet special evils; as that of vagrancy, when warning would be given that "contraveners" who chose to entertain improper people, who could not produce satisfactory "testificats" would be dealt with as "scandalous persons" themselves; and such occasions as penny bridals had to be legislated upon by Synod, Presbytery, and Session, with a view to restrain the undue jollities to which they led; or otherwise suppress the institution altogether.

When moral lapses of the kind with which Kirk-Sessions have all along been but too familiar had to be dealt with, the discipline was proportioned to the gravity of the offence. A money penalty of four to six pounds Scots, equal to as many shillings sterling, was the current pecuniary mulct, and the "public appearances" of the defaulters for rebuke might be few or many, according to circumstances. For single offences that bore no special aggravation once or twice was deemed sufficient, if the parties "carried" themselves properly. In more complicated cases the Session studied the effects; and where due tokens of penitence seemed wanting, or merely in the incipient stage, they, like faithful men, could only exhort the defaulters to "continue the profession of their repentance" in a becoming spirit, they freely according them ample opportunity for so doing. And the end desired was often not attained very soon. Concerning a woman who was a "trelapser" in a country parish in 1720, we find this brief entry in the Session minute:—"Compeared in sacco. *pro* 7mo., and was rebuked;" that is, she appeared for the seventh Sunday in sackcloth. On her eighth appearance she is "examined *coram*, and, appearing to be weighted with a sense of her sin," the Session "gave it as their advice that absolution should be allowed her upon her next appearance. She payed four lib. penalty," and was then handed over to the Presbytery for final absolution. The case is an illustrative one, and such cases were by no means of exceptional occurrence.

In some instances the boundary line between the ecclesiastical and civil jurisdictions was curiously traversed. When a case of infanticide had occurred, and the deed had been discovered by the dead body of the murdered bairn being got, the Kirk-Session would occasionally set itself to find out who the unnatural mother was. The mode adopted was to order all the "free" or unmarried women to "compear" at the kirk; and there, for the honour of the parish, individually to satisfy a jury of midwives that none of them had given birth to the defunct infant, with certification that any "free woman" who chose to disobey the order would be held as taking guilt to herself. Reversing the maxim of law which says that every person shall be held innocent till proved guilty, the Session boldly announced the principle of holding those guilty who did not adopt the prescribed means to prove their innocence. And then in return for the Session thus, in its own way, taking up what was clearly the duty of the Civil Court, the Civil Court reciprocated at times by recognising the function of the Session in what would seem a rather odd fashion. At the Aberdeen Quarter Sessions in May, 1750, Adam Lind, in Tarves, pleads guilty to giving insulting and abusive language to a county Justice of the Peace at a private Session. He is sent to jail for fourteen days, and fined £5; and also "to appear first Sunday after his liberation within the Kirk of Tarves immediately after divine service, and in presence of the congregation convened for the time, make acknowledgment of his insulting the said Justice, and to procure a report and certificate under the hand of the Session-clerk and two elders, of his having made such acknowledgment." Expenses were given against him too, and £10 demanded in security of performance.

The Session interested itself in such matters as the

building of bridges, which, properly enough, it recognised as "a pious work," and would readily order a collection to be made to help on an undertaking of that kind. And if a farmer got his "steading" burnt down, not only the Session of his own parish, but those of other surrounding parishes would agree to render him aid in the same way. But indeed there was no interest, temporal or spiritual, in which the Session might not intermeddle. An illustration of this of a rather peculiar sort is found in the records of the Kirk-Session of Chapel of Garioch. It was in the autumn of 1737, about the time when John Skinner, as a youthful tutor at Monymusk House, in the neighbouring parish of that name, was inditing his " Christmas Ba'in." The well-to-do tenant in the pleasant farm of Bridgend, on the banks of the Ury, who had been among the first to build a pew for himself in the parish kirk in 1718, had died leaving a family of seven sons, still alive, for two of whom he had been able to provide separate farms, leaving the rest together in family at Bridgend. His widow had followed him to the grave in the bygone spring, and now it was noised through the parish that her ghost had been seen; and indeed was causing no little terror about Bridgend. The Session being convened on a certain date, the minister, Mr. Gilbert Gerard, reported that he had something to lay before them concerning the " said pretended spirit." His statement, in substance, was that he, as minister of the parish, had been asked by George Watt from Bridgend, to come and " converse with the spirit, who, ever since about three or four weeks after the death of his mother in the preceding February, had frequently appeared and spoken to him and his brothers without the windows of the rooms where they lay, to their great terror and amazement." On being " posed" as to its identity by George Watt and his brothers, the ghost, with a superabundance of sanctions, "solemnly averred and swore" that "it was a good spirit; yea, the very spirit of their glorified mother," sent from heaven to "reveal several things to them for their temporal and eternal good, which they were to behove and do at their highest peril." But while the spirit—" which spoke always with a shrill and heavenly voice," making the beds and house where they lay to " shake and tremble again " — " gave them very good instructions and counsels," and even told them " the very secrets of their hearts," the main burden it had been charged to deliver was " that it was the will of the great God that Geordie Watt should marry Tibbie Mortimer (who then was the only woman-servant in that family), because that Tibbie was now in a gracious state, and had been predestinated to glory from all eternity."

This somewhat incongruous revelation had first been made to George Watt when he was lying in bed all alone; whereupon George, like a prudent man, objected, as he alleged, to a marriage so unequal in point of worldly circumstances, and so contrary to his inclination, until it should be made clear to him and others that what he was desired to do really was the will of God. The accommodating spirit undertook to satisfy him on that point; and the seven brothers having, according to compact settled beforehand, duly assembled in the same room, the ghost appeared at the window and repeated its commission, with the portentous threat that " unless Geordie Watt should marry Tibbie Mortimer, he and all his brothers, and all things belonging to them, should certainly be consumed with fire from heaven !" Geordie himself at least having, in addition, nothing to look for thereafter but everlasting punishment. By all this, and similar revelations and threats oft repeated, George Watt had, as he averred, got so " frightened and straitened " that he felt impelled to come to the minister, who, in following out George's request, had gone to Bridgend on the previous Thursday evening, taking with him a member of the Session and his own servant. His first care was to pray with the family of seven sons, and the next to take what precautions he could with a view to prevent being imposed upon, and, if possible, to unravel the matter. After some hours waiting, a voice was heard at a little window of the bedroom in which Geordie Watt slept, " pronouncing with a very wild and vehement tone " that its owner was come in the name of the Trinity to speak to them all—"to men, minister, and all, 'Speak, George Watt, speak, men and minister ! Come here and I will discourse you all,'" said the irrepressible ghost. On hearing the " bold and blasphemous expressions" used, the company were in " the greatest consternation ;" all but the wide-awake parson, who started to his feet and ran outside, making his way to the corner of the house nearest to where the ghost seemed to be. " The appearance which first presented to his view," says the Session minute, " was about the bulk of ane ordinary woman, covered with white clean linnen head and arms down to the middle of the body before, and somewhat farther behind. Then, willing to unravel the matter whatever the event should be, he made such a trial of the apparition as he thought agreeable to the principles of the Christian revelation and true philosophy ; and by its resistance to the end of a small rod which he had in his hand, he soon found it to be a material substance. And immediately the pretended spirit took itself to its heels, and he running after it a few paces, caught it by the neck, and his servant coming up at the same time on the other side, caught it by the arm. The apparition was brought flat to the ground, and then, being charged as a base imposter to speak, it was silent till he pulled the white vail from its face, whereupon (it being a bright moonshine), he clearly saw that it was the above-named Isobel Mortimer."

Alas, poor Tibbie ! What a collapse of her skilfully-devised plot! She was remorselessly led into the "firehouse" in presence of the seven brothers Watt, where the minister held forth to her "at some length" on "the blasphemy, devilish tricks, and mischievous pranks" of which she had been guilty; when, sad to say, in place of becoming penitence, Tibbie "discovered" such a "surprising boldness and impudence, obdurateness, and obstinacy," that the minister was restrained from handing her over to the civil magistrate only by the entreaty of the family, whose servant she had been for a considerable time. He contented himself, however, with seeing her "march off, bag and baggage, before he left that place."

What the Session did was to pass a set of formal resolutions, wherein they found that "this vile, base, and impudent woman" had gone on "in a course of horrid blasphemy;" had "prescribed charms and suspicious things," disturbing that "sober and orderly family" by her imposture, frightening them "to the great prejudice of their health, yea, to the endangering of their lives;" doing what she could to set the brothers by the ears, and moreover, venting as revelations from God "most false, malicious, and black calumnies against several persons of an untainted character and reputation." In regard the case of "this wicked wretch" was "altogether very complex and of a singular nature," the Session reserved it as it stood for the advice of the Presbytery.

The lapse of a little time seems to have shed new light on the matter, and brought the demure Geordie Watt into the foreground in another guise. Some ten months thereafter it was recorded that Isobel Mortimer had been before the Presbytery, and by them convicted "of the sin and scandal of fornication with George Watt in Bridgend, as also of acting the part of a ghost and blaspheming the holy name of God." She was ordered to appear in sackcloth before the congregation; and threatened at first to be contumacious; but by and by promised to satisfy discipline, and entered on the profession of her repentance by appearing "in *sacco*" for the first time on 3rd December, 1738. Meanwhile there had been strenuous dealing with Geordie Watt. On account of "the several presumptions that lay against him of his being in less or more conscious of, or having a hand in ye abominable part yt Isa. Mortimer acted," Geordie had also been ordered to appear before the congregation in sackcloth; but he protested against the award, vowing that "he would never satisfy in sackcloth for yt which he knew nothing about." He was willing to "satisfy" in the ordinary way for what we suppose we may, in his case at least, call the major charge. Geordie, who had not been altogether a simpleton evidently, offered to pay 100 merks for behoof of the poor, on condition of being liberated from the sackcloth; and as the Session had got into the way of listening favourably to such proposals by defaulters of substance, his bribe obtained him that indulgence. He simply appeared three Sundays "in his own seat," and paid the statutory penalty of four pounds Scots. As for poor Tibbie Mortimer, she, in fulfilment of the Presbyterial order, had no choice but don the sackcloth and sit in public four Sundays at Chapel of Garioch. She was then called in "and exhorted to continue the profession of her repentance" at Monymusk, which probably had been her native parish. So long after as March, 1740, she is again remitted to the Chapel Session "to do with her as they shall see cause," and "as they were of opinion yt her oftener appearing there could be of little edification," they agreed that she should be dismissed "after sitting one Sabbath more in sackcloth and paying one guinea for the use of the poor." Next month she appeared and paid 12 lb. 12 sh. penalty, and was absolved.

CHAPTER XXVI.

IN CONCLUSION—SUMMARY OF THE SOCIAL, MORAL, AND RELIGIOUS STATE OF THE PEOPLE.

AN impartial survey of the life to which these illustrations refer, is fitted to suggest various reflections more or less to the purpose. On its material side, as compared with the life of the present day, it was poor; and that poverty permeated the "commonality" more or less in all its sections. In the measure of absolute wealth owned by the comparatively well-to-do amongst the rural population, the thousands of to-day may almost literally be said to have been represented by hundreds in the time at which we have glanced; and the hundreds by tens. And though the relative value of money has very much decreased, the social conveniences and comforts enjoyed, or that could be commanded, by even the "bein" householder of the eighteenth century, were meagre indeed in comparison with those in which a large part of the population now participate without difficulty, and as a matter of course.

The condition of the labouring population at any given period affords a reliable index to the general civilisation and social well-being of the community of which they form an indispensable part. And although the separation of classes was not by any means so distinctly marked seventy or a hundred years ago as now—the farmer and his helps, male and female, ordinarily eating their meals at the same table, while the weaver, the smith, and the tailor, could meet either class on a common footing—yet was it the case that those whose lot it was to earn a livelihood by the labour of their hands were alike indifferently housed, and meagrely fed at all times. Before the progress of agricultural improvement had so far mended matters, they also suffered severely from unsanatory natural conditions, such as the abounding marsh vapours that rose from stagnant undrained swamps, and crept about many of their habitations. Ague was a common complaint in many parts of Scotland during a considerable portion of the past century; indeed, it was so common in some districts among the peasantry, in spring and autumn particularly, that farmers occasionally found it difficult to get through the ordinary operations of the season for want of labourers. And when a special piece of work had to be executed it was not unusual, we are told, "to order six labourers instead of four, from the probability that some of them, before the work could be finished, would be rendered unfit for labour by an attack of this disorder. Indeed, in several parishes," it is added, "the inhabitants, with very few exceptions, had an annual attack." And when Sir John Sinclair wrote one of his later papers early in the present century, he deemed the fact that ague had become less common, and had been entirely banished from a number of districts, " so highly honourable to agriculture," that he says he could not mention it without "a high degree of pride and pleasure." Malignant fevers too ravaged country localities now and again, with a severity unknown to the living generation, elder or younger, at times almost literally decimating the population of a parish. And of course small-pox, when it came, had its way unchecked; killing not a few, leaving its indelible impress on many a countenance, and often producing blindness, where the attack was not fatal.

Touching the religious and moral aspects of the question, it were perhaps easier than it is desirable, or quite wise, to make sweeping statements on the one side or the other. Where the sense of religious obligation was really felt the theological opinions of the time were no doubt severe, and the prevailing notions concerning Christian liberty narrow and restricted. It does not, however, betoken any great depth of insight, nor is it indicative of a true and adequate comprehension of facts in their due relations or a really cosmopolitan philosophy, to misapprehend totally the distinction between earnest piety of even the gloomier sort, and simple fanaticism or pure hypocrisy. In the regions to which we have had reference, and during the time under notice, an actively religious spirit was certainly not a prominent feature. With considerable show of reason it might be said the very reverse was the case. The dominant Presbyterianism managed parish affairs creditably; supplied a reasonable proportion of passable sermons, prevailingly of the type of theology known as "Moderate," as contra-distinguished from "Evangelical," weekly; carried on the stated diets of catechising, yearly, and took oversight of the schools; its ministry yielding a man here and there destined to eminence more or less, as occasionally, too a brother with pronouncedly erratic tendencies, who ruled his diocese after his own queer fashion, and left his corresponding moral impress upon a generation of parishioners when he had disappeared from the scene. Episcopalians, who, in due course "suffered" for their non-jurant principles, did not bulk largely; neither did the followers of the first or second Secession. The feelings of contempt and aversion with which Seceders were regarded were very general; as one can readily understand from occasional references made to them by contemporary writers. A sufficiently pointed example of the estimation in which they were held by the landowning class is furnished by the articles and conditions of tack for his lands, registered in the Sheriff Court books of Aberdeenshire, in February, 1781, by Alexander Fraser, of Strichen. In the second Article, in which are specified the various offences for which tenants shall be held to have forfeited their tacks, such as their becoming bankrupt or the like, it is *inter alia* specified—" or, *eighthly* shall knowingly or wilfully take into their service, or harbour, or set ground to any Seceders or thieves, vagabonds or beggars, or any other person who has not sufficient testimonials of their former good and honest behaviour, to the satisfaction of the said Alexander Fraser, or his foresaids, or to such as are suspected to harbour any of the above-mentioned." We may possibly look upon the laird of Strichen, himself a Roman Catholic, as somewhat extreme in his intolerance, yet putting it in a mildly negative form, one cannot, at anyrate, regard such facts as that Seceders were very limited in number, and that they were held in general contempt, as furnishing evidence of any deep or wide-spread interest in religious questions. Thus far, at least, we may safely go.

The question of the comparative morality of the people may be handled with all requisite freedom, even should it be at the risk of challenge on some points. The idea that degeneracy, in point of morals, has crept in amongst our rural population within the past half century or so, and that if a greatly higher standard was not uniformly maintained in the time immediately preceding, a sort of Arcadian innocence and simplicity prevailed very generally at least, finds acceptance with some who profess to have knowledge of the subject. Unhappily the records of the time do not seem to bear out such ideas in the very least. In their everyday life rude roystering, drinking, quarrelling, and fighting were the too frequent recreations of the common people a hundred years ago. Even then there were complaints that the people were not what they had been in the previous times of fancied guilelessness and primitive virtue. Only they did not gather up and tabulate the details of crime as is now done, and in so far as mere personal outbreaks went, if the offenders escaped the notice of the Kirk Session, the Civil Court would hardly interfere unless the fray had been so savage as to involve actual loss of life or very serious damage "to lith or limb." The character of those whose position placed them above the common people was not always indeed regarded as entitling them to be spoken of with unqualified respect. The writer of a letter of date 1750, discussing the agriculture of the time, gives his opinion of Aberdeenshire landlords, and the relations between them and their tenants in these words—"The landed gentlemen, many of them, look upon religion as below them, morality as an unnecessary incumbrance, economy as sordid, and their tenants as a species of animals, made to be abused and oppressed—to labour and spend their strength to maintain their luxury and riot." Like enough the writer desired to put in his tints strongly, but what nineteenth century Radical has ever denounced the territorial shortcomings of his time in more unsparing terms?

Nor even in relation to the sore subject of bastardy did the people of last century in the north-east of Scotland hold a greatly more favourable position than their descendants do. Possibly the actual percentage of illegitimate births may have been somewhat less. We have no available statistics of a comprehensive sort to compare with the Registrar's figures of the present time. But the Kirk-Session records serve the end in a rough, yet reasonably reliable way. And a careful scrutiny of some of these records does not encourage the belief that even the proportional number of bastards to population was always very appreciably less—the number of aggravated and specially bad cases that needed severe dealing, and where the Session had to call in the aid of the Presbytery, was certainly as great or greater than now. Any inquiry bearing on the causes of a high rate of bastardy in these districts would lead us into irrelevant and probably fruitless discussion of a vexed question. But of one thing we may hold ourselves assured—that at no period known to history was the proportion of bastard births other than considerable. Starting on that basis and keeping clearly in view that so it has been all through, we can at least more readily understand how the result of a traditional and inherited moral sentiment all too deadened and dormant, should serve to take the edge off the feeling of shame and blunt the sense of honour in the sex amongst whom chastity is properly deemed the crown of all the virtues. Born into and nurtured from childhood in a pervasive social atmosphere of this sort it becomes readily intelligible how women whose characters otherwise one would be sorry to impugn in the least barely realise it as any permanent stain on their womanhood to have been the mother of a bastard. And here, doubtless, we touch the most formidable phase of a species of immorality that has gained for the common people of these regions an unenviable notoriety. We need not contrast it with the measure of the like vice as it exists among the classes where purity in one sex is demanded and valued; and, indeed, such contrast or comparison cannot be made. Only this much may be said with truth that while the women who sadly fail in virgin modesty ordinarily prove true and faithful wives when married, even the men who join with them in wedlock do also as a rule act with conjugal fidelity thereafter. With them the vice as it exists is gross and open; we see it in its full extent, and may know its limits; and in this way the common people of the rural community probably suffer some considerable injustice when their sins in this respect are sought to be contrasted with those of certain other classes more highly civilised it may be, and enjoying far greater social advantages.

Generally viewed then the life of last century, in so far as it has come under our notice, cannot be regarded as strongly typical of the "good old times." Confining our retrospect to that period we should certainly be compelled to say—

> Those times were never
> Airy visions sat for the picture.

Along with abounding poverty of means and resources, we find that industry was stagnant, and unprogressive, and that the ordinary rural life of the time was strongly tinctured with superstition, or simply in the state of uninquiring indifference as regards its spiritual beliefs. It had nevertheless its own features of attraction, as contrasted with the life that has followed it. There was a sense of quiet leisureliness about the manner in which each man held his position and transacted the business of his daily life; an absence of hurry and headlong competition, and a feeling of neighbourliness and hospitality amongst the constituent membership of each small community that did much to make life not merely tolerable, but rationally enjoyable. The changes that have occurred in these respects, we may warrantably say, have not all been in the nature of an unqualified social gain.

APPENDIX.

1.—LIST OF BOOKS REFERRED TO.

Domestic Annals of Scotland from the Reformation to the Revolution. By Robert Chambers. 3 vols. 1859.

Lectures on Scotch Legal Antiquities. By Cosmo Innes. 1872.

Spalding Club Publications—
  List of Pollable Persons within the Shire of Aberdeen in 1696.
  Collections for History of the Shires of Aberdeen and Banff.
  Miscellanies, &c.

The Statistical Account of Scotland, drawn up from the communications of the Ministers of the different Parishes. By Sir John Sinclair, Bart. 21 vols. 1782-94.

Memorials for the Government of the Royal Burghs in Scotland. By Baillie Alexander Skene of Newtile. 1685.

General View of the Agriculture and Rural Economy of the County of Aberdeen, with Observations on the means of its Improvement, drawn up for the consideration of the Board of Agriculture and Internal Improvement. By James Anderson, LL.D. 1794.

The Bee; or Literary Weekly Intelligencer. By James Anderson, LL.D. 17 vols. 1791-3.

General View of the Agriculture of Aberdeenshire, drawn up under the direction of the Board of Agriculture. By George Skene Keith, D.D., Minister of Keith-hall and Kinkell. 1811.

General View of the Agriculture of Kincardineshire or the Mearns. By George Robertson, landsurveyor. 1807.

General View of the Agriculture of the County of Banff. By David Souter, farmer. 1812.

The Political Works of Andrew Fletcher, Esq. of Saltoun. Glasgow, 1749.

Letters from a Gentleman in the North of Scotland (Captain Burt), to his friend in London. 1726-30.

A True Method of Treating Light Hazely Ground; or an exact relation of the practice of farmers in Buchan: containing Rules for Infields, Outfields, Haughs and Laighs. By a small Society of Farmers in Buchan. Edinburgh, 1735.

A General Description of the East Coast of Scotland, from Edinburgh to Cullen. By Francis Douglas. 1827.

Present State of Husbandry in Scotland, extracted from Reports made to the Commissioners of Annexed Estates (by Mr. Andrew Wight), and published by their authority. Edinburgh. 1778.

Memoirs of the Life and Works of the late Right Honourable Sir John Sinclair, Bart. By his Son, the Rev. John Sinclair, M.A., Pembroke College, Oxford. 2 vols. 1837.

Buchan. By Rev. J. B. Pratt, LL.D., Cruden.

An Echo of the Olden Time, from the North of Scotland. By Rev. Walter Gregor, M.A.

2.—EARLY ABERDEENSHIRE ROADS AND POST TOWNS.

In June, 1739, a meeting of the Commissioners of Supply was held, and the minute bears *inter alia* :—

"As to the Kintoir road recommend to the town of Aberdeen the management thereof, so far as their freedome goes; and recommend to Dr. Gordon; Auchmull; Stonywood, younger; Invercauld, and the factors of Caskieben and Craig, or any two of them to take upon them the management and direction of the Kintoir road from the place where the freedome of Aberdeen ends, untill it comes to the head of the Hill of Tyrebagger; and recommend to the Earle of Kintoir's factor and the Magistrates of Kintoir to take the management and direction of the said road from the head of the Hill of Tyrebagger to the town of Inverury; and recommends to the Magistrates of Inverury to carry on said road through the whole of their freedome; and recommends to the laird of Pittodery; John Innes of Tillyfour, and John Leslie of Afforsk, to carry on said road from Inverury to the west corner of the park dykes of Pittodery; and recommends to Overhall; Westhall; Premnay; Dunnydeer; and the laird of Law, or any two of them to carry on said road up through the Garioch. And as to the branch of the Inverury road which leads to Strathbogie, the Commissioners recommend to Inveramsay; Coldwalls; Threefield; Gight; Shellagreen, and Rothney, or any two of them to take upon them the management and direction of the said branch from Inverury to Strathbogie, and particularly orders a cassey to be made at Leggatsden; and appoints Inveramsay to deburse the charges thereof, and to be repayed at the next generall meeting."

In constructing roads, what they did was simply to level out the site where the ground was hard and firm: and lay a causeway of rough stones in the low-lying and soft parts that could not otherwise be got over. The Legatsden Causeway

A lang mile frae Harlaw,

Appendix. 217

where a burn came down the Den and a hamlet stood, was a case in point.

Statute labour unwillingly given, and amateur overseership made but a poor business of it, arrange it as the county would. And in April 1759 "all the plans hitherto proposed having proved inefficient," eight separate Road Districts were formed in the county, corresponding with the eight Presbyteries. And here we may as well give the Districts, valued rental and rating as they stood in 1770.

Names of Presbyteries or Districts.	Total valued rent of each Presbytery Scots.	Proportion of Highway Money to each District Scots.	Proportion in sterling.
Deer,............	£40,233 17 4	£188 8 6	£15 14 12
Ellon,............	39,191 2 6	183 11 0	15 5 11
Garioch,.........	34,238 12 10	159 16 0	13 6 4
Turriff,...........	27,835 13 8	129 15 0	10 16 3
Aberdeen,......	26,160 5 0	121 14 0	10 2 10
Kincardine,.....	32,271 13 6	149 4 0	12 8 8
Alford,...........	22,292 18 10	103 7 0	8 12 3
Strathbogie,.....	11,224 11 9	52 11 0	4 7 7
	£233,448 15 5	£1088 6 6	£90 13 10

The sum of £90 odds as Highway money for the whole county was not a large sum.

The turnpike from Stonehaven to Aberdeen was made in 1797; and that from Stonehaven by Durris to Banchory-Ternan in 1800.

In appendix to a report prepared in 1863 for the Aberdeenshire Committee on Road Reform, by the late Mr. George Marquis, accountant, a list of the turnpike roads in the county of Aberdeen, in the order in which they were opened, and the number opened in each decade after 1790, and other particulars, are given. The following figures are from Mr. Marquis's statement:—

Name of Road.	Year when opened.	Length. M. F. Y.
Deeside, ...	1798	13 4 0
Ellon, Peterhead, and Fraserburgh,	1799	52 4 0
	Carry forward,	66 0 0

Name of Road.	Year when opened.	Length. M.	F.	Y.
Brought Forward,		66	0	0
Inverury, ...	1800	15	4	0
Turriff, ...	1802	20	6	0
Charleston, ...	1802	16	6	120
Gardensmill, ...	1803	13	2	0
Oldmeldrum, ...	1803	14	1	14
Skene, ...	1803	17	4	0
Huntly, ...	1804	22	0	0
Newburgh, ...	1804	11	1	209
Fyvie, ...	1806	7	6	73
Echt and Midmar, ...	1807	13	2	97
Longside, ...	1807	12	0	0
		164	2	73
Alford, ...	1810	8	4	0
New Pitsligo, ...	1810	7	4	0
Cortiebrae, ...	1813	12	0	0
Boyndlie, ...	1816	10	5	3
		38	5	3
Bridge of Dee, ...	1821	1	4	0
Buchan, ...	1821	13	0	0
Tarland, ...	1822	11	0	202
Insch and West Foudland, ...	1823	14	0	0
Rhynie, ...	1825	10	4	1
Raemoir and Lumphanan, ...	1825	17	1	22
Donside, ...	1826	19	7	117
Kintore and Alford, ...	1826	11	2	117
Udny, ...	1828	11	5	20
		110	2	10
Kennethmont, ...	1833	9	1	71
Corgarff, ...	1833	6	1	84
Sheelagreen, ...	1835	11	4	83
Strichen, ...	1837	7	7	197
Inverury and Forgue, ...	1839	22	1	70
		57	0	65
Strichen and Fraserburgh, ...	1849	7	7	$102\frac{1}{2}$
Kemnay, ...	1855	3	3	$167\frac{1}{2}$
Total length of Turnpike, ...		447	4	201

The total amount of original subscriptions for the foregoing 447 miles of road was £108,857 19s. 3¼d., but this did not suffice for their construction; preferable subscriptions, or borrowed monies, were needed in all but six or seven cases; and, adding these amounts, the total sums raised for construction of turnpike roads in Aberdeenshire amounted to £176,678. The total debt upon the various trusts (only two roads, the Inverury and Bridge of Dee being free of such burden) was no less than £409,433 9s. 3d.; and in 1863, the estimated value of this large amount of debt was, at twenty years' purchase, only £39,521 9s. 6d., the revenue being in many cases seriously affected by the opening of railway lines. The average cost of construction (calculating by the amounts raised) was £394 per mile.

About 1787-8 there were only eight post towns in Aberdeenshire, viz., Ellon, Peterhead, Fraserburgh, Kintore, Old Rain, Old Meldrum, Turriff, and Huntly. After the establishment of the mail coach to Aberdeen, Post Offices were opened at Banchory-Ternan, Kincardine O'Neil, Aboyne, Tullich, Tarland, Strathdon, Braemar, Old Deer, Mintlaw, Strichen, New Pitsligo, Keith-hall, Monymusk, Skene, Alford, and Rhynie.

3.—THE ABERDEENSHIRE CANAL.

The Aberdeenshire Canal, the total length of which, from the river Don to the Shorelands of Aberdeen, was nearly eighteen and one-fourth miles, was designed by Telford. It reached the summit level, 168 feet above low-water mark, at Stoneywood. There were on it seventeen canal locks, five aqueduct bridges over considerable streams of water, and fifty-six accommodation bridges. By the first Act, obtained in 1796, the Company were authorized to raise £20,000, in £50 shares. The Corporation of Aberdeen subscribed £1000; James D. H. Elphinstone, £1000; and the Earl of Kintore, £1000. A few other county gentlemen subscribed to half that amount, and others in less sums; but only £17,715 in all was realised. A second Act was obtained in 1801, under which a farther sum of £11,421 10s. was raised. The difficulty of completing the undertaking was, however, found to be very formidable. The monies subscribed under the second Act (and which were placed as preference shares), proved quite inadequate, and a further mortgage loan of £10,000 was raised upon the credit of revenue. At the close of 1808, the total expenditure had been £43,895 18s. 10d.; the super-expenditure above capital, at that date, being £17,259 8s. 10d., and the original design had not then been completed by formation of a lock and basin connecting the canal with the tide-way at Aberdeen Harbour. The canal was opened for navigation, in the beginning of June, 1805; but again completely stopped in a few days, on account of no fewer than fourteen of the locks having failed, through insufficiency of the mason work. Before this was completely got over, the season of 1806 even was partially interfered with. Next season, 1807, a revenue of £339 2s. 11d. was drawn, and in season 1808, £706 12s. 11d., irrespective of rent for the passenger fly-boats. The average revenue does not seem to have much increased for fully twenty years. In 1834, it had risen to £1141 ; in 1844, to £1619 ; and in 1853, when the canal was superseded by the Great North of Scotland Railway, the revenue was £3062.

4.—CONTRACT BETWEEN MILL SUPERIOR AND SUCKENERS.

In a contract between a mill superior and certain burghal and other suckeners, of date 1790, the parties, under a penalty on either side of £100 sterling, bind and oblige themselves as follow :—"*Primo*, the said—— hereby becomes bound at all times to keep a sufficient qualified miller at the foresaid mill for the service of the sucken, and to be at all times ready to discharge his duty as a millart at the said mill, particularly to carry the clean shilling from the shilling hill to the said mill. *Secundo*, On the other part, the said—— for themselves and their successors, &c., hereby become bound to continue thirled and astricted to the said mill of ——, in all time coming, and to grind their hail corn, including pease, of the growth of their said lands at the said mill, and to pay the 25th peck to the tacksman of the said mill therefor, in name of insucken multure, and a peck of each six bolls of shilling, in name of knaveship, and no more ; as also to grind all their malt at the said mill, and to pay the 25th peck, in name of multure and knaveship therefor ; and further to pay the 25th peck for all grain of whatsover kind of the growth of their said lands, that shall be sold by them or any of them without the bounds of the said sucken. They also further become bound to grind all grain of whatsoever kind at the said mill which they shall purchase and bring within the bounds of the foresaid thirlage, and which they shall have occasion to manufacture, and to pay the usual outsucken dues therefor, being the 48th peck, besides the usual knaveship. It being in all cases understood that the dust and shilling seeds is to be at the disposal of the suckeners. *Tertio*, The said —— become further bound, as said is, to bigg and uphold their just proportions of the mill house and mill damms, and to cast the water gang or lead, and trail or carry stone, yeird, and tree for upholding of the said mill, mill water, and mill house, as oft as the same shall be necessary, and that they be required so to do. The tacksman of the said mill being always obliged and subjected to furnish the timber upon his own expenses, and to cart and win the yeird for upholding of the said mill, mill water, and mill house upon the most commodious part

Appendix.

adjacent to the said mill without the corn grounds. And further, it is agreed upon betwixt the said parties that in case the millart to be employed at the foresaid mill shall be complained upon as not sufficient for grinding of the corn or discharging the other parts of his duty thereat, and the same being tried in a Court to be holden by ——, with the advice and concurrence of the said [superior], and the said millart being convicted thereon shall be fined to double the skaith which any of the inhabitants within the sucken shall happen to suffer through his default, and shall be removed at the term of Whitsunday thereafter, and another sufficient millart placed in his stead."

5.—MALCOLM GILLESPIE'S BOOTY.

At the close of his Memoir, Malcolm Gillespie appended an abstract of his seizures during his career as an exciseman; and which, being made up officially, is probably correct. It will be more intelligible if it is borne in mind that his period of service was divided thus—Collieston, 1801-1807; Stonehaven, 1807-1812; Skene, 1812-1827. The abstract is as follows:—

Foreign Seizures while stationed at—

	Seized.	Destroyed.
Colliston,	10,000 gals. 15 horses, 15 carts,	1000 gals.
Stonehaven,	4,000 gals. 18 horses, 13 carts,	800 gals.
Skene,	291 gals.	
Other places,	100 gals. 4 horses, 2 carts,	25 gals.

British Seizures made while stationed at—

Colliston,	300 gals. 7 horses, 4 carts.	
Stonehaven,	500 gals. 17 horses, 12 carts.	
Skene,	3,759 gals. 92 horses, 33 carts.	
Other Places,	1,000 gals. 12 horses, 3 carts.	

British Seizures destroyed while stationed at—

Colliston,	17 stills, 20 gals. aqua,	900 gals. wash.
Stonehaven,	20 stills, 100 gals. aqua,	1,000 gals. wash.
Skene,	330 stills, 500 gals. aqua,	60,000 gals. wash.
Other places,	40 stills, 150 gals. aqua,	500 gals. wash.

Seized since date of last Seizure referred to in the Memoir, from May 9 to May 19, 1826—

206 gals. aqua, and 3 carts.

The following Books are now ready or preparing for Publication:—

I.

ON POETIC INTERPRETATION OF NATURE. By Principal SHAIRP, St. Andrews.
[*In May.*

II.

In the Press, in One Volume, Folio.

SOLIMAN THE MAGNIFICENT, AND THE TURKS IN THE SIXTEENTH CENTURY. By Sir WILLIAM STIRLING MAXWELL, Bart., K.T. and M.P. Illustrated by numerous Facsimiles of rare contemporary Drawings and Portraits.

III.

In Crown 8vo. Price, 7s. 6d.

LETTERS OF THOMAS ERSKINE OF LINLATHEN, FROM 1800-1840. Edited by WILLIAM HANNA, D.D., LL.D.
[*Now Ready.*

IV.

In One Volume, Crown 8vo., 6s.

THE LANGUAGE AND LITERATURE OF THE SCOTTISH HIGHLANDS. By JOHN STUART BLACKIE, Professor of Greek in the University of Edinburgh.

"The way to a mother's heart is through her children; the way to a people's heart is through its language."—*Jean Paul Richter.*
[*Now Ready.*

V.

In One Volume, Extra Fcap. 8vo., 2s. 6d.

SELF-CULTURE: INTELLECTUAL, PHYSICAL, AND MORAL, A VADE MECUM FOR YOUNG MEN. By JOHN STUART BLACKIE, Professor of Greek in the University of Edinburgh. Tenth Edition.
[*Now Ready.*

VI.

In One Volume, Crown 8vo., 6s.

SERMONS. By the Rev. JOHN KER, D.D. Eleventh Edition.
[*Now Ready.*

VII.

In One Vol. 8vo. with Maps, 15s.

CELTIC SCOTLAND : A HISTORY OF ANCIENT ALBAN. By WILLIAM F. SKENE. Vol. I.—History and Ethnology.

[*Now Ready.*

VIII.

In One Volume, Demy 8vo. with Maps.

THE CELTIC CHURCH. By WILLIAM F. SKENE, LL.D. Forming the Second Volume of "Celtic Scotland, a History of Ancient Alban."

[*Immediately.*

IX.

In One Vol., Crown 8vo., 5s.

BOWEN'S DAILY MEDITATIONS, WITH AN INTRODUCTORY NOTICE. By Rev. WILLIAM HANNA, D.D., LL.D. A New Edition,

[*Now Ready.*

X.

In the Press, in One Volume Ex. Fcap. 8vo., 6s.

HORÆ SUBSECIVÆ. By JOHN BROWN, M.D. A New Edition, with a Portrait by James Faed.

XI.

Dedicated by Special Permission to Her Majesty the Queen. Now Ready, in Two Volumes, 4to, with 16 Full-Page Illustrations, Six Guineas.

RECORDS OF THE COINAGE OF SCOTLAND, FROM THE EARLIEST PERIOD TO THE UNION. Collected by R. W. COCHRAN PATRICK, of Woodside.

"The most handsome and complete Work of the kind which has ever appeared in this country."—*Numismatic Chronicle, Pt. IV.*, 1876.

Only Two Hundred and Fifty Copies Printed.

[*Now Ready.*

XII.

In the Press, in One Volume, Demy 8vo.

TALES FROM THE NORSE. By Sir GEORGE WEBBE DASENT, D.C.L. Third Edition, with Introduction and Appendix.

XIII.

In the Press, in One Volume, Fcap. 8vo.

JOHNNY GIBB OF GUSHETNEUK. Fourth Edition.

EDINBURGH :
DAVID DOUGLAS, 9 CASTLE STREET.

9 CASTLE STREET,
EDINBURGH, *May* 1877.

LIST OF BOOKS
PUBLISHED BY DAVID DOUGLAS.

BLACKIE—Lyrical Poems.
By JOHN STUART BLACKIE, Professor of Greek in the University of Edinburgh. Crown 8vo, cloth, 7s. 6d.

BLACKIE—The Language and Literature of the Scottish Highlands. In 1 vol. crown 8vo, 6s.

"The way to a mother's heart is through her children; the way to a people's heart is through its language."—*Jean Paul Richter.*

* "Ein Buch, das ich auch deutschen Lesern, und zwar in einem beträchtlich weitem Umfange, nicht angelegentlich genug empfehlen kann. . . . Eingehend wird von den Wurzeln und ihrem Verhältnisz innerhalb der groszen Sprachenfamilie, von Vocalen und Consonanten insbesondere, von der Regeln der Wort- und Satzbildung gehandelt, wobei viele sprachliche Alterthümer und einige Ueberreste an den Tag kommen, welche in den englisch-schottischen Dialekten fortleben. . . . Mit F. A. Wolfs lebendiger Auffassung vom Ursprunge der homerischen Epen vor der Seele weisz er die echten lyrischen Schöpfungen der Vorzeit mit ihrem Ansatz zu epischer Fassung zu erkennen und greift aus den Resten des wahren Ossian einige köstliche Perlen heraus, wie sie zu Anfang des 16. Jahrhunderts der Dechant Macgregor von Lismore aufzeichnete. . . . Das letzte Capitel enthält eine Reihe anziehender Beispiele gaelischer Dichtung aus den letzten hundert Jahren. . . . Auch über die kümmerlich gedeihende Prosa werden lehrreiche Angaben hinzugefügt."—*Dr. Reinhold Pauli.*

BLACKIE—Four Phases of Morals : Socrates, Aris- totle, Christianity, and Utilitarianism. Lectures delivered before the Royal Institution, London. Fcap. 8vo, second edition, 5s.

BLACKIE—Songs of Religion and Life.
Fcap. 8vo, 6s.

"The poems in this volume may be regarded as a Second Edition of the second part of my 'Lays and Legends of Ancient Greece,' which has long been out of print, along with other Poems not hitherto published, and a few from a volume of 'Lyrical Poems' previously published, all having one common object, viz., 'the cultivation of religious reverence without sectarian dogmatism, and of poetical sentiment tending not so much to arouse the imagination or to take the fancy, as to purify the passions and to regulate the conduct of life.'"—*Preface.*

BLACKIE—On Self-Culture: Intellectual, Physical,
and Moral. A *Vade-Mecum* for Young Men and Students. Tenth edition. Fcap. 8vo, 2s. 6d.

"Every parent should put it into the hands of his son."—*Scotsman.*

"Students in all countries would do well to take as their *vade-mecum* a little book on self-culture by the eminent Professor of Greek in the University of Edinburgh."—*Medical Press and Circular.*

"An invaluable manual to be put into the hands of students and young men."—*Era.*

"Written in that lucid and nervous prose of which he is a master."—*Spectator.*

BLACKIE—On Greek Pronunciation.
Demy 8vo, 3s. 6d.

BLACKIE—On Beauty.
Crown 8vo, cloth, 8s. 6d.

BLACKIE—Musa Burschicosa.
A Book of Songs for Students and University Men. Fcap. 8vo, 2s. 6d.

BLACKIE—War Songs of the Germans.
Fcap. 8vo, price 2s. 6d. cloth ; 2s. paper.

BLACKIE—Political Tracts.
No. 1. GOVERNMENT. No. 2. EDUCATION. Price 1s. each.

BLACKIE—Homer and the Iliad.
In three Parts. 4 vols. demy 8vo, price 42s.

BOWEN—Daily Meditations by Rev. G. Bowen of Bombay. With Introductory Notice by Rev. W. HANNA, D.D., Author of "The Last Day of our Lord's Passion." Third edition, small 4to, cloth, price 5s.; or limp roan, red edges, price 7s. 6d.

> "Among such books we shall scarcely find another which exhibits the same freshness and vividness of idea, the same fervour of faith, the same intensity of devotion. . . . I count it a privilege to introduce in this country a book so fitted to attract and to benefit."—*Extract from Preface.*

> "These meditations are the production of a missionary whose mental history is very remarkable. . . . His conversion to a religious life is undoubtedly one of the most remarkable on record. They are all distinguished by a tone of true piety, and are wholly free from a sectarian or controversial bias."—*Morning Post.*

BROWN—John Leech and other Papers.
By JOHN BROWN, M.D., F.R.S.E. Crown 8vo. [*In the Press.*

BROWN—Locke and Sydenham, and other Papers.
Extra fcap. 8vo, 7s. 6d.

BROWN—Horæ Subsecivæ.
Ninth edition. Extra fcap. 8vo, 7s. 6d.

BROWN—Letter to the Rev. John Cairns, D.D.
Second edition. Crown 8vo, sewed, 2s.

BROWN—Arthur H. Hallam;
Extracted from "Horæ Subsecivæ." Fcap. sewed, 2s.; cloth, 2s. 6d.

BROWN—Rab and his Friends;
Extracted from "Horæ Subsecivæ." Forty-ninth thousand. Fcap. sewed, 6d.

BROWN—Rab and his Friends.
Cheap Illustrated edition. Square 12mo, ornamental wrapper, 1s.

BROWN—Rab and his Friends.
With Illustrations by Sir George Harvey, R.S.A., Sir J. Noel Paton, R.S.A., and J. B. New edition. Demy quarto, cloth, 6s.

BROWN—Marjorie Fleming: A Sketch.
Fifteenth thousand. Fcap. sewed, 6d.

BROWN—Our Dogs;
Extracted from "Horæ Subsecivæ." Nineteenth thousand. Fcap. sewed, 6d.

BROWN—"With Brains, Sir;"
Extracted from "Horæ Subsecivæ." Fcap. sewed, 6d.

BROWN—Minchmoor.
Fcap. sewed, 6d.

BROWN—Jeems the Doorkeeper: A Lay Sermon.
6d.

BROWN—The Enterkin.
6d.

CAMPBELL—My Indian Journal,
Containing descriptions of the principal Field Sports of India, with Notes on the Natural History and Habits of the Wild Animals of the Country. By Colonel WALTER CAMPBELL, Author of "The Old Forest Ranger." 8vo, with Illustrations, 16s.

CUMMING—Wild Men and Wild Beasts. Adventures in Camp and Jungle. By Lieut.-Colonel GORDON CUMMING. —With Illustrations by Lieut.-Col. BAIGRIE and others. Second edition. Demy 4to, price 24s.

Also, a cheaper edition, with *Lithographic* Illustrations. 8vo, 12s.

CHALMERS—Life and Works of Rev. Thomas Chalmers, D.D., LL.D.

MEMOIRS OF THE REV. THOMAS CHALMERS. By Rev. W. HANNA, D.D., LL.D. Cheap edition. 2 vols. crown 8vo, cloth, 12s.

DAILY SCRIPTURE READINGS. Cheap edition. 2 vols. crown 8vo, 10s.

ASTRONOMICAL DISCOURSES, 1s.

COMMERCIAL DISCOURSES, 1s.

SELECT WORKS, in 12 vols., crown 8vo, cloth, per vol., 6s.

- LECTURES ON THE ROMANS. 2 vols.
- SERMONS. 2 vols.
- NATURAL THEOLOGY, LECTURES ON BUTLER'S ANALOGY, ETC. 1 vol.
- CHRISTIAN EVIDENCES, LECTURES ON PALEY'S EVIDENCES, ETC. 1 vol.
- INSTITUTES OF THEOLOGY. 2 vols.
- POLITICAL ECONOMY, WITH COGNATE ESSAYS. 1 vol.
- POLITY OF A NATION. 1 vol.
- CHURCH AND COLLEGE ESTABLISHMENTS. 1 vol.
- MORAL PHILOSOPHY, INTRODUCTORY ESSAYS, INDEX, ETC. 1 vol.

CHIENE—Lectures on Surgical Anatomy.

By JOHN CHIENE, Assistant-Surgeon, Royal Infirmary, Edinburgh. In 1 vol. 8vo. With numerous Illustrations drawn on Stone by BERJEAU. [*In the Press.*

CONSTABLE—Archibald Constable and his Literary Correspondents: a Memorial.

By his Son, THOMAS CONSTABLE. 3 vols. 8vo, 36s., with Portrait.

"The cream of a generation of interesting men and women now gone from among us—these are the subjects of this important memoir."—*Saturday Review.*

"These three volumes are decidedly additions to our knowledge of that great and brilliant epoch in the history of letters to which they refer."—*Standard.*

"He (Mr. Constable) was a genius in the publishing world. .... The creator of the Scottish publishing trade."—*Times.*

"These three volumes are of a singular and lasting interest."—*Nonconformist.*

"The third volume (Sir Walter Scott) of this elaborate and interesting history is almost an independent work."—*Athenæum.*

"We heartily commend this book to the notice of all readers."—*Guardian.*

DASENT—Tales from the Norse.
By Sir GEORGE WEBBE DASENT, D.C.L. Third edition, with Introduction and Appendix. In 1 vol. demy 8vo. [*In the Press.*

DUN—Veterinary Medicines; their Actions and
Uses. By FINLAY DUN. Fourth edition, revised and enlarged. 8vo, 12s.

DUNBAR—Social Life in Former Days;
Chiefly in the Province of Moray. Illustrated by Letters and Family Papers. By E. DUNBAR DUNBAR, late Captain 21st Fusiliers. 2 vols. demy 8vo, 19s. 6d.

ERSKINE—Letters of Thomas Erskine of Linlathen, from 1800 till 1840. Edited by WILLIAM HANNA, D.D., Author of the "Memoirs of Dr. Chalmers," etc. In 1 vol. crown 8vo, 7s. 6d.   [*Now ready.*

"Here is one who speaks out of the fulness of a large living human heart; whose words will awaken an echo in the hearts of many burdened with the cares of time, perplexed with the movements of the spirit of our time, who will speak to their deepest needs, and lead them to a haven of rest."—*Daily Review.*

"It does one good to come in contact with so saintly a man, and Dr. Hanna has certainly conferred a benefit on the Church at large by editing this volume."—*Edinburgh Courant.*

"'How high must that peak have been which caught the light so early' were the words with which a writer in the *Contemporary Review*, in sketching the life of Thomas Erskine, shortly after his death, characterised his position, his spirit, and his influence."—*Nonconformist.*

> "It is impossible by brief quotation to communicate the beautiful spirit which the letters breathe, but we may indicate what Dr. Hanna has so well done to make the letters answer as nearly as practicable the purposes of a biography. We take leave of the volume with a hearty commendation of the purity of spirit it is fitted to impart."—*Banffshire Journal.*

ERSKINE—The Unconditional Freeness of the Gospel. New edition revised. Crown 8vo, 3s. 6d.

ERSKINE—An Essay on Faith.
Fourth edition. 12mo, 3s.

ERSKINE—The Spiritual Order, and other Papers selected from the MSS. of the late THOMAS ERSKINE of Linlathen. Second edition. Crown 8vo, cloth, 5s.

> "It will for a few have a value which others will not the least understand. But all must recognise in it the utterance of a spirit profoundly penetrated with the sense of brotherhood, and with the claims of common humanity."— *Spectator.*
>
> "Very deserving of study."—*Times.*

FINLAY—Essay to which was awarded the First Mackenzie Prize for the best Essay on the best means of Improving the Relations between Capital and Labour. By JAMES FAIRBAIRN FINLAY, M.A. Demy 8vo, 1s.

FLETCHER—Autobiography of Mrs. Fletcher (of Edinburgh), with Letters and other Family Memorials. Edited by her Daughter. Second edition. Crown 8vo, 7s. 6d.

> "This is a delightful book. It contains an illustrative record of a singularly noble, true, pure, prolonged, and happy life. The story is recounted with a candour, vivacity, and grace which are very charming."—*Daily Review.*

FORBES—The Deepening of the Spiritual Life.
By A. P. FORBES, D.C.L., Bishop of Brechin. Fifth edition. 18mo, cloth, price 1s. 6d.; or paper covers, 1s.; calf, red edges, 3s. 6d.

FORBES—Kalendars of Scottish Saints, with Per-
sonal Notices of those of Alba, etc. By ALEXANDER PENROSE FORBES, D.C.L., Bishop of Brechin. 1 vol. 4to, price £3, 3s. A few copies for sale on large paper, £5, 15s. 6d.

"A truly valuable contribution to the archæology of Scotland."—*Guardian*.

"We must not forget to thank the author for the great amount of information he has put together, and for the labour he has bestowed on a work which can never be remunerative."—*Saturday Review*.

"His laborious and very interesting work on the early Saints of Alba, Laudonia, and Strathclyde."—*Quarterly Review*.

GAIRDNER—On Medicine and Medical Education.
By W. T. GAIRDNER, Professor of the Practice of Medicine in the University of Glasgow. Three Lectures, with Notes and an Appendix. 8vo, 3s. 6d.

GAIRDNER—Clinical and Pathological Notes on
Pericarditis. By W. T. GAIRDNER, Professor of the Practice of Medicine in the University of Glasgow. 8vo, sewed, 1s.

GIBSON, C. P.—Cheerfulness.
By CHARLES P. GIBSON. In 1 vol. fcap., 3s. 6d.

"It depicts, in very graphic and glowing terms, much of the scenery of this northern district of England, and is therefore sure to be prized very highly by those Northumbrians into whose hands it may happen to fall. Apart, however, from its local interest, it has peculiar merits of its own, and no one can read it without feeling that his own spirit has been enlivened and elevated by so doing. Its pictures remind us very forcibly of those of Thomson, Cowper, and Burns. In fact, since Thomson wrote his 'Seasons,' no poem has appeared in this country that so graphically and beautifully describes the pursuits of rural industry. 'His Muse,' writes Dr. John Cairns of Berwick, 'at home amidst every glimpse of rural beauty and sweetness, gilds the living processes of husbandry and sheep-tending rather than the raids and sieges of other days, and turns away from the death-scenes of romance to pour the blessed light of a pure and loving sympathy over the humble abodes scattered all up and down the lovely borderland.' These words truthfully describe the nature of the poem."—*Newcastle Daily Journal*.

GORDON—The Home Life of Sir David Brewster.
By his Daughter, Mrs. GORDON. Second edition. Crown 8vo, 6s.

> "With his own conntrymen it is sure of a welcome, and to the *savants* of Europe, and of the New World, it will have a real and special interest of its own."—*Pall Mall Gazette.*

GORDON—Workers.
Fourth thousand. Fcap. 8vo, limp cloth, 1s.

GORDON—Work; or, Plenty to do and How to do it.
Thirty-fifth thousand. Fcap. 8vo, cloth, 2s. 6d.

GORDON—Little Millie and her Four Places.
Cheap Edition. Fifty-fifth thousand. Limp cloth, 1s.

GORDON—Sunbeams in the Cottage; or, What Women may do. A Narrative chiefly addressed to the Working Classes. Cheap edition. Forty-fourth thousand. Limp cloth, 1s.

GORDON—Prevention; or, An Appeal to Economy and Common Sense. 8vo, 6d.

GORDON—The Word and the World.
Twelfth edition. Price 2d.

GORDON—Leaves of Healing for the Sick and Sorrowful. Fcap. 4to, cloth, 3s. 6d. Cheap edition, limp cloth, 2s.

GORDON—The Motherless Boy;
With an Illustration by Sir J. NOEL PATON, R.S.A. Cheap edition, limp cloth, 1s.

> "Alike in manner and matter calculated to attract youthful attention, and to attract it by the best of all means—sympathy."—*Scotsman.*

GRAHAM—"Mystifications."

By Miss STIRLING GRAHAM. Fourth edition. Edited by JOHN BROWN, M.D. With Portrait of "Lady Pitlyal." Fcap. 8vo, 3s. 6d.

HANNA—The Life of our Lord.

By the Rev. WILLIAM HANNA, D.D., LL.D. 6 vols., handsomely bound in cloth extra, gilt edges, 30s.

> Separate vols., cloth extra, gilt edges, 5s. each.
>
> 1. THE EARLIER YEARS OF OUR LORD. Eighth thousand.
> 2. THE MINISTRY IN GALILEE. Third edition.
> 3. THE CLOSE OF THE MINISTRY. Sixth thousand.
> 4. THE PASSION WEEK. Fifth thousand.
> 5. THE LAST DAY OF OUR LORD'S PASSION. Forty-seventh thousand.
> 6. THE FORTY DAYS AFTER THE RESURRECTION. Ninth thousand.

HANNA—The Resurrection of the Dead.

By WILLIAM HANNA, D.D., LL.D., author of "The Last Day of our Lord's Passion," etc. Second edition. One vol. fcap. 8vo, 5s.

JOHNNY GIBB of Gushetneuk, in the Parish of

Pyketillim: with Glimpses of the Parish Politics about A.D. 1843. Fourth edition, with a Glossary. 12mo. [*In the Press.*

"It is a grand addition to our pure Scottish dialect; . . . it is not merely a capital specimen of genuine Scottish northern *dialect;* but it is a capital specimen of pawky characteristic Scottish humour. It is full of good hard Scottish dry fun."—*Dean Ramsay.*

Notes and Sketches Illustrative of Northern Rural

Life in the Eighteenth Century, by the Author of "Johnny Gibb of Gushetneuk." In 1 vol. fcap. 8vo, 2s.

KER—Sermons by the Rev. John Ker, D.D., Glasgow. Eleventh edition. Crown 8vo, 6s.

"This is a very remarkable volume of sermons. We have not seen a volume of sermons for many a day which will so thoroughly repay both purchase and perusal and re-perusal. And not the least merit of these sermons is, that they are eminently suggestive."—*Contemporary Review.*

"The sermons before us are indeed of no common order; among a host of competitors they occupy a high class—we were about to say the highest class—whether viewed in point of composition, or thought, or treatment."—*British and Foreign Evangelical Review.*

LAING—Lindores Abbey, and the Burgh of Newburgh: their History and Annals. By ALEXANDER LAING, F.S.A. Scot. 1 vol. small 4to. With Index, and thirteen Full-page and ten Woodcut Illustrations, 21s.

"This is a charming volume in every respect."—*Notes and Queries.*

"The prominent characteristics of the work are its exhaustiveness and the thoroughly philosophic spirit in which it is written."—*Scotsman.*

"It will repay attentive and minute study on the part even of those who may be well acquainted with the subject with which it deals. Any one who peruses it will gain no imperfect idea of the whole past history of religion and civilisation in this country."—*Fifeshire Journal.*

"The real value of the volume is certainly not indicated by its title. Lindores Abbey and Newburgh are but the centre around which are clustered masses of historical, antiquarian, and genealogical lore."—*Dundee Advertiser.*

"The contents of the volume are full of interest, do the utmost credit to the author, and give it a strong claim to a place on the shelves of all who have a taste for reading in the line of his researches."—*Daily Review.*

"Out of scattered ancient records, both literary and sculptured stones, the author has produced a most interesting and instructive work."—*Dundee Courier.*

"It merits a place beside the standard historical works on our country."—*Perthshire Advertiser.*

"The author treats in several very interesting chapters on the subject of witchcraft, industrial pursuits, and old customs and folk-lore."—*Courant.*

"We have the pleasant duty of giving unqualified commendation of the author's valuable work."—*Perth Constitutional.*

"It is a most valuable contribution to Scottish history."—*Ayr Advertiser.*

"The thanks of all who are interested in Scottish antiquities and history are due to the author."—*Spectator.*

MACLAGAN—The Hill Forts, Stone Circles, and other Structural Remains of Ancient Scotland. By C. MACLAGAN, Lady Associate of the Society of Antiquaries of Scotland. With Plans and Illustrations. 1 vol. fol., 31s. 6d.

"We need not enlarge on the few inconsequential speculations which rigid archæologists may find in the present volume. We desire rather to commend it to their careful study, fully assured that not only they, but also the general reader, will be edified by its perusal."—*Scotsman.*

MACKAY—Memoir of Sir James Dalrymple, First Viscount Stair, President of the Court of Session in Scotland, and Author of "The Institutions of the Law of Scotland." A Study in the History of Scotland and Scotch Law during the Seventeenth Century. By Æ. J. G. MACKAY, Advocate. 8vo. 12s.

MACPHERSON—Omnipotence belongs only to the Beloved. By Mrs. BREWSTER MACPHERSON. 1 vol., extra fcap., 3s. 6d.

MAXWELL—Soliman the Magnificent, and the Turks in the Sixteenth Century. By Sir WILLIAM STIRLING MAXWELL, Bart., K.T. and M.P. Illustrated by numerous Facsimiles of rare contemporary Drawings and Portraits. In 1 vol. folio. [*In the Press.*

MILN—Researches and Excavations at Carnac (Morbihan), the Bossenno, and Mont St. Michel. By JAMES MILN. In 1 vol. royal 8vo, with Maps, Plans, and numerous Illustrations in Wood-Engraving and Chromo-Lithography.

PATRICK, R. W. COCHRAN—Records of the Coinage of Scotland, from the earliest period to the Union. Collected by R. W. COCHRAN PATRICK of Woodside. Only Two Hundred and Fifty Copies printed. Now ready, in 2 vols. 4to, with 16 Full-page Illustrations, Six Guineas.

"The future Historians of Scotland will be very fortunate if many parts of their materials are so carefully worked up for them and set before them in so complete and taking a form."—*Athenæum.*

"When we say that these two volumes contain more than 770 records, of which more than 550 have never been printed before, and that they are illustrated by a series of Plates, by the autotype process, of the coins themselves, the reader may judge for himself of the learning, as well as the pains, bestowed on them both by the Author and the Publisher."—*Times*.

"The most handsome and complete Work of the kind which has ever been published in this country."—*Numismatic Chronicle, Pt. IV.*, 1876.

Popular Genealogists;
Or, The Art of Pedigree-making. Crown 8vo, 4s.

RENTON, W.—Oils and Water Colours.
By WILLIAM RENTON. 1 vol. fcap. 5s.

"The book is obviously for the Artist and the Poet, and for every one who shares with them a true love and zeal for nature's beauties."—*Scotsman*.

"To have observed such a delicate bit of colouring as this, and to have written so good a sonnet in the 'strict style,' as that we have quoted, shows that our author has no common powers either as an observer or a writer."—*Liverpool Albion*.

"To those minds that really hold this joy in beauty, Mr. Renton's book will undoubtedly give delight."—*Northern Ensign*.

ROBERTSON—Historical Essays in connection
with the Land and the Church, etc. By E. WILLIAM ROBERTSON, Author of "Scotland under her Early Kings." In 1 vol. 8vo, 10s. 6d.

ROBERTSON—Scotland under her Early Kings.
A History of the Kingdom to the close of the 13th century. By E. WILLIAM ROBERTSON. In 2 vols. 8vo, cloth, 36s.

"Mr. Robertson's labours are of that valuable kind where an intelligent and thorough sifting of original authorities is brought to bear upon a portion of history handed over hitherto, in a pre-eminent degree, to a specially mendacious set of Mediæval Chroniclers, and (not so long ago) to a specially polemical and uncritical class of modern Historians. He belongs to the school of Innes and Skene and Joseph Robertson, and has established a fair right to be classed with the Reeves and Todds of Irish historical antiquarianism, and the Sharpes, and Kembles, and Hardys in England."—*Guardian*.

SHAIRP—Studies in Poetry and Philosophy.

By J. C. SHAIRP, LL.D., Principal of the United College of St. Salvator and St. Leonard, St. Andrews. Second Edition. 1 vol. fcap. 8vo, 6s.

SHAIRP—On the Poetic Interpretation of Nature.

By J. C. SHAIRP, LL.D., Principal of the United College of St. Salvator and St. Leonard, St. Andrews. In 1 vol. crown 8vo.
[*In the Press.*

SHAIRP—Wordsworth's Tour in Scotland in 1803,

in company with his Sister and S. T. Coleridge; being the Journal of MISS WORDSWORTH, now for the first time made public. Edited by PRINCIPAL SHAIRP, LL.D. Second Edition, 1 vol. crown 8vo, 6s.

"If there were no other record of her than those brief extracts from her Journal during the Highland Tour, which stand at the head of several of her brother's poems, these alone would prove her possessed of a large portion of his genius."—*North British Review.*

SKENE—The Four Ancient Books of Wales,

Containing the Cymric Poems attributed to the Bards of the Sixth Century. By WILLIAM F. SKENE. With Maps and Facsimiles. 2 vols. 8vo, 36s.

"Mr. Skene's book will, as a matter of course and necessity, find its place on the tables of all Celtic antiquarians and scholars."—*Archæologia Cambrensis.*

SKENE—The Coronation Stone.

By WILLIAM F. SKENE. Small 4to. With Illustrations in Photography and Zincography. 6s.

SKENE—Celtic Scotland.

A History of Ancient Alban. By WILLIAM F. SKENE. Vol. I. Book 1, History and Ethnology. Illustrated with Maps. 15s.

"It is a book of solid and good work, and which ought to be thankfully welcomed by all who are engaged in any minute study of the early history of Britain."—*Pall Mall Gazette.*

"This volume is the first instalment of a work which will bring the early history of Scotland out of the clouds and mists of artificially constructed systems of history, exaggerated tradition, and legendary fiction, and into a real, if still somewhat dim, historic light."—*Edinburgh Courant.*

"Da ist es denn in der That ein Fortschritt, wenn ein Gelehrter, der sich die schwierigen, aber unerläszlichen Sprachkenntnisse erworben und seit Jahren mit Sichtung der vertrauenswerthen Ueberlieferung von den Truggebilden, welche alles Keltische so leicht bedecken, befaszt hat, die bedeutende Aufgabe in die Hand nimmt nach strenger Methode die wirklichen Thatsachen jener Anfangsjahrhunderte hinzustellen. Er hat sich gründlich mit der einheimischen Literatur von Wales und Irland bekannt gemacht und steht durch Kenntnisz des Deutschen in verbindung mit den Fortschritten der sprachvergleichenden Wissenschaft überhaupt. . . . . Ungemein lehrreich mit Hülfe einiger Kärtchen, deren wissenschaftliche Begründung wohl verdient von der neuen Ausgabe des Historischen Atlas von Spruner-Menke für die britannische Abtheilung ernstlich in Betracht gezogen zu werden, ist Alles, was ein so genauer Kenner seiner Heimath, wie Skene es ist, hinsichtlich der physikalischen und ganz besonders der geschichtlichen, Geographie derselben beibringt. . . . . Linguistik, Ethnographie, Topographie und Kritik der historischen Quellen greifen für diese wichtige Epoche des Uebergangs wirkungsvoll in einander, wie es meines Wissens bisher in keinem anderen Werke geschehn ist."—*Göttingische gelehrte Anzeigen.*—Dr. R. PAULI.

SKENE—Celtic Scotland.
A History of Ancient Alban. Vol. II. Book 2, Church and Culture. In 8vo. With Maps, 15s.

SKENE—Celtic Scotland.
A History of Ancient Alban. Vol. III. Book 3, Land and People. [*In preparation.*

SMALL—Scottish Woodwork of the Sixteenth and
Seventeenth Centuries. Measured, Drawn, and Lithographed by J. W. SMALL, Architect. In one folio volume with 100 Plates. [*In the Press.*

SMYTH—Life and Work at the Great Pyramid.
With a Discussion of the Facts ascertained. By C. PIAZZI SMYTH, F.R.SS.L. and E., Astronomer-Royal for Scotland. 3 vols. demy 8vo, 56s.

SMYTH—An Equal-Surface Projection for Maps of the World, and its Application to certain Anthropological Questions. By C. PIAZZI SMYTH, F.R.SS.L. and E., Astronomer-Royal for Scotland. 8vo, 3s.

SOUTHESK—Britain's Art Paradise; or, Notes on some Pictures in the Royal Academy, 1871. By the EARL OF SOUTHESK. 8vo, sewed, 1s.

SOUTHESK — Saskatchewan and the Rocky Mountains. Diary and Narrative of Travel, Sport, and Adventure, during a Journey through part of the Hudson's Bay Company's Territories, in 1859 and 1860. By the EARL OF SOUTHESK, K.T., F.R.G.S. 1 vol. demy 8vo, with Illustrations on Wood by WHYMPER, 18s.

SOUTHESK—Herminius.
A Romance. By I. E. S. Fcap. 8vo, 6s.

STRACHAN—What is Play?
A Physiological Inquiry. Its bearing upon Education and Training. By JOHN STRACHAN, M.D., Jun. In 1 vol. fcap.

> Reasoning at every step he treads,
> Man yet mistakes his way,
> While meaner things, whom Nature leads,
> Are seldom known to stray.

WILSON—Reminiscences of Old Edinburgh.
By DANIEL WILSON, LL.D., F.R.S.E., Professor of History and English Literature in University College, Toronto, Author of "Prehistoric Annals of Scotland," etc. etc. 2 vols. post 8vo.

www.ingramcontent.com/pod-product-compliance
Lightning Source LLC
Chambersburg PA
CBHW020806230426
43666CB00007B/879